Ninety
Story
Sermons
for Children's Church

. . . and they shall call his name Emmanuel, which being interpreted is, God with us (Matt. 1:23)

Ninety Story Sermons
for Children's Church

Marianne Radius

Linoleum cuts by Frederick J. Ashby

BAKER BOOK HOUSE
Grand Rapids, Michigan

Paperback edition issued by
Baker Book House
with permission of copyright owner

Formerly published under the title,
God With Us

ISBN: 0-8010-7641-2

First printing, August 1976
Second printing, March 1978
Third printing, September 1979
Fourth printing, May 1981

FOR
MY HUSBAND
WHO HELPED ME WRITE THIS BOOK

Preface

All that we know about the life of Jesus on earth is found in the four Gospels. Yet the plan of salvation, of which Jesus is the center, is not confined to the Gospels. It is the subject of the entire Bible. And so we see the Old Testament saints looking forward to Him with eager longing, even as we look back to Him in wondering amazement. The author who writes to the Hebrews says of the Old Testament saints, "These all died in faith, not having received what was promised, but having seen it and greeted it from afar." Peter, writing to the early Christians in Asia Minor, says similarly, ". . . whom, not having seen, ye love." This is God's plan of salvation, which Paul calls the great mystery of godliness, and which Peter tells us even the angels desire to look into.

In this book I have tried to set the life of Jesus into the perspective of the Old Testament prophecies and into its apostolic fulfillment. This is in accord with what Jesus Himself does, for He speaks repeatedly of the Old Testament people and events which illumine the meaning of His ministry and, again, predicts the future mission outreach of His church. When Jesus mentions these events and persons, past and future, I have set the stories themselves into the text,

7

to show God's over-all plan of salvation: the ladder which connects the holy God and sinful Jacob, the Passover lamb sacrificed for the sins of God's people, the brazen serpent lifted up so that whoever looks at it in faith is saved, the drowning Jonah crying to God "out of the belly of Sheol," and the wedding feast of the Lamb where guests from the far corners of the earth will be present.

However, this is not intended to be just a book about the life of Jesus in its total Bible setting. For it is really of no use to us to know the life of Jesus unless it has an impact on our own lives. This is not just a book *about* Jesus. It is an invitation to the young reader to open his heart to the Saviour, to put his hand in God's hand, and to walk with Him in love and trust. For the person who is old enough to sin is old enough to meet his Saviour. John tells us that if everything Jesus said and did were to be written down, the world itself could scarcely contain the books. But even if we had all these books, it would serve no purpose unless we — and our children — understood that these things were written "that ye may believe that Jesus is the Christ, the Son of God, and that believing ye may have life in his name."

—MARIANNE RADIUS

Contents

10

12

1

Waiting for Jesus

t here is a strange thing about the days of December — they seem to pass more slowly than the days of any other month. As Christmas comes nearer and nearer, the days get longer and longer, until at last they drag past so slowly that you wonder if Christmas will ever come.

If this is the way you feel, then I ask you to come with me on a journey — a journey across an ocean to a strange land, and a journey back in time to a world that had never heard of Christmas.

How would you feel if you had to wait for Christmas not a few short days or weeks, but hundreds, no, thousands of years? You have known whose birthday Christmas is as far back as you can remember. But in the world we are going to visit, though the people longed for Christmas, and hoped for it, and prayed for it, they did not know when or how it would come. For these people Christmas was only a promise. It was a very old promise. It was a promise given by God.

God first gave this promise when the gate into the garden closed tight against Adam and Eve because of their sin. Somehow, God promised that He Himself, through one of their children, would win back for the man and the woman that wonderful friendship with God which they had so carelessly thrown away when they disobeyed God and ate the forbidden fruit. Adam and Eve did not understand how this could happen. They did not know when. They had only the promise of God, but that was enough for them. They trusted in God's promise. Someday they were going to walk and talk with God again.

God repeated the promise to Abraham. Someday, through one of his children, all the nations of the earth would be blessed. Abraham did not understand how. He did not know when. He had only the promise. He trusted in that.

And David — he, too, trusted in the promise, the promise that one of his children would rule over a kingdom that would never end. And Isaiah, and Jeremiah, and the other prophets — all of them longed and hoped and prayed for the Saviour who God had said would someday come. They did not know when He would come. They did not know where. They had only the promise.

"The Lord whom you seek will suddenly come in his temple." This was again the Christmas promise, repeated by God in the very last book of the Old Testament, the book of Malachi. But since that last time when God had spoken this promise, more than three hundred years had passed. The Saviour had not come. All those three hundred years God had sent no message. There was only silence. And the heavens above seemed as brass!

Three hundred years is a long time to wait. I do not know your family, but I can guess that your grandfather was born not more than eighty years ago, and your great-grandfather about a hundred and ten years. So you see in this world we are visiting, the last person who had actually heard God's promise spoken was the great-grandfather of the great-grandfather of the great-grandfather of the people who lived now. It would have been at least nine generations ago. Not many of us can count our ancestry that far back, much less know anything about those people who lived three hundred years ago. And would you stake your life on a promise made that long ago and still not come true?

And then, just as God had promised, the Saviour came suddenly.

2
The Man Who Saw an Angel

Luke 1:5-23

Zacharias saw an angel, and he could hardly believe his eyes. And when he heard the angel's message, he *didn't* believe his ears. "But that is impossible," he said to himself, "quite impossible."

Zacharias was an old man when this strange thing happened to him. He was a priest, and he served in the temple in Jerusalem. He served one week out of every twenty-four, and while he served he lived in a little dormitory on the temple grounds. The other twenty-three weeks he was free to go home.

Home was a small white house in the hill country of Judaea. But, most of all, home was his wife Elisabeth. Zacharias and Elisabeth had spent most of a lifetime together. They were even distantly related, for they both belonged to the family of the first great high priest, Aaron, who, long before Zacharias and Elisabeth lived, had helped his brother Moses bring the children of Israel out of Egypt and back to the Promised Land.

But Zacharias and Elisabeth had much more in common than this family ancestry. Each of them felt a deep longing in his heart for the Saviour God had promised. They prayed for the coming of the Saviour, they hoped, they clung to God's promise. There were some people who laughed at their hope. It was more than three hundred years since any prophet had brought a message from God. For three hundred years God had been silent. Some said that God must be dead. Zacharias and Elisabeth did not listen to this wicked talk. They just went on hoping, and praying, and trusting God, even when the silent heavens seemed to mock at their belief.

They shared a common sorrow too. For they had no child. No one who has not experienced their trouble can understand their heartbreak. How many anguished prayers they had sent to God! Year after year they prayed, they hoped, they prayed again. At last they realized that God was not going to give them what they wanted so much. They were both too old now to have a child.

They did not strike out in anger and rebellion at God. No, they recognized God's right to plan their lives. They accepted God's refusal of their prayer. They prayed now for grace, instead of for a child; for submission, that God's Holy Spirit would work His will in their hearts. And most of all they prayed that God would look with pity on His suffering people, and send the promised Saviour.

But I was going to tell you about the angel. When this happened, Zacharias was not at home; he was serving his week in the temple. And this week he had been chosen to offer the incense to God in the holy place behind the curtain. This was a great honor. It happened to a priest only once in his lifetime, and to many priests the honor never came at all. The great crowd of worshipers stood in the temple court, praying. Zacharias took the incense in his hand and went behind the curtain into the holy place. There he placed the sweet-smelling incense on the glowing coals of the altar that stood just in front of the holy of holies, where God Himself dwelt among His people. As the perfume of the incense ascended to heaven, the prayers of the worshipers outside went with it.

And this was just when it happened. There, at the right side of the altar of incense, stood the angel. Zacharias knew that when he lifted the curtain and entered the holy place, he came into the very presence of God; but he certainly had not expected this messenger from God to appear before his eyes. He was frightened. The angel spoke to him: "Do not be afraid, Zacharias. Your prayers have been heard. You and Elisabeth are going to have a son. You must call him John. He will bring joy to you, and also to many other people, for he will be great in the sight of God. He is not to drink any wine or strong drink. He will be filled with the Holy Spirit from the day he is born, and he will turn the hearts of many back to God, to prepare the way for the Lord."

All his life long Zacharias had trusted and believed God's promises.

But this, coming so suddenly, was too much for him, was more than he could believe. "How can I be sure of this?" he asked. "My wife and I are much too old to have a baby!" And the angel answered, "I am Gabriel, who stand in the presence of God. I was sent to bring you this good news. And now you will not be able to speak until the day that all this happens, because you did not believe my message."

The crowd of worshipers outside was waiting for Zacharias. They wondered why he stayed so long inside the holy place. And when at last he came out, he could not speak at all, but had to make signs to them with his hands. And so they knew he must have seen a vision.

At the end of the week Zacharias went home. I am sure that that night there must have been great joy in that little white house in the hills of Judaea. Joy that they were really to have a son at last, long after they had given up hope. But joy even more because of this marvelous evidence of the love and faithfulness of God. For God had indeed heard all those anguished prayers. And, as He so often does, He had prepared for them an answer far more wonderful than anything they would ever have dared to ask for.

3

His Name Is John

Luke 1:57-79

When I was your age, my mother used to say to me, "Do be quiet, Marianne, I can hardly hear myself think!" Perhaps your mother says the same thing to you. But there was once a little house in the hills of Judaea where no one ever had to say, "Be quiet." There had never been any children's shouts and laughter in that house. Just two grown-up people who would have thought a baby's cries the sweetest sound they had ever heard. And then, after many long years of heart-sick disappointment, two *old* people, who knew they would never hear a child at play.

Twice a year Zacharias was gone from home to serve his week in the temple. It was even quieter those two weeks, of course. But when he came back there was always a lot to talk about. He brought news from the big city, what was happening in Jerusalem. And Elisabeth had things to tell about their neighbors and relatives in the village.

And then one day he came back from Jerusalem and could not talk at all. Did Elisabeth guess something had happened as soon as she saw him coming down the road? Did his old hands shake with excitement, as he hunted for a tablet and a pen, and tried to write down the news? I imagine Elisabeth must have trembled, too, when she read his message. For when God reaches right down into our lives, and does something for us so far beyond what we have dared to hope, then we are, every one of us, shaken with amazement and with awe.

Sometimes I try a little experiment — and you can try it too, if you like. I close my eyes tight, and try to see if I can find my way around without them. It gives me a little glimpse of what it must be like to be blind. And if you would like to have some idea of how Zacharias felt those ten long months that he could not speak, you can try that too. Just for one hour, sometime when your whole family is around you talking, just for one hour pretend you cannot talk. If there is something you *have* to say, you must write it down, or try to explain it in sign language. Pick out an hour when something exciting is happening. For those ten months were certainly the most exciting of Zacharias' whole life.

I do not want you to think that Zacharias was struck dumb as a punishment for his disbelief. God *never* punishes those who put their trust in Jesus. He could not, for Jesus bore *all* their punishment when He died on the cross. No, Zacharias' silence was a lesson. And I want you to notice how wonderfully God suited the lesson He assigned to the need of His pupil. Zacharias had prayed for perhaps thirty years. And then, when God suddenly answered his prayer, he started back, saying, "No, no, that is impossible!" Now Zacharias will be silent. He will watch God doing what is impossible before his very eyes. And perhaps you and I ought to keep him company. We, too, should watch in silent amazement how mighty our God is, and how faithful! "Be still," God says to us, as He said to Zacharias, "and know that I am God."

Even when you cannot talk, you can still think. Indeed, you will think harder if you cannot speak. And you can pray, although you cannot say one word out loud. Surely that was part of the lesson too. What did they think about, Zacharias and Elisabeth, those ten months? What did they pray for? Surely they prayed for the baby, that God would watch over him, and lead him, and teach him to love God and to trust only in his Saviour. And they must have prayed for themselves, that God would teach them to be good parents, would give them wisdom for this new trust. You may have never thought about it, but your parents prayed these things for you before you were born. Day by day, night by night, as soon as they knew God was going to give them a baby, they besought God to care for you, to lead you, to save you.

And then they thought about what the baby would become. What would he do when he grew up? Just as your parents wonder where God will call you to serve. John was a very special baby, of course. Gabriel had told them he was to prepare the way for the coming of the Saviour. The angel quoted to Zacharias the last two verses of the Old

Testament: "And he shall go before his face, to make ready a people prepared for the Lord." There were other prophecies in the Old Testament about the one who prepared the way for the Saviour. I am sure Zacharias and Elisabeth must have searched for these texts, and pondered them in their hearts. They did not own a Bible, of course. Bibles were rare and very expensive in those days. But they knew most of the Bible by heart. They had learned it in school, and now it had precious new meaning for them.

And then the wonderful day arrived. Elisabeth held a baby boy in her arms. All their neighbors and relatives came to celebrate with them this unexpected goodness of God. "The baby," they said, "must be called Zacharias, for his father." But Elisabeth objected, "No, no! His name is John!" The relatives were puzzled. "Nobody in your family has that name," they said. They made signs to Zacharias, as to what he wanted to call the baby. He motioned for a tablet, and wrote down, "His name is John." That very instant his mouth was opened and, filled with the Holy Spirit, he spoke a song of praise and gratitude to God, who had not forgotten the promises made so long ago.

Blessed be the Lord God of Israel.
He has remembered the promise He made to our father Abraham.
And you, child, shall go before the face of the Lord.
The light of the Saviour is going to shine on us who sit in darkness
    and in the shadow of death.
He will guide our feet in the way of peace.

4

The Christmas Gift

Luke 1:26-38

her name was Mary, and she was hardly more than a child, only a year or two older than some of you. She lived with her father and mother in the little town of Nazareth that was perched on the side of a hill in southern Galilee. Her home was a simple, one-room shelter, with clay walls, and a flat roof covered with rushes. Half of the room was fenced off, to provide shelter for the family animals. It would have seemed a poor sort of house to you, but to Mary it seemed very pleasant. Everyone she knew lived in such a house.

Mary no longer played with the younger children in the market place. For Mary was going to be married. For some months now she had been engaged to the carpenter, Joseph; and the wedding date had been set for next year. Even a little girl helps her mother with the work. But when you are almost grown up, and soon to have a home of your own, then you help, not because Mother asks you to, but because you yourself want to know how to be a good wife, and perhaps, if God is good to you, a good mother. And so Mary worked hard at learning how to bake a light, fragrant loaf of bread, and how to weave a fine, smooth piece of cloth.

As she and her mother worked together, they talked of many things. They talked of where Mary and Joseph were to live, of the equipment she would need — a water jug, a kneading trough to make bread in, cups to drink from — of the furniture Joseph would make for their home — a chest to hold their clothes, stools to sit on, perhaps even a table. They would not need much.

They talked of more serious things too. Mother told about times in the past when the family had had serious trouble — a sick child, or Father out of work — and they had prayed to God, and He had heard them. And they talked about all the long, wonderful history of their people, all the times the nation had been in desperate trouble, and had turned to God in desperate prayer, and how God had never failed His people. They talked, too, about the greatest promise of all God's promises, the promise that some day He would send them a Saviour. How long, how eagerly they had waited for this promise to be fulfilled!

"Do not forget," Mother said, "to pray for the Saviour."

"No, I will not forget," Mary promised. She was a quiet, thoughtful girl. She did not say much, but she thought a great deal. When she was by herself, working at her loom or kneading the dough, she turned over and over in her mind the promises of God that Mother and Father had taught her. Did she sometimes wonder whether perhaps, if she had a child, he might be the promised Saviour? Perhaps she did. For she was a descendant of the great King David, and she knew that the Saviour was to be born in his family. But she was a modest girl. Was it likely that God would send His special Saviour into such a simple home as hers would be? Mary did not think so.

One day Mary was alone in the house. I do not know whether she was weaving, or whether she was just sitting quietly thinking about her new life that lay ahead. Suddenly a strange person stood beside her.

"Hail, you who are specially blessed by God," he said to her. "The Lord is with you."

Mary wrinkled her forehead in perplexity. She had never heard of anyone being spoken to like this. Who could this person be? What ever did he mean?

Before she had time to think this out, or even give a polite answer, the angel (for this was the angel Gabriel, sent direct from God, though Mary did not recognize him, having never seen an angel before) went on: "Do not be afraid, Mary. God has a special blessing for you. You are going to have a baby, and you must call Him Jesus. He will be the Son of God Most High, and God will give Him the throne of His father, David. He will rule over God's people forever. There will never be any end to His kingdom."

Mary did not really understand all this, but she did recognize that this was a message from God Himself. She asked just one question: "How can I have a baby? I am not married yet."

"The Holy Spirit will come upon you," Gabriel answered, "and the power of the Most High will overshadow you. That is why the holy child that is your baby will be called the Son of God. What is more, I have a sign for you from God. Your cousin Elisabeth — you know how all her life long she has prayed for a son? And now that she is an old woman, much too old to have a baby any more, God has answered her prayer. Because you see, Mary, nothing is impossible for God."

Can you imagine the thoughts, the feelings, the amazement that flooded through Mary's mind? But she did not trouble Gabriel with any of this. She was too overcome by awe. This person who spoke to her came direct from the presence of God Himself. She bowed her head and said, "I am God's servant. Let Him do with me whatever He chooses."

Mary was not the only one who saw an angel before her baby was born. God sent a message to Joseph too. One night, while he was sleeping, Joseph had a dream. An angel stood beside him and spoke to him.

"Take care of Mary," the angel said. "The baby she is going to have will be the Son of God. You must call Him Jesus, because He is going to save His people from their sins."

Then Joseph woke up, and it was a dream. But Joseph did as the angel had commanded him. He married Mary and took her into his house to live.

Joseph was a carpenter. As he went about his work, sawing and nailing and building, he had many things to think about. He and Mary were going to have a baby to care for, such a baby as had never been born before. Mary was the baby's mother, but God Himself was the baby's father. A tiny baby with curled-up fingers and a toothless smile, a baby who had to be cared for and trained and taught, but this baby was God Himself as well as man. Who ever heard of anything so wonderful! It was hard to understand. I am sure, too, that Joseph wondered if he and Mary would know enough to do the right things. I think each of them must have breathed many a prayer to God for help while they waited.

5

The Son of God Becomes Man

Luke 2:1-20

When you were born, your mother went to the hospital. She had a pleasant room and a comfortable bed. Girls from the diet kitchen brought her tempting meals on a tray, and her room was filled with flowers. You had your own bed too: an immaculate white crib, softly padded so that you would not bump your tiny head. All day long, and all night long, too, a nurse watched near your bed, to be sure you had everything you needed, to bathe you and feed you, and even to hold you up so that your proud father could look at you through the nursery window.

Once, long before you and I were ever thought of, another baby was born. This was not an ordinary baby, like you and me. This was a king's son; indeed, He was king Himself. Even more than this, this baby was the great God of heaven and earth. He was not born in a hospital. He was not born in a palace either, as a king's son ought to have been. He was born on a journey.

It is seventy-five miles or more from Nazareth to Bethlehem. Not so very far, you say. You could drive it in an hour and a half in your car. But it is a long way to walk. The roads are rough. There are many hills to climb. In the day the sun beats down upon your head. At night there is a sharp chill to the air.

Mary was in no condition to make such a journey, expecting her baby now any day as she did. But she had to go just the same. The Roman emperor had ordered a census. Every person must go back to his birthplace to be counted. Now of all times Mary would have liked to be at home with her mother, and among friends. But the emperor cared nothing about this.

Joseph was a poor man, but perhaps he was able to scrape together enough money for a donkey for Mary to ride. Even so, the trip would take at least four days—four long days of dust and heat and endless hills, of bumping through the ruts and over the rocks. Have you ever ridden on a donkey? It is not much like riding in your car.

Where was God when all this happened? Why was He not taking care of His Son and of Mary? He was. It was not really the emperor who ordered the census. It was God, God who became poor for our sakes — so that His Son was not born in a hospital, not in a palace, not even in the humble home where Mary lived in Nazareth. No, God's Son was born on a journey.

At last they came to Bethlehem. Mary was weary to her very bones, so tired that she did not see how she could go any further. Joseph walked beside her, his arm around her waist to support her. He tried to encourage her; he reminded her of the faithful promises of God.

At the edge of the little town there was an inn. Not such an inn as you are used to. This was a big field that had been fenced in. The middle was filled with animals belonging to the travelers, camels and donkeys. Around the field was an open porch. Here travelers could sleep, their coats thrown on the ground for a bed, but with at least a roof over their heads. There were a few rooms to rent too, but they were reserved for the very rich. The rent was much more than a poor man could pay. The bellowing of the animals and the shouting of the travelers mingled with the smoke of many fires and the hot smell of frying food. What a place for a king's son to be born!

But even this was too good for God's Son. When Joseph knocked at the gate, the innkeeper opened it only a crack. "You can't stay here," he said roughly. "We are filled up. Haven't you heard about the census?"

"But I have to come in," Joseph said. "Can't you see my wife is expecting a baby?"

The innkeeper peered at Mary. Then he shrugged his shoulders. "There is a cave over there on the hillside, where sheep are sheltered when it is too cold for them to be outdoors at night. Take her there."

Mary began to cry softly. Joseph helped her off the donkey and into the cave. He piled up a little hay for her to lie on.

"Do not be afraid, Mary," he said. "God has been with us all this time. He will not forsake us now."

So that is how it happened. The Saviour of the world, the King of kings, the Son of Almighty God, was born in a cave used to shelter the sheep. There was a little hollow scooped out of the ground, to hold the grain for the animals. Joseph padded the hollow with hay, and laid the baby there to sleep.

None of the crowds of people there in Bethlehem guessed what had happened. None of them dreamed that the Saviour whom God had promised had been born right there among them. Only Joseph and Mary knew the secret.

But God did send a message to earth about the birth of His Son. He did not send it to the rich and the powerful, to the king or the high priest. Jesus was born in a cave used to shelter the cattle, not in the palace. And the people God told about it were poor people, ordinary folk.

Outside of Bethlehem, in the fields, there was a flock of sheep. Among them, watching them so that they would not get lost, or be harmed by the wild beasts who roamed at night, there were shepherds. The shepherds sat around the fire, talking quietly among themselves. This was an ordinary night, and it followed an ordinary day. So they thought. But actually this was a very special night.

This was the night all the people of God had been waiting for ever since that unhappy day in the beautiful garden when Adam chose to disobey God. This was the night you and I will remember all our life long — the night God spoke to us in a little, helpless, crying baby; the night God showed us something about what our God is like, which we could never have guessed otherwise; the night we began to understand a little bit about the marvelous love and mercy and goodness of Almighty God. And about His justice, His hatred of sin, His willingness to sacrifice His own Son so that our wickedness could be undone, and our hopeless account settled.

Suddenly an angel stood before the shepherds. Around him shone the dazzling light of the glory of God. The shepherds were terribly frightened. They were used to darkness, and storms, and wild animals. But they had never seen anything like this before.

"Do not be afraid," the angel said. "I bring you wonderful news that will make you happy. Your Saviour has been born in Bethlehem this very night. Would you like to know how you can recognize Him?

You will find Him sleeping on the hay in a manger."

Suddenly there was a great crowd of angels in the sky. They all began to sing: "Glory to God in the highest. And on earth peace among men, whom God has chosen to help."

After the angels had gone back to heaven, I think it must have been a little while before any of the shepherds dared to speak. They had seen a sight such as no man had ever seen. They had heard music such as no man had ever heard — the heavenly music of the angel choir. At last one of them said, "Let us go to Bethlehem and see this thing God has told us about." They got up quickly. They did not wait till morning. They left their sheep. They hurried to find the baby Jesus.

When they got to Bethlehem they found it was just as the angel had said. There in the cave were Mary and Joseph, and lying asleep on the hay was the baby Jesus, God's own Son.

Does it seem strange to you that when God wishes to tell us what He is like, He sends a little baby who is born in a cave, and sleeps in the feed trough on the hay? If it does, you need to look again, to look more closely. This *is* the measure of how much God loves us. It is the first page of that wonderful book Jesus has given us, the book about our God. For Jesus is the Word of God, sent to us with a precious, life-giving message.

6
The Prayers That Were Answered

Luke 2:22-38

*t*he people who had crowded into Bethlehem for the census did not stay long. As soon as they had registered, they went home again. Now there was plenty of room in the town. Joseph found a little house for himself and Mary and the baby, where they could be more comfortable than they had been in the cave.

Joseph was a carpenter, and he soon was busy making tables and chairs, building sheep pens and cattle sheds. Mary kept the house clean, cooked the meals, and cared for the baby, just as your mothers do. But as she went about her work, she thought about everything God had said about the baby. He was her Saviour. But how was He going to save His people? She did not know. Would He become a carpenter, like Joseph? Or would He, as most of the Jews expected, become a great general, and drive out the hated Roman conquerors? Would He became a powerful king, like His great ancestor David? Where would He live? What would He do? She did not know. She could only wonder.

Long before all this, when the Israelites were slaves in Egypt, on the night of the first Passover, all the first-born sons of the Egyptians died; but God saved alive all the first-born sons of the Israelites. After that He commanded His people to bring every first-born son to the temple, and there to pay a ransom price for him, as a sign that these children belonged first of all to God, not to their parents, and that it was God who gave them the precious gift of life. So when the baby Jesus was about six weeks old, Joseph and Mary brought Him to the temple in Jerusalem, to pay the ransom price to God. In the temple something very strange happened, something that gave Mary another thing to wonder about.

Living near the temple in Jerusalem there were two very old people, Simeon and Anna. Both of them had lived a long time, and now there was just one thing left in all the world that they wanted. They wanted this one thing so much that each of them spent most of his time in the temple, praying to God. What was it they prayed for, so long and so earnestly? It was the Saviour. This Saviour seemed so desirable, so precious, to these two old people, that He outweighed everything else God could give them.

So far God had not answered their prayers. But He had given to each of them another gift, the gift of the Holy Spirit. The Holy Spirit of God was so real, so close to Simeon that he could hear Him speaking in his heart. And the Holy Spirit had given Simeon a promise. "Your prayers will be answered," the Holy Spirit said to him. "Before you die you are going to see the Saviour with your very own eyes." And on this day, when Mary and Joseph and the baby Jesus came to the temple in Jerusalem, the Holy Spirit spoke to Simeon again. "To-day," He said, "you must go to the temple." And so it happened that Mary and Joseph and Simeon and Jesus met each other in God's temple that morning.

Simeon took the little baby in his arms. "I have watched a long time, Lord," he said, "for You commanded me to watch all through the long dark night, and I am Your slave, and live to do Your will. But now my watch is over. I can die peacefully. For I have seen the salvation You have prepared for all nations, the light that is going to end the darkness, and bring the joy of day to all Your people."

Mary and Joseph listened in amazement to these words. Then Simeon turned to Mary. "This child," he said, "will make many who think they are strong fall down, and others who think they can never walk again, rise up and run. Yes, and a sword will pierce your heart too, Mary, and the secret thoughts of many people will be revealed."

While Simeon was saying these strange, puzzling words, Anna also came into the temple. Once, long, long before this, Anna had had a husband and a home of her own, when she was just a young girl, about the age Mary was now. She and her husband had lived to-gether just seven short years, and it seemed God had never given them any children. Then, when Anna was scarcely twenty years old, her husband had died. It was all so long ago now that it seemed more like a dream than anything that had actually happened. Anna had never married again. She was eighty-four years old now; and, like Simeon, the one thing she still longed for was the promised Saviour. She spent most of her time in the temple praying, praying all day, and far into the night.

When Anna saw the baby Jesus she bowed her head and thanked God — our faithful God who always answers the prayers of His children. And she spoke to everyone she knew, every one of her friends who were also hoping and praying for the Saviour, telling them how God had had mercy on His people, how He had remembered the promise first given thousands of years ago, and had at last sent the Saviour.

Simeon and Anna — just two old people, two people so old they were almost on the edge of the grave. Yet who of us shall say what part their prayers played in the coming of Jesus? Perhaps you yourself have a grandmother, or a grandfather — someone so old they cannot run and play with you any more. Yet, while you are busy about your own affairs — your school work, your home chores, your friends, your fun — your aged grandparents, who totter on the edge of the grave, are busy praying for you. It is a great blessing to have godly grandparents, and you and I ought to thank God for it every day.

7

The Seekers

Matthew 2:1-18

They call them *magi,* and if that name seems strange to you, just remember that the word is related to *magic* and *magician.* Of course, they were not the kind of magicians you and I know. They did not stand in front of an audience and pull rabbits out of a hat. No, they sat at night in lonely towers studying the stars. But you cannot call them astronomers either. For it was not science that interested them, but religion.

These were troubled men, men who searched for answers to the problems of life, men hungry for the true bread that satisfies, but not knowing where to turn to find it. And so, desperately, they hoped to discover in the stars the answers to the problems that troubled them: What is the meaning of life? Why are we here on earth? What does the unknown future carry in its hands?

These are questions God has planted in the mind of every man. But many of us run away from them. We bury them by filling our lives so full of activities that we have no time left to think. Not so the magi. They were deeply concerned. They were earnestly seeking an answer. And God — who has promised that every man who seeks shall find — God had prepared an answer for these men that was beyond their wildest hopes.

And so the magi sat in their lonely towers and studied the stars. Above their heads stretched that dazzling oriental nighttime sky which you and I, used to our western sky, can only imagine. And God spoke to them in the very last place you and I would have expected — He spoke to them in the sky. One night they saw a star so much more brilliant than any other star that they knew at once this was a message from God. A king must have been born that night, a king so much greater than any other king that only a dazzling new star was a fit celebration of His birth. And in their hearts these magi felt a strange desire, an irresistible pull to go to see this newborn king.

They did not understand that what they felt was the prompting of the Holy Spirit of God. And how did they know where to find the new king? Was this, too, the secret working of the Holy Spirit? However it was, they set out for Jerusalem. Not at once, you understand. This was a hard journey; it took careful preparation.

The pictures show three of them, but this is only the artists' guess. There may have been more, or fewer. At any rate, they must have had a large train of servants and camels. It was a long, wearisome journey, but at last they reached Jerusalem. If they had expected to find the city wildly celebrating, they were disappointed. No one seemed even to have heard of the birth of a new king. When they inquired at King Herod's palace — surely the likeliest place for a baby prince — Herod, too, was astonished. He called in the Jewish priests to ask where the Saviour was expected to be born, and they answered readily, "Bethlehem." But not one of them was interested enough to go along with the magi, to see whether the story was false or true.

If a prize should be given for the cruelest, most jealous man that ever lived, I guess Herod would receive the award. He had killed many members of his family, including several of his own sons and his favorite wife, for fear they might be plotting to seize his throne. This talk of a newborn king threw the aged Herod into a panic. But he was not too frightened to be crafty. "When you have found the king," he told the magi, "come back and tell me about it, so I can come and worship him too."

So the magi set out for Bethlehem, and then a wonderful thing happened. The same star they had seen before appeared again. It led them down the road, and at last it stopped right over the house where Jesus and Mary and Joseph lived. The magi went into the house, and there they saw at last the new king they had come so far to worship. This new king did not live in a palace, with silken clothes, and servants to wait on His every wish. But the magi recognized that He *was* a king. They fell down on their faces before Him and worshiped Him. Then they opened their packs and brought out gifts for the new king. They gave Him gold, and frankincense and myrrh, sweet-smelling and very costly perfumes.

That night, before they started back home, the magi had a dream. "Do not go back to Herod," God told them in the dream. So the magi went home by another route. After they had gone, God's angel appeared to Joseph. "Get up," the angel said to Joseph, "and take Jesus and Mary and flee to Egypt. Herod is planning to kill the young child." So Joseph and Mary got up, packed a few things, and, in the darkness of the night, they escaped to Egypt. He was the King of heaven and earth, but He had to flee for His life in the middle of the night — and He did all this for love of you and me.

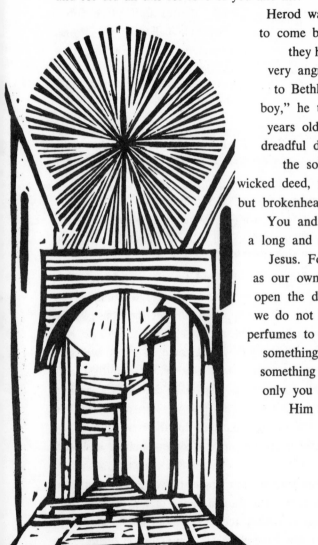

Herod was waiting for the magi to come back. When he saw that they had fooled him, he was very angry. He sent his soldiers to Bethlehem. "Kill every baby boy," he told them, "who is two years old or under." That was a dreadful day in Bethlehem. After the soldiers had finished their wicked deed, you could hear nothing but brokenhearted crying on all sides.

You and I do not have to take a long and difficult journey to find Jesus. For He is as close to us as our own hearts, if we will only open the door to His knock. And we do not have gold and precious perfumes to give Him. But there is something you can give to Jesus, something Jesus wants, something only you can give. You can give Him the love of your heart.

8

The Boy Jesus

Luke 2:40-51

*N*azareth was a little town to the north of Jerusalem, perched on a hillside. The streets were lined with fig and olive trees, and in the center of town was a fountain that supplied the people with water. This is where the boy Jesus grew up. Perhaps someday you can go to Nazareth and see the streets where Jesus played.

He was the oldest of a large family of boys and girls, so their home must have been a busy one. He went to the synagogue school, where He learned to read and write, and especially to know the Old Testament well. He learned a good deal of the Old Testament by heart, as did all Jewish children. Joseph was a carpenter, and Jesus helped in the carpenter shop, and gradually, as He grew older, learned the trade.

His childhood was like yours in many ways. He played, and He helped His parents. He studied and learned, and He grew taller and stronger every year. But there was one way in which He was different from you. He never did anything wrong. This was not because His life was easier than yours. He had to obey His parents whether He felt like it or not. Sometimes He thought they were unfair. His brothers and sisters argued, and quarreled, and took advantage of Him. But Jesus loved God so much that He wanted more than anything else in the world to do God's will.

There was still another reason why Jesus always did what was right. He did it for you, because He loved you so much. No matter how hard you try, you cannot ever live a sinless life. And that is because you have a sinful heart. So Jesus lived a perfect life for you. That is just why He came into this world. He lived and died to pay for all the wrong things you have done. If you trust in Jesus, then when God looks at you He does not see the wrong things you have done. Instead He sees the perfect life Jesus lived, and His death on the cross to pay for all your wrongdoing.

Once every year Joseph and Mary went to Jerusalem for the feast of the Passover. It was about eighty miles to Jerusalem, and that took several days of walking. They did not travel by themselves. A large group of friends from Nazareth went together. When He was twelve years old, they took Jesus along with them.

The Passover celebrated the wonderful deliverance God had given His people when He brought them out of slavery in Egypt. The ceremonies lasted several days. Perhaps this was the first time Jesus had seen the beautiful temple of God in Jerusalem since He was brought there as a baby.

After the feast the people from Nazareth started home again. Joseph and Mary did not notice that Jesus was not with the other boys His age. They looked for Him when it was time to sleep at night, and they could not find Him. They were alarmed. Early the next morning they started back to Jerusalem. They searched in all the places they had stayed. When they could not find Jesus they were more and more worried.

Where was Jesus all this time? He was just where you would expect Him to be, in God's house. The priests who taught God's law were sitting together, and Jesus sat at their feet, listening to what they said, and asking them questions. Everyone who listened was surprised at how much He understood, and how well He could answer the teachers.

After Joseph and Mary had looked many places for Jesus, at last they came to the temple. They were amazed when they saw Jesus talking to the teachers.

"Why have you treated us like this?" Mary asked Him. "Your father and I have hunted everywhere for you." And Jesus answered, "Why did you hunt for me? Didn't you know I must be in my Father's house?" Jesus knew that He was God's Son, and that He had special work to do, God's work. But Mary and Joseph did not really understand what He meant.

But Jesus did not stay in the temple. It was not yet time for Him to begin His great work. He still had many years of training and preparation to finish. He did not start to preach until he was about thirty years old.

Now He went back to Nazareth with Joseph and Mary and took His place in the family. Even though He was the almighty Son of God, He honored and obeyed His parents. Not because they were perfect; not because they were always right. He obeyed them because God had commanded, "Honor thy father and thy mother." This was part of the perfect obedience He offered to God in our place.

Do you ever have times when it seems as if no one understands you; when no one seems to realize the spot you are in, and the problems you have? You would probably be surprised if you knew how hard your parents try to understand. But it is a long time since your mother was a girl, and your father a boy. No matter how hard they try, they often have forgotten how they felt when they were your age.

But Jesus has not forgotten what it was like to be a boy. He understands just how you feel because He Himself has been where you are. He knows your difficulties, your problems, your temptations. He knows them because He has shared them Himself. And so you need never hesitate to bring your problems to Him. The Bible says that you can draw near to Him with boldness, because He understands.

And He cares what happens to you. He gave up His glorious home in heaven and became a child Himself because He loves you. He has paid for all your sins. And if you trust in Him, He will give you a new heart, and help you live a life of obedience to God.

9

Jesus Shares Our Baptism

Matthew 3

At the very end of the Jordan River, just before it spills its waters into the Dead Sea, lies the ford of Bethabara. Here the river can be waded, and here, for many thousands of years, traders and travelers from Arabia and Persia and India have crossed the river on their way to Jerusalem, and Egypt, and Africa. It is not a friendly spot. Some terrible catastrophe has pressed the earth in this region deep down towards its flaming center. The ground is more than a thousand feet beneath the level of the ocean, the lowest place on all our planet.

During the summer the heat is terrific; the air is heavy; the surface of the Dead Sea is the color of lead. Here, so we are told, were located, in a happier time, the lost cities of Sodom and Gomorrah. Indeed, the smell of sulphur still hangs in the air, as if to remind men forever after that God's patience is not inexhaustible, that wickedness will be punished by the Judge of all the earth.

During the winter a cooling breeze blows down the Jordan valley in the evening. Then, for a month or two, the heat can be endured. It was at this ford, in the middle of this desolate landscape, that there appeared one day a messenger from God. He was a strange, rough-looking man. His one garment was a camel-skin, caught at the waist by a strip of leather. His food was the locusts and the wild honey which he found in the scrub trees that languished at the river's edge.

His message was hardly more attractive than his appearance. "The reign of God is about to begin," he cried to everyone who passed by and stopped a moment to listen. "Right now God has His axe set ready at the base of the tree of your life. Unless you repent of your wicked ways, and submit your life to His rule, He will chop you down and throw you into the fire." But there was a happy side to this preaching too. Everyone who truly repented would be forgiven. How forgiven? The preacher did not explain all this. Instead, he led his hearers to the river's edge, and dipped their sweaty, dust-covered bodies into the refreshing water. Just as the water of the Jordan cleaned their bodies, so God would clean their filthy, sin-stained souls.

Yes, he baptized them. That is why we call him John the Baptist.

It was more than three hundred years since the last prophet had spoken the frightening and yet comforting words, "Thus saith the Lord." For three hundred years God's people had been waiting and hoping and praying for the Saviour that God had promised so long ago. Some had fallen into despair. Many had fallen into sin. And now the word spread like lightning through the land: "There is a new prophet preaching at the Jordan ford. A message has come from God."

They came from far and near to hear the new prophet. The rich came, and the poor — important officials of the church and government, and plain, ordinary folk like you and me. They came in great crowds. And as they listened, their hearts were stirred. Their consciences awoke from sleep. They remembered all their past sins, their selfishness and greed and meanness and disobedience. They streamed into the water to be baptized, to be assured that God was willing to forgive even such sinners as they were — just as He is willing to forgive even such sinners as you and me.

Then someone asked the man beside him, "Can this be the promised Saviour?" Soon everyone was asking this question. John was quick to answer. "I am only a voice crying in this wild place," he said, "a voice preparing you for the coming of the Saviour. Soon someone will come after me, someone so much greater than I am, that I am not fit to

untie His shoes. He will baptize you, not with water, but with the fire of the Holy Spirit."

Among the crowds who came to listen there was a stranger from far-off Galilee. He, too, stepped into the water to be baptized, to claim for Himself the promise that God would forgive His sins.

There is something you should especially notice as this Man wades into the Jordan River. For this Man alone, of all the men that ever lived since God set the first man in the beautiful garden, this Man has no sins. This is the only Man who has no need to be baptized, no need to beg for God's mercy.

Why then does He join the wicked and the disobedient at the water's edge? If you look with eyes of faith you can see why. This Man is carrying into the river a heavy burden. On His back rest the sins of all those who have ever lived or will ever live who trust in God's salvation. Yes, this is our Saviour, Jesus Christ, and it is for your sins and mine that He is claiming God's promise of mercy and forgiveness.

There is something else even more amazing here which you can perhaps see if you look very closely. Jesus is not only bent beneath the heavy load of our sins. He is the very reason why there is mercy and forgiveness at all. He is, as John the Baptist exclaimed, the Lamb of God who is going to lay down His own life to pay for our wickedness. Willingly, and out of love for us, He steps into the water to begin His wonderful work as our Sin-Bearer.

And then, as He climbs back up the bank, something else amazing happens. Suddenly above His head the veil of the sky — which separates you and me from God and heaven — is torn in two, and the astonished people standing there see the Holy Spirit Himself coming down from heaven in the shape of a dove, and resting on our Saviour's shoulder. And then God Himself speaks from heaven above.

"This is my beloved Son," He says, "in whom I am well pleased." Yes, that is how it was at the Jordan River ford when our Saviour began His work for you and me.

10
The Lamb of God

Exodus 12:21-33

By eleven o'clock the land of Egypt was asleep. Pharaoh slept on a bed that was beautifully carved, ornamented with fine gold, and spread with soft linen sheets. The merchant and his family spread their blankets on the floor of the little room behind the store. The farmer and his wife and children lay on the bare floor of their mud hut. The streets were dark. The towns were silent.

Only the Hebrew slaves were still awake. They were busy about some strange new religious ceremony. That afternoon the Hebrew women had driven a great flock of lambs, bleating and baaing, through the streets. They left one in front of each of the slaves' huts. As darkness gathered, and the men came stumbling home from their work gangs, the animals were killed. With a crude brush made of twigs they painted the blood of the animals on their doorways. Then a great smell of roasting meat rose from the slave quarters.

Now it was close to midnight. Inside the Hebrew huts the flickering lamps cast strange shadows on the walls. The family stood around the table, dressed as if ready to start on a journey. They were eating the roast lamb, together with bitter-tasting herbs. There was bread too, not the usual kind, but a sort of cracker, such as you bake when you are in a hurry and cannot wait for yeast to rise. Indeed, there was a feeling of haste about the whole ceremony, as if they might have to rush off at any moment.

Outside in the streets there was a strange, indescribable smell of horror. The Egyptians slept on, not even dreaming. But even as they slept, God's destroying angel was going up and down the streets, in and out of the houses. Silently, wordlessly, he entered every house. Every house, that is, except where he saw the blood smeared on the doorway. These blood-marked houses he passed over.

It was half-past midnight. The Egyptians stirred in their sleep. Pharaoh turned over, too, on his carved bed. He lay still a moment, and then he got up softly and went to look at his little son, the crown prince, who slept in the next room. The child slept quietly. Suddenly terror clutched Pharaoh's heart. Did he lie too quietly? He put his hand on the child's side. No breath stirred his little chest; there was no heart beating within. Pharaoh's oldest son was dead!

The shriek of grief that went up as Pharaoh roused the palace was picked up and echoed on every side. For in every Egyptian home there was a dead child. The oldest son of every family lay cold and still. Only the houses with the blood on the doorway had been spared.

In the darkness of the night Pharaoh sent for Moses. "Wake up your people," he cried, "and leave Egypt at once. Get out of my country before we all become dead men!"

That was how God rescued His people from their cruel Egyptian masters. Always afterwards the Jewish people remembered that night. Once a year they stood again around a table, and ate the roasted lamb and the bitter herbs, and the crackerlike bread which had not had time to rise.

They called it the Passover, because God's destroying angel had *passed over* the houses where he saw the blood. The Egyptians died because they had sinned against God. In the end everyone who sins against God must die. The Hebrew slaves had sinned too. Like the Egyptians, they deserved to die. But they did not die because someone else died in their place. The lamb died instead, and the angel passed over every house where he saw the lamb's blood.

Of course, the blood of a little lamb cannot pay the price of my sins and of yours. That lamb was just a sign. He pointed to another Lamb, who would be born long afterwards, to live and die to pay for our sins. The Jews did not know when this Lamb would come. They did not know where. They had only the promise of God, and they trusted in that promise.

11
Jesus Finds His First Disciples

John 1:35-51

One day out of every year belongs especially to you. On this day you get presents. There are special things to eat, perhaps even a party. Your family and your friends are all celebrating, because this is the day on which you were born.

But there is another day that is even more important to you. This is the day Jesus comes to you, and you come to Jesus, the day He asks you to put your trust in Him because of what He has done for you, the day you put your hand in His to walk with Him through all the rest of your life.

Perhaps you can hardly remember when you first heard about Jesus. Perhaps your mother taught you stories about Him and how to talk to Him in prayer when you were still a very little child. As you have grown older, you have learned from day to day to trust in Him, to ask Him for forgiveness when you have done wrong, to turn to Him for help when you are in trouble.

Still, if you try hard, perhaps you can imagine what it would be like to need Jesus, to long for Him, and yet not to know Him. And then one day you actually meet Him, and your whole life is changed. Our story is about five men who had this experience.

Of course, God's people had known for hundreds and hundreds of years that God was going to send them a Saviour. But they did not know who this Saviour would be, nor what He would be like. Those who loved God just trusted in God's promise without being able to understand how it would happen.

But all of God's people longed for the day when the Saviour would really come. Year after year and century after century, when God seemed to delay, when some people said God had forgotten, still those who trusted God prayed and waited for the promised Saviour.

And then one day John the Baptist came out of the desert. He was wearing a camel-skin coat with a strip of leather tied around his waist. John told the people to be sorry for their sins and to change their wicked lives. He led them to the Jordan River and baptized them, to show that their sinful hearts needed to be washed.

Great crowds of people followed John the Baptist. Many of those who were hoping for a Saviour thought that this man might be the one God had promised. But John kept telling them that someone was coming after him, someone much greater than he was.

Andrew and his friend were fishermen. They had left their boats and their nets to listen to John's preaching. They wondered about the strange things John said about the one who would come after him. One day as he was preaching to the people, John looked up and saw Jesus walking nearby.

"Behold the Lamb of God," John said to Andrew and his friend.

The two fishermen had never spoken to Jesus, but they felt drawn to Him by a strange attraction. They followed Him. Jesus turned around and said to them, "What are you looking for?"

The two men hardly knew what to answer.

"Teacher, where do you live?" they finally asked Him.

"Come and see," Jesus said.

So Andrew and his friend went along with Jesus, and they spent the night with Him. What did they talk about that afternoon and evening? God has not told us. But we do know that, before the evening was over, they knew for sure that they had met the one they longed for, the Saviour whom God had promised.

Early the next morning Andrew went to find his brother Simon.

"We have found the Saviour," he told him. Andrew brought Simon to Jesus.

When you and I look at someone, we can only guess what he is like inside and, often as not, we are wrong. But Jesus could read a man's thoughts and his heart. He looked at Simon and said: "Your name now is Simon, but you are going to be called Peter." Peter is the Greek word for a rock or a stone. Later on Peter really became a rock of strength and courage to the early church.

When Jesus was ready to leave the Jordan and go back to Galilee, He met Philip.

"Follow me," He said to Philip.

Did Philip answer, "Why?" or, "Who are you?"? No, he got up and followed Jesus. He, too, had been looking and hoping for the Saviour, and when he met Jesus he knew that his prayers had been answered. Like Andrew the day before, Philip could not wait to share the good news. He went at once to find his friend, Nathanael.

"We have found the Saviour whom Moses and the prophets wrote about," he said. "His name is Jesus, and He comes from Nazareth." Nathanael found this hard to believe.

"Has anyone important ever come from Nazareth?" he asked.

"Come and see for yourself," Philip answered.

Jesus saw Nathanael coming. "Here is a true son of Israel," He said, "an honest man."

"How do you know me?" Nathanael asked, surprised.

"Before Philip called you, I saw you sitting under the fig tree," Jesus answered.

Nathanael was startled that Jesus could read his thoughts and knew what he had been doing.

"Teacher," he said, "You are the Son of God! You are the King of Israel!"

Though the Bible does not tell us this, I think that perhaps Jesus smiled at Nathanael's words.

"Do you believe in me," He said, "just because I said I saw you under the fig tree? You will see much greater things than this. You will see heaven opened, and the angels of God ascending and descending upon me."

This is how these five men met Jesus, and each of them found that his life was changed forever afterwards. And they did indeed see many amazing things, as Jesus had promised they would.

12
The Dream

Genesis 28:10-17

*t*he angels of God ascending and descending! Heaven opened, and a ladder reaching from God down to man, and from man up to God! Only one man had ever seen such a sight. And he saw it in a dream.

He saw this amazing sight, and dreamed this extraordinary dream, at an unlikely moment. He saw it when he was neck-deep in sin.

He had stolen his brother's blessing. He had lied to his blind old father. He had tried to force God's hand. And now he was running for his life!

He could still hear his brother's angry threats echoing in his ears: "I will kill him for this trick!" It was this that had driven Jacob on through all the heat of the day, weary step after weary step, until he came at last to this lonely spot.

Here he sank exhausted to the ground. He ate a few mouthfuls of the bread his mother had given him, drank a little water from the skin slung over his shoulder, and then stretched out on the bare ground, resting his head on a rock.

Worn out as he was both by grief and by exertion, he should have fallen asleep at once. But this was such a lonely place! He was so homesick! His conscience tormented him too. Would he ever see his mother again? Would he ever get a chance to throw himself at his blind father's feet, and beg, "Forgive me!"? No, it was not likely he would ever be able to go home.

At last he fell into a troubled sleep. The brilliant stars wheeled above his head, but they did not notice the lonely figure, wrapped in his coat against the night chill, lying there among the stones.

And then he had the dream. He saw a ladder set between earth and heaven. Up and down the ladder went the angels of God. What were the angels doing there? They were carrying the desperate needs

48

of this sleeping fugitive up to God, and bringing back to Jacob the forgiveness, the love, the tender, watchful care of God.

At the top of the ladder stood God Himself. "I am the God of your father Isaac," God said to him, "and of your grandfather Abraham. I am going with you wherever you go, and I will take care of you. I will also bring you back again to this place. For I am going to give this very place where you are sleeping to your children's children. And through one of them all the families on the earth will be blessed."

And then he woke up, and he was afraid. "Surely," he said to himself, "God is in this place, and I never knew it. This place is nothing less than the house of God. This is the very gate of heaven!"

How could there be a ladder joining the holy God with a man as sinful as he was? Jacob did not know. He only knew that he had seen it. He did not know who it would be among his descendants who would some day bring a blessing to every family in the world. He did not know when this would happen, or where. He did not know how God would bridge the terrible gulf between heaven and earth. Or why the ladder, and God's forgiveness, and the One who would be a blessing even to you and to me were all mysteriously joined together. But he had heard God's promise. And that was enough for him.

13
Jesus Resists Satan's Temptation

Matthew 4:1-11

You have often, I am sure, said a prayer of thanks for the death of Jesus for our sins. But have you ever thought to thank God for Jesus' life? Jesus lived thirty-three years, and every single one of those more than twelve thousand days He lived for your sake and mine.

When Jesus died on the cross, He paid for all the sinful deeds you and I have done, for all the times we have been angry and disobedient and selfish and quarrelsome. But He did much more than this for us. All the days of His life He did good deeds. He was loving and unselfish and obedient to God. And all these good deeds were for us, because we, who have wicked hearts, could not do what was right ourselves. When God figures up our bill, He puts down not only the payments Jesus has made for our sins, but also the good deeds He has done in our place. He does so, that is, if Jesus is our Saviour and we trust only in His work.

When Jesus was baptized, and took our sins on Himself, the Holy Spirit came down from heaven and sat on Jesus' shoulder in the form of a dove. And God the Father spoke from heaven. "This is my beloved Son," He said, "in whom I am well pleased."

But there was one person who was not pleased that Jesus was about to start His work. That person was the devil. Long, long ago Satan had rebelled against God. He had been thrown out of heaven — out of the happy fellowship of the angels who stood always in the presence of God — out into the terrible outer darkness. Now Satan hated God. The one thing he wanted was to get even with God, to pay Him back. As a result, Satan hated men too. That was why he sneaked into the Garden of Eden, disguised as a snake. He wanted men, too, to sin against God, to be on his side, to share in his terrible punishment.

Adam listened to Satan, and he sinned. After that, all men were born with sinful hearts, and all of them disobeyed God. But now Jesus had come to pay for these sins, and to do for men the good deeds, pleasing to God, they could not do themselves.

Satan saw what was happening. He was determined to prevent it if he could. He was lying in wait for Jesus in the wilderness, not far from where Jesus was baptized.

Jesus was not afraid of Satan. He was ready for the battle that He knew was coming. He went to the wilderness to meet the devil.

The Holy Spirit of God, who had come down on Him like a dove when He was baptized, went with Him, to help Him and to strengthen Him.

When Jesus came into the wilderness, He fasted for forty days and forty nights. He had nothing at all to eat. At the end of that time He was weak and tired; He was on the edge of starvation. This was the time Satan chose to attack Him.

"If you really are the Son of God," Satan said, "you are all-powerful. Change these stones into bread. Why should you die of hunger?"

"No," Jesus answered. "I will trust in God. He is able to keep me alive by His powerful word."

Then Satan tried again. He took Jesus to the topmost tower of the temple, so high you could hardly see the ground far below.

"You say you trust in God," Satan said. "Let us try Him out and see if He will take care of you. He has promised to keep you from harm. Jump off, and test His promise." Again Jesus refused to yield to the temptation of Satan.

"It is forbidden to experiment with the promises of God," He said. "I do not need a test to prove that He will care for me. I know He can be trusted."

Then Satan tried once more. The years Jesus had ahead of Him were years of suffering and trouble. Satan knew this. Jesus knew it too. He had chosen of His own free will to suffer for our sakes, because He loved us so much.

"There is a much easier way to rule the world than the way you have chosen," the devil said. "The world belongs to me, and I will give it to you free, if you will just bow down once and worship me."

But Jesus knew that the way to our salvation, the only way, was the way of obedience to God, of suffering and dying, of Himself paying the dreadful price of our sins.

"Go away, Satan," He said. "The Bible says that God, and only God, is to be worshiped."

When Satan heard these words, he knew he was beaten. He left Jesus alone for a time. And do you know what happened then? Angels from God came to Jesus. They brought Him food and rest and comfort.

I am sure you also know the temptations of Satan. There are times when he whispers his wicked lies to you — just as he lied to Jesus — when he tries to persuade you to do what is wrong, to distrust the promises of God. Do you know where to go for help when this happens? One of the reasons Jesus submitted to the dreadful temptations of the devil was so that He would understand what you go through when you are tempted, so that He would really sympathize with you when you have a struggle to do what is right. Jesus has conquered Satan for you, and He will help you, too, to resist temptation, if you turn to Him in prayer.

14

The House of God

John 2:13-17

When we last saw Jesus, He was resting in the desert. Satan had slunk away, ashamed. No, he was not ashamed that he had tried to tempt our Saviour. He was only ashamed that his clever plot to get Jesus to sin against God had failed. He planned to try again later. But, for the moment, all he wanted was to get as far away as possible from the scene of this humiliating defeat.

Jesus was resting, and the angels of God were caring for Him. They were bringing Him something to eat, and cool, refreshing water to drink. They brought Him comfort, and rest, and encouragement.

This is the very thing that sometimes happens in our own lives. After a time of trial, God sends His angels to us with rest, refreshment, and encouragement. True, you cannot see them with your eyes. But they are there just the same, as Jacob saw them in his dream, climbing up and down the ladder between heaven and earth, bringing help, and rest, and fresh strength, from God to you.

But Jesus could not stay long in the desert. There was work to do, people to be taught, sermons to be preached, the sick to be healed, the commands of God to be obeyed — for your sake, and for mine; in your place, and in mine.

One of the first things Jesus did after leaving the desert was to go to Jerusalem for the Passover. This was the great feast the Jews held every year to celebrate the wonderful way God had rescued them when they were slaves of the Egyptians. Every Jewish man who could, and many women and children too, even those who lived far away in foreign lands, went to the city of Jerusalem to thank God for this deliverance.

And so Jesus, too, and His disciples, went to Jerusalem and visited the temple where God dwelt among His people. Jesus had been in the temple often before, and He had not liked what He had seen. In fact, what He had seen had made Him angry.

Have you ever thought what the entrance of a church ought to be like? It ought to seem quiet and beautiful, don't you think, so that when you come in you feel reverent — so that you remember you are stepping into a sacred place, a place where the great God of heaven and earth meets with His people.

In the time of Jesus the entrance to the temple was not like that. Far from it! Have you ever been to a Penny Social? You need a big room for a Penny Social. A gym will do just fine. All around the walls you put up booths. In one booth hot dogs are for sale; in another, candy bars; in still another, cookies and cake and pies. There will be a fish pond, and a place to have your picture taken. But everywhere there are crowds of people, and loud talk, and laughing and joking.

That is something like what Jesus saw as He came into the temple. All around the outside court there were booths. You could buy oxen or sheep or doves to be sacrificed. There was oil for sale, and salt, and many other things. There were still other booths where you could change your foreign money into the right sort of coins to give the priests. There were crowds of people everywhere, arguing with the merchants about prices, shouting that they were being robbed. The cows were mooing, the sheep bleating, the doves cooing. There was hay and grain piled about for the animals to eat, and over it all the smell of manure. This was God's house. You can see why Jesus was angry.

Jesus was very angry. He did not stop to argue. He did not stop to explain. He twisted some rope together into a whip, and He drove the sheep and cows out of God's house. With one push He upset the tables of the money-changers, scattering coins in every direction.

"Take these things out of here," He said sternly. "Do not make my Father's house into a market place!"

It is true, somebody had to provide animals for those who came from far away and wished to offer a sacrifice to God. Somebody had to change the foreign money. It was not wrong to do these things. It was *the place* that was wrong. It is good to talk to your friends. But it may be that the church service is the wrong place to do this. I think you can guess why.

Your best friend has come to spend a week while her parents take a trip. You give her your bed to sleep on. You sleep on the couch. You and Mother talk over what specially nice things you can have to eat while she is here. Perhaps you plan a picnic. But when she comes, she does not talk to you. She spends most of her time playing with the children next door. One noon she even goes there to eat. How would you feel?

There may be many reasons why you and I go to church. But there is only one good reason — we go there to meet our God. And while we are there, we ought to give God — who has invited us to His house — all our attention.

I am sure you have tried this and have found out for yourself that it is not easy. It is very hard. It is so hard that it is impossible. You and I cannot worship God as we ought. This is one more thing that Jesus has done for us because we could not do it for ourselves. But just because He has done so much for us, we are eager to show our love for Him. And so, when we go to church, we say a short, secret prayer to God, who hears what we say in secret: *Holy Spirit, fill my heart with love, and teach me to worship as I ought to worship. Amen.*

15

A Visitor at Night

John 3:1-16

It was desolate country through which the Israelites were traveling. No trees, no green grass, no drinking water either. Nothing but rocks and sand. The Israelites had spent nearly forty years in this desert. God was teaching them a dreadfully hard lesson. He was teaching them that they must trust in Him.

God had never forsaken them through all these weary years. He had led them with a pillar of cloud in the daytime, and a pillar of fire at night. He had brought water out of the dry rock for them to drink, and had sent them manna from heaven to eat. In all those long years their clothes had not grown ragged and their shoes had not worn out.

Were the Israelites learning to trust in God? Some of them were. But many refused to learn. They were tired of the desert. They complained about the way God treated them. They wished they were back in Egypt again, where they had been slaves.

The sinner who does not trust in God must die. So God punished the people for their sins. He sent fierce snakes to bite them. Those that were bitten died. The people came running to Moses.

"We have sinned," they admitted. "Pray to God to take away the snakes."

Moses prayed for the people. And God answered him.

"Make a snake of brass," God told Moses. "Set it up on a pole. Everyone who has been bitten by the snakes, if he looks at the brass snake, will live and not die." So the people looked up to the brass snake, and they lived, and did not die.

Was the brass snake magic? Could it cure the deadly snake bite? No, it was just a piece of metal. It was God who cured the snake bite, God who forgave the sins of the people, God who gave them life instead of death. Only God can do these things. But the brass snake was a picture of how God was going to save His people. The brass snake pointed to Someone else, who was also going to be lifted up. It pointed to Jesus, who died for our sins on the cross.

* * * * *

The brass snake had happened long, long ago. Now Jesus had actually come to earth to save men who were dying because of their sins. He was going up and down the roads of Palestine, teaching the people. The common people followed Him in crowds, listening to every word He said. But the leaders of the Jews were suspicious. They were not at all sure that Jesus was the kind of Saviour they wanted.

One of them was especially interested. His name was Nicodemus. He did not dare to follow Jesus publicly in the daytime, so he came to Him secretly one night, after it was dark.

"Teacher," Nicodemus said, "we know that God must be with You. We can tell that from the miracles You are able to perform."

Jesus was able to read the thoughts of Nicodemus, just as He can read your thoughts and mine. He knew that Nicodemus was looking for a Saviour who would raise an army and drive out the Roman rulers. He saw that Nicodemus was proud of how good a man he was, of how well he obeyed all the hundreds of rules the priests had set up.

"Nobody can even see God's kingdom," Jesus said, "unless he is born again." Nicodemus was shocked at this answer. Did a good man like himself need to be born again? To start all over from the beginning?

"How can a man be born again when he is old?" he asked Jesus.

"You cannot enter God's kingdom," Jesus answered, "unless you are born of the Spirit of God."

When you and I were born, we were born with sinful hearts. We cannot possibly be part of the kingdom of Jesus, and serve Him as loyal subjects, unless we are born a second time. God must give us a new heart.

How can this happen? Nicodemus was puzzled, and you and I wonder too. We can never entirely understand it, because it is a miracle, done by the almighty power of God. But Jesus told us a little about it.

"You hear the wind," He said, "and you see its power and what it does, but you do not know where it comes from, or goes to. The work

of God's Spirit is like this. You cannot see the Spirit of God, you cannot understand how He works, but you can feel His power in your heart."

How do you get that new heart which you so badly need? Jesus explained this to Nicodemus too.

"Just as Moses lifted up the brass snake in the desert, so I am going to be lifted up on the cross, and whoever trusts in my work will be saved. God loved the world so much that He gave His only Son. Everyone who trusts in God's Son will not die, but instead will live forever."

Nicodemus had a lot to think about after he went home. He had thought he was a good man. Now he realized he was a sinner. He could not possibly save himself. He must trust in the saving work of Jesus and ask God for a new heart.

Nicodemus never forgot what Jesus had told him. He thought about it and thought about it. After Jesus died, Nicodemus was one of the two men who dared to come forward and bury the body of Jesus. He was a rich man, and he brought precious spices to anoint Jesus' body.

These words of Jesus were not spoken just for Nicodemus. They are for us too. You and I, too, need to be born again; we need a new heart. We need to pray: "God, who loved me so much that You gave Your own Son for my sake, give me a new heart. I know I cannot save myself. I trust only in the death of Jesus on the cross."

You are not too young to pray this prayer. God hears your prayers just as surely as He hears the prayers of grown-ups. If you trust in Jesus, if you ask God for a new heart, He will surely hear and answer you. I know that this is true, because God has promised.

16
The Great Encounter

John 4:5-42

It was just a small village, a handful of low white houses clustered along a dusty road. If the people who lived there ever thought they would be remembered, they would have said, I suppose, "It is because of our well." The well was a short distance down the road. The shaft ran a hundred feet straight down, and the water they pulled up in their buckets was cold, and clear, and sweet. It had been dug, so they said, by the great patriarch Jacob himself, almost two thousand years ago.

But it is not for the well that we remember these people. There was a woman in this village who was a great sinner, sunk so deep in sin that decent folk wanted to have nothing to do with her. She had changed husbands five times, and now, discarding even this pretense of decency, she lived openly with a man to whom she was not married at all. It is this sinful woman that has made the village famous.

Other women went to the well to fill their jugs in the early morning, and again after the sun had set. But when she went with them, they turned their faces aside, and drew their robes tightly about themselves, as if her shadow might dirty those it fell on. She had to listen to their half-whispered jokes, their cruel snickers of laughter. After that she began to fetch the water that she needed in the heat of the day, when her neighbors were indoors.

And so, on this particular day, she lifted her jug to her shoulder and set out down the road to the well, the dust swirling in little eddies about her feet. It seemed just an ordinary day to this woman whose name we do not even know. But it was not. Even now she was on her way to an encounter that would turn her life upside down.

The person who was going to meet her knew she was coming. Indeed, He had planned this meeting. For a day and a half now He

had been on His way to meet this woman at the well. Pilgrims returning from Jerusalem to the northern part of their country did not usually travel by this road. For this road led through Samaritan country. Jews and Samaritans were distantly related. They worshiped the same God, and hoped and prayed for the same Saviour. But the Samaritans had intermarried with heathen people; they had lost the pure faith the Jews guarded so jealously. There is no hatred so bitter as the hatred of brothers who have quarreled.

Jesus knew all this, but it did not stop Him. This woman was a great sinner who desperately needed a Saviour, and He had come into this world to save such people as this. He reached the well first. He was hungry and very thirsty. He sat down beside the well to rest and to wait, and His disciples went into the village to see if they could buy something to eat.

When the woman reached the well and saw a strange man sitting there, she was startled. But she did not speak to Him; in her country a woman did not speak to a man in public. She lowered her bucket, and then, hand over hand, she pulled it back up. Jesus said to her, "Give me a drink." Now the woman stared at Him in disbelief. "You, a Jew, ask a drink of me, a Samaritan woman!" she exclaimed.

"If you knew about the gift of God," Jesus answered, "and who it is that asks you for a drink, *you* would have asked *me,* and I would have given you living water."

The woman looked at Him scornfully. "You do not even have a bucket, and this well is deep. How can you give me 'living water'? Are you greater than our father Jacob, who gave us this well?"

"Everyone who drinks this water will get thirsty again," Jesus answered. "Whoever drinks the water I give him will never be thirsty again. For the water I give him will be like a spring of water inside him, always bubbling up to eternal life." Now the woman was interested, though she still did not understand what kind of thirst, and what kind of water, Jesus meant. "Give me this water," she said, "so that I will never thirst again."

"Go home and fetch your husband," Jesus said. "I do not have a husband," the woman answered. "You are right," Jesus said. "You have had five husbands, and the man with whom you are now living is not your husband." The woman was overcome with confusion that this man had discovered her shame. She tried to change the subject. "I can see," she said, "that you are a prophet. Our fathers worship on this mountain, but you Jews say God should be worshiped in Jerusalem."

"Believe me," Jesus said, "the time is coming when true worshipers will not come to this mountain, nor to Jerusalem, to worship God. The time is already here when true worshipers will worship God with their hearts, with sincerity, for this is the kind of worshipers God desires." The woman was not quite sure what He meant. "I know," she said, "that the Saviour is going to come, and when He comes He will make everything clear and plain." And Jesus answered, "I, who speak to you, am He." As He said this, His disciples returned. They were astonished to find Him talking to a woman, but not one of them dared to ask Him, "Why are you talking to her?"

The woman left her water jug forgotten on the ground. She hurried back to the village. She could hardly wait to share this wonderful news with her neighbors — those very neighbors who had treated her

so cruelly. "Come and see a man who told me everything I ever did,"
she said. "Can this be the Saviour?" They were just Samaritans, only
part Jewish, sinners every one of them, not just this one woman. But
the Holy Spirit had awakened in their hearts a longing for the Saviour.
They forgot that this woman was not fit company for decent folk. They
listened with growing excitement to what she said. They hurried to
the well. They begged Jesus to come and stay with them. He stayed
two days. Many of those despised Samaritans became Christian be-
lievers.

17
Jesus Goes to a Party

John 2:1-11

everyone loves a party — the fun, the games, the delicious
things to eat. But — perhaps you have never stopped to think about
it — the nicest thing about a party is the guests. Doing these things
alone is no fun. It is doing them with your friends that makes the day
special.

This is because you are made that way. God made you a part of a
family, not all by yourself. He made you so that you want companionship, so that you need friends. Long, long ago, in the very beginning
of things, God Himself said, "It is not good that man should live alone."

Jesus was like you in this. He was a real man, with the same needs
as you and I. He wanted companionship; He needed friends to share
His life. Jesus liked people, all kinds of people — the rich and the
poor, the educated and just plain ordinary folk like you and me. He
liked to be with them and to talk to them.

Once He went to a party. Perhaps He went to many parties, but
this one God has told us about. It was at the beginning of His work.

Jesus had been very busy. He was tired. Yes, Jesus got tired, just as you and I do. He needed rest and relaxation. And just when He needed a change, He was invited to this party.

The party was a wedding. We do not know who the bride and groom were who were so honored as to have Jesus at their wedding. They must have been friends, or relatives of His family, because His mother, Mary, was there helping to look after things.

In Palestine a girl was usually engaged to a boy for twelve months before they got married. When the wedding day finally came, the bridegroom took his friends and went to get his bride. She was waiting and she wore a crown of flowers on her head. The young people made a little procession, and they carried the bride to her new home. When they got there, there was a great feast. There was music and merry-making. Often the party lasted a whole week.

So there they all were enjoying themselves — the bride and her new husband, their young friends and Mary, and Jesus and His new disciples too. There was a Master of Ceremonies in charge of things, whom they called the Ruler of the Feast.

And then something went wrong, something threatened to spoil the fun. There were so many guests that there wasn't enough wine to go around. Mary noticed what was happening, and she turned to Jesus for help.

"There isn't enough wine," she told Him.

Jesus made a very strange answer. "Woman," He said to His mother, "what have I to do with you? It isn't my hour yet."

Perhaps Mary wanted Jesus to show who He was right now by some great sign. Jesus was reminding her that He, and He alone, must choose the time to reveal Himself. It was not time for that yet.

Do you think Mary should not have bothered Jesus about such a little thing as there not being enough wine? That is where you are wrong. Jesus is concerned about the little things in our lives as well as the big ones. He is concerned about our having fun and friends, yes, and parties too.

Mary knew this. She said to the servants, "Do whatever He tells you."

Nearby there were six big water jars standing. The water in them was used to wash the guests' hands before they ate.

"Fill the pots with water," Jesus said to the servants. They filled them right up to the top.

"Take some out now," Jesus went on, "and serve it to the Ruler of the Feast." The servants must have wondered what would happen when they served water instead of wine to the Ruler of the Feast. But they did not argue. They did as Jesus commanded.

The Ruler of the Feast tasted what was offered him. It was delicious wine. He was very much surprised, so surprised that he called the bridegroom.

"Most people," he said, "serve their best wine first, and then, when that is gone, they serve cheaper wine. But you have kept the best wine till the last."

The Ruler of the Feast did not know that Jesus had changed water into wine. The bridegroom and the bride and the guests did not know either. Only the servants and Jesus and His disciples knew what a wonderful thing had happened.

Those new disciples already knew that Jesus was the Saviour sent by God. Nathanael had even called Him the Son of God and the King of Israel. But when they saw Jesus perform this wonderful miracle, they learned something more about His power. Jesus was teaching them that He was God Himself, and that He had power to create.

This was the first miracle Jesus did. Do you know why I think He did this first? It was because He wanted us to know that we must serve Him first of all in our daily lives. You do not have to go to Africa as a missionary to serve Jesus. Perhaps some day He will call you to go to Africa. And if He does, He will give you the special rewards He has promised to all those who leave family and home for His sake. But you must not wait till that day comes to start serving Him. He wants you to love Him, and obey Him, and to enjoy Him too, right now, beginning today, at home, at school, yes, and in your play and fun, and even at your parties.

18

The Sick Child and the Heavenly Doctor

John 4:46-53

Johnnie was sick, so sick that he didn't even care that it was Saturday and all the other children were out playing. He felt hot and cold at the same time. His head ached. His throat hurt. He didn't want any breakfast.

He was so sick that Mother had called the doctor. "I don't want to see the doctor," Johnnie complained crossly. "Hush!" Mother said. "The doctor won't hurt you. He is going to make you well again."

The doctor stuck a little glass thermometer in Johnnie's mouth. He looked at Johnnie's throat, and peered into his ears with a special flashlight thing. Then the doctor plugged his stethoscope into his ears and listened to Johnnie's heart and his breathing. He took a bottle out of his bag and poured some pills into an envelope. *Take two every four hours with a full glass of water,* he wrote on the envelope. "We'll have you right as rain in a day or two," he said to Johnnie.

And sure enough! The next morning Johnnie was hungry. By afternoon he was following Mother about the house. Monday he went back to school, boasting just a little about how sick he had been. That night he said to Mother, "Maybe I'll be a doctor myself when I grow up."

There was once a doctor who didn't need any little white pills; who didn't have to listen to your heart, and look at your ears and throat to find out what was wrong; who didn't have to come to see you at all, but could make you better just by speaking a word, even though He was miles away. That, you say, would be like magic. Only it wasn't magic. For this doctor was the One who had made the whole earth. And so it should not surprise us that He could make a little boy well again just by a word. "In him," the Bible tells us, "was life." And He Himself said, "I came that they might have life."

The little boy was very sick, much sicker than Johnnie. The doctor had been called to see him, but had just shaken his head sadly and gone away again. He didn't have any medicine that would make this little boy better. Day by day the little boy grew thinner and paler and weaker. His father and mother sat helpless beside his bed. They hardly dared to meet each other's eyes. They knew in their hearts their child was going to die.

One day someone — was it a friend? or perhaps a servant? — someone told the father, "Jesus has come to Cana." The despairing father got up. He called for his horse. He left his wife watching beside his dying son. He went to look for Jesus.

How did he guess that Jesus could do what no doctor could? He was desperate, of course, ready to snatch at any straw. But there was more than this. The Holy Spirit was working the first faint tremblings of faith within his heart. And though this frantic father never dreamed it, one reason Jesus had come to Cana was because of this sick little boy.

It was about twenty miles from Capernaum, where the sick child lived, to Cana. I am sure the father rode those twenty miles as fast as his horse could go, scarcely stopping for a bite to eat or a drink of

water. And when he got to Cana, he threw himself at Jesus' feet, and begged Him, "Come with me, and heal my son, for he is at the point of death!"

Jesus heard the anguish in that prayer. He felt pity for the father's grief. We might have expected He would immediately set out for Capernaum. But He did not. For He intended to give this man something far better than he had asked for.

"You people," He said to the grief-stricken father, "do not believe in me unless you see all sorts of signs and wonders." Perhaps you think this was a strange answer to a heartbroken father's prayer. Jesus did not speak out of indifference, or even in reproach. He wanted to encourage that flickering little flame of faith in the man's heart. He wanted the father to see that it was not necessary for Jesus to go to Capernaum to lay His hand on the sick child in order to heal him. For Jesus was God Himself. He had only to speak and the child would live. And to discover this marvelous fact was even more important for this frantic father than that his little son should get well again.

"Sir," the man said pitifully, "come quickly, before my child dies." And Jesus answered, "Go home again. Your child lives." And now, wonder of wonders, the man began to understand! He believed Jesus. He trusted His promise. He turned around and started home without another word. Late that night, as he hurried towards home, he met one of his servants on the road. "I was sent to bring you news," the servant said. "Your son is going to live." Then the father asked, "When did he begin to get better?" The servant answered, "Yesterday, at one o'clock." And the father said to himself, "It was the very moment that Jesus said to me, 'Your child lives.' "

And so the little boy got better. But, more than that, the whole family learned to know their Saviour. They all became Christians.

When I was your age, I used to wish that I had lived when Jesus did, that I might have seen His face, and listened to His teaching. Perhaps you have wished the same. And then, as I grew older, I, too, learned the lesson Jesus taught that heartsick father. An ordinary doctor has to examine you before he can cure you. Not Jesus. He does not need to stand bodily beside our bed. For He is the very Son of God Himself, and He is always with us. He cares what happens to you and me, just as He cared what happened to that little boy so long ago. He knows when we are sick, and He hears our prayers. But much more. He offers us, as He offered that father, the much greater gift of salvation. And if we accept this gift in faith, nothing can harm us.

19
How Can We Recognize Him?

Luke 4:16-30

*t*he Carpenter came into the meeting hall and sat down. No one turned his head to stare at Him. That would have been improper, for this was a service to worship God. And yet His arrival caused a stir of excitement among all the assembled people.

They had known this man for thirty years. He had grown up among them. They had played with Him in the streets. They had wandered with Him through the fields and over the hills. They had sat beside Him day after day in this very hall — for this building was school as well as church.

As soon as He had finished His elementary schooling, He had become a carpenter, learning His trade from His father Joseph. For more than fifteen years now He had built their tables and chairs, repaired their fences, helped lay the roof beams of their one-room clay houses. Yes, they knew Him well.

Recently He had been gone for a short time, south, to where their great temple was, at Jerusalem. Strange stories had filtered home about Him. Some said He had cured people who were seriously sick. Others had heard that He had spent two days with the hated Samaritans, and had actually slept and eaten with these worse-than-heathen neighbors to the south.

But now He was home again. It seemed quite natural to see Him sitting there among them as He had every Sabbath since He was a little boy. Would He come forward later in the service and speak to them? Would He deny the rumors? Or perhaps even perform a miracle of healing just to satisfy their curiosity?

The service began. The congregation tried to think only about God. The leader of the synagogue got up to pray. Then the chest on the platform was opened, and from it the leader took the scroll of the law. He unwrapped it carefully — for these scrolls, which contained the Word of God, were the most precious possession of the people of Nazareth. He unrolled it, and read a few verses from the Law, one of the five books of Moses. Then he carefully replaced the scroll in the chest. He sat down on the chair on the platform and explained the meaning of the verses he had read. There was a second prayer.

Then the leader took out the scroll of one of the prophets. It was the custom for some member of the congregation to read this part of God's Word. There was an expectant hush in the building. Jesus stood up and came forward. He took the scroll and opened it to Isaiah. He read the words:

The Spirit of God is upon me. He has sent me to preach good news to the poor; to proclaim liberty to those who are captive, and new sight to the blind; to tell everybody that this is the year of the Lord.

These verses were familiar verses, for they told about the coming of the promised Saviour. Many of that congregation knew them by heart. Over and over they had prayed for this Saviour. Jesus rerolled the scroll and put it back in the chest. He sat down in the teacher's chair. The people sat attentive, wondering what He would say.

"Today," He said, "this prophecy has been fulfilled in your ears." At first they were pleased to think one of their own boys could speak with such grace. And then suddenly it dawned on them — He was claiming to be the Saviour Himself. They stared at Him, unbelieving. "Who does he think he is?" they said to each other. "This is only the carpenter, Joseph's son."

Jesus knew what they were thinking. They were His own people, and He had come to bring the message to them first of all. But He knew that if they turned away from God's Good News, God would turn away from them. And then others, men from the east and the west and the north and the south, would be gathered into the kingdom of God. "No prophet," He said sadly, "is honored in his own home town. Remember how in Elijah's days there was no rain for three years and six months. There were many widows among God's chosen people then, but Elijah was not sent to any of them, but instead to a widow in Sidon. And in the days of Elisha there were many lepers in Israel, but none of them was healed, only Naaman, the Syrian general."

Now the people were furious. How dare He speak such insults? What had been a congregation worshiping God became an angry mob. They drove Jesus out of the city. They tried to throw Him over the cliff at the edge of town. But the time had not yet come for Jesus to die. He passed right through their hands, and went on His way.

He came unto his own, and his own received him not. He offered them comfort, and liberty, and salvation. He offered them the friendship of God Himself. And they turned it down. They had prayed for a Saviour, but when the Saviour came, they did not recognize Him. They tried to murder Him instead.

And you and I? Do we recognize Him? Or do we, like those unhappy people of Nazareth, turn our backs on the Gift of God? Perhaps you ask, "How can we know for certain this is our Saviour?" There is only one way to be sure. Only the Holy Spirit speaking to your heart can give you this certainty. And where can you get the Holy Spirit? You pray for Him, pray humbly, pray earnestly. And if, when you are hungry, your mother gives you a sandwich, not a stone, how much more will your Father in heaven give His Holy Spirit to all who ask Him! This is the promise of Jesus, our Saviour.

20
Turned Upside Down

Luke 5:1-10

*t*he best time to catch fish is after the sun has gone down. During the heat of the day the fish lie quiet in the deeper water. But as it begins to get dark, they come up to the shallower water to feed.

And so it was dark when my partners and I, Peter, pushed our boats out from the shore. We were not fishing for fun; fishing was our work. We sold the fish we caught to provide the things our families needed.

We had not been working as regularly lately as we usually did. Somehow, earning a living had not seemed as important as it used to. Has it ever happened to you that things in your life seemed to turn upside down? That what you thought was most important no longer seemed to matter? That something else which you had hardly ever thought about before became the most important thing of all?

But I started to tell you about that night. It was like many other nights, as any fisherman can tell you. We shoved our boat off from the shore. We took off our outer clothes, so as to be ready to work. We threw our net into the water on one side of the boat. After a short wait, we hauled it in again. The net was empty. We threw it out again, this time on the other side of the boat. We waited, and hauled it in again. It was still empty.

We moved the boat and tried once more, first on this side, then on the other side. No fish this time either. But fishermen are used to this. They do not get discouraged easily. A lot of fishing is just waiting patiently. If you cannot wait, you will not catch many fish. So we kept on trying. The stars came up, grew bright above our heads. And then, as the night wore on, they grew dim again, and the first morning light glimmered in the east.

At last we gave up. The night's work was a failure, so it seemed. And yet it turned out not to be a failure after all. But I am getting ahead of myself.

We ran our boats up on the beach and took out the nets to wash them and to look for broken places. As we sat there, not talking much because we were discouraged, we heard a sound in the distance. We could not be sure just what it was. And then, as it grew louder, we saw a great crowd of people coming toward the lake, and ahead of them walked the new Teacher.

The Teacher was not a stranger to us. He had been teaching nearby for some time. But there was something about Him that was different from other teachers. My brother, Andrew, and my partner, John, had even spent a night with Him at His house. They had talked a long time that night, and the next day Andrew had introduced me to Him. It was the Teacher who had given me my new name, the name by which I was always known later on. He called me Peter, which means *rock*. I did not know what it was the Teacher saw in me that made Him choose this name, but I did know that when He looked at me He saw right into my heart. He knew my thoughts, and all my feelings too.

We had talked a great deal about this Teacher among ourselves since that day. Sometimes we left our fishing to listen to His words. We wondered if He could possibly be the Saviour God had promised so long ago.

This morning, as He came toward us on the beach, there was a great crowd of people following Him. Those who were on the outside pressed in so as to hear Him better, but those who were near Him would not give up their place. I thought for a moment He would be crushed in the middle. He came down the beach and got into my boat.

"Row out a little way," He said to me. So I rowed out a few yards, and He sat there in my boat and talked to the people on the beach. And I sat there beside Him and listened to the things He said. I thought that I could never hear enough. It was as if I had been thirsty for a long, long time and had suddenly found a wonderful well of water.

I do not know how long He talked, but at last He said to me, "Pull out a little further, and we will catch some fish."

"Master," I answered, "we fished all night, and caught nothing. But if You say so, we will try again." So I rowed the boat out and let down a net. But I knew well enough you can't catch fish in the heat of the early morning.

But when I tried to pull the net back up, it was so full of fish I thought it would break. I called excitedly to my partners, James and John, to come with their boat. When at last we got the net in, our two boats were so heavy with fish that they were at the point of sinking.

And then a great conviction flooded into my heart. Only the power of God Himself could have brought that great multitude of fish into my net. This was indeed God's Saviour. And who was I to be in the same boat with the Saviour?

I felt terrified. I remembered all the wicked things I had ever done. I fell down at His feet, and I cried out, "I am not fit to be near You, Lord; I am a great sinner." He spoke to me reassuringly. "Do not be afraid," He said. "From now on you are going to catch men, not fish."

Yes, that was how it happened. That was how my whole life was turned upside down. Before this I had wanted to work hard, to make a little money, to get ahead in the world. Now I no longer cared about these things. I knew I could trust all this to Him. He would provide whatever was needed, just as He had provided the fish that very morning. The one thing I wanted now, more than anything else,

was to follow Him. I wanted to hear more of those wonderful words, to satisfy my thirst with more of that wonderful water. I wanted God's Son to become my Saviour.

21
Jesus Binds the Strong One

Mark 1:21-34

Don't look now, but there is someone close behind you. Behind you, and above you, and beside you. It is your angel, the one appointed by God Himself to care for you, to carry your needs up to God, and to bring God's grace and loving protection down to you.

You cannot see him with your eyes, for he is a spirit who has no body. Only on rare occasions does God roll back the veil that hides from us the spirit world. And when He does, then we see an angel leading Lot and his family by the hand to bring them out of Sodom before the fire and brimstone fell. We see an angel showing Hagar the well of water that will save young Ishmael's life. We see an angel carrying a live coal from the altar to cleanse Isaiah's lips. We see Elisha's servant standing with open mouth as he stares at the angels of God, ranged rank on rank, to protect God's prophet. We see an angel carrying the soul of dead Lazarus to Abraham's bosom. We see an angel touching the chains of Peter in prison, and Peter standing up free. Yes, the air around us is filled with spirits we cannot see. Not all of them are friendly, of course. Some of them are demons. But we do not need to be afraid of the demons either. And that is why I want to tell you a special story today.

Long, long ago, before God made the earth, and hung the sun and moon in the sky, God made the angels. The angels were servants of God, messengers. They watched Him working, and they sang His praise. But among their great ranks there was one who did not wish to be a servant. Satan rebelled against the loving rule of God. He persuaded other angels to join in his revolt. And so Satan and all his followers were thrown out of heaven. They were separated from God — and there is no more terrible punishment than this, for God is the only source of joy, and light, and love.

Then God created man. Satan could not bear to see the man walking and talking with God. Somehow he must separate them. Then he would have the man as company in the lonely, dark hell where he now lived. If he could not be happy himself, he did not want anyone else to be happy either.

I am sure you remember the story of how he disguised himself as a snake, and by his lies persuaded Adam and Eve to disobey God. When Eve bit into that forbidden fruit, Satan must have known a moment of devilish triumph. But it was hardly more than a moment. For that very evening God promised Satan's final doom: "Some day a child of the woman will crush your head, Satan, even though for now you may bite his heel."

For hundreds of years the children of Adam and Eve longed and prayed for the coming of the promised Saviour. But Satan trembled at the very thought. When Jesus was born, Satan might have given up in despair, but he did not. Instead, he unleashed fresh outbursts of devilish fury. He tempted Jesus Himself to give up the path of suffering for our salvation. And upon men, too, the devil loosed new attacks.

And so it happened that, during the life of Jesus on earth, we find men in whom Satan made his home. Never asking whether or not these poor persons wished to have a guest like this, the devil simply took over their lives. He screamed from their mouths. He drove them away from friends and family to live in caves, or even among the tombs. He compelled them to tear off their clothing, and even to shatter to pieces the chains with which their friends tried to confine them. These unhappy victims we call demon-possessed.

At the time of our story it is the Sabbath morning. Jesus is staying with Peter and Andrew in Capernaum. They go together to the synagogue, and Jesus gets up to read the Bible and explain it. His listeners are amazed at His preaching. For He teaches as if the words come straight from God.

Suddenly there is a commotion in the audience. A man stands up right in the middle of the service, and he (or, rather, the demon who had taken possession of him) cries out, "What have we to do with You, Jesus from Nazareth? Have You come to destroy us? I know who You are, the Holy One of God!" The synagogue officials hurry forward to get this man out of the building. But before they can seize him, Jesus speaks to the demon: "Be quiet, and come out of him." The demon, in his fury, convulses the man, and throws him down. But he cannot resist the power of Jesus. With a loud cry the demon flees, leaving the man well and whole. Everyone is amazed. "Who is this miracle-worker?" they say. "He commands even the evil spirits, and they obey him!" The story spreads like wildfire through the city.

That evening, after the sun has set and the Sabbath rest is over, the people of the whole city crowd around Peter's house. They bring to Jesus all those who are sick, and all those possessed by demons. And Jesus heals them all.

76

Yes, He had come to bind the strong one, our great enemy, the devil, and He did exactly this. It was not easy to bind Satan, and to rescue those whom Satan had enslaved. Jesus had to die to do it; it cost Him his very life. And so, when Satan whispers in your ear, when he tempts you to join him in his rebellion against God, remember this story. For God has set it down in His Word so that you and I can always know for sure that God is stronger than the devil, and that Jesus conquered Satan for us when He died so long ago.

22
What Does a Paralyzed Man Want Most?

Luke 5:17-26

Susie was a tomboy — perhaps because she had no sisters, but only three brothers to play with. Susie did not care for dolls. But she could run faster, jump further, and climb higher trees than any boy she knew.

It was the trees that got her into trouble. "Do be more careful, Susie," Mother had said over and over. Susie did not mean to disobey. It was just that she and Mother had different ideas about what being careful meant when it came to climbing trees. And that is how she came to be in the doctor's office that lovely spring afternoon, where the doctor wound row after row of gauze around her leg, and added layer after layer of plaster.

At first Susie's broken leg was the center of attention at school. All the children signed her cast. They even quarreled about who was to carry her books. But after school, when everyone else went to the park, Susie sat at home alone, day after day. One day she threw her crutches on the floor. "Hateful old things!" she said. Mother looked at her thoughtfully.

"You know, Susie," she said, "nothing happens to a child of God by accident. Have you thought at all what Jesus might be trying to teach you by this broken leg?"

"What could I learn from a horrid pair of crutches?" Susie answered.

"Perhaps Jesus is trying to stretch your heart."

"Stretch my heart?" Susie stared at her Mother. "Yes," Mother said, "so that there will be room in it for someone else besides Susie. Perhaps He wants you to sit still a little while to think about other people. There are some people, you know, who have to walk on crutches all their lives, and some who cannot walk at all."

"How awful!" Susie said. And to herself she thought, "Never to be able to climb a tree again! How could I stand it?" And then her conscience whispered to her, "And how do you think they stand it? They have feelings too, just like yours."

Mother came and sat down by her daughter. "Let me tell you a story," she said, "about a man like that. This man was paralyzed. He could not move at all.

"This all happened long ago, when Jesus was on earth. I do not know how long this man had been paralyzed. But I do not think he had been born that way. He could remember what it was like to walk and run and play. And that made it all the harder. Long ago this man had given up all hope. He knew he was going to have to lie on this bed until he died.

"And yet God had not forgotten this man. God had sent him a special gift. He had given the paralyzed man four friends. These friends could all walk and run and jump. But somehow they understood what it was like to be paralyzed. Perhaps sometime or other God had made them sit down to think what it was like not to be able to walk and to work. And because of that, they had room in their hearts for the paralyzed man.

"They came to see him, I suppose, and they brought him news, and perhaps even little presents. And sometimes they must have taken him with them different places.

"And then they heard about Jesus. 'He has healed so many,' one of them said. 'Perhaps He can even heal our friend.' The sick man was not hopeful. 'It is just money thrown away,' he said gloomily. 'No man can cure me.'

" 'This one does not ask for money,' his friend replied. 'He must be someone specially sent by God to help us, I think. Only God could do the things He does.' And so they encouraged each other and the sick man.

"The four of them picked up the sick man's bed, each holding one corner, and they went to look for Jesus. But when they came to the house where our Saviour was, there was such a crowd already there that they could not even get near the front door. But this did not stop them. There was a staircase on the outside of the house, which went up to the flat rooftop. Up this staircase the four friends carried the sick man, walking carefully so as not to drop him. They put him down on the roof, and then they set to work to lift up the roof tiles one by one. As soon as they had a hole that was big enough, they tied a rope to each corner of the sick man's bed, and they slowly let him down through the hole, right in front of Jesus.

"Jesus looked at the man, and saw how much he wanted to be able to walk again. He even saw something the man needed much more but did not realize himself. 'My child,' Jesus said, 'be of good cheer. Your sins have been forgiven.'

"Does this seem to you a strange thing to say? Let me tell you something. When God stops you in your work, or in your play, and makes you sit down to think a bit, then you remember all the things you have ever done that are wrong. You have forgotten God so often! Can you expect Him to remember you now? This is what you ask yourself. And so the paralyzed man did not say to Jesus, 'But I want to walk again.' No, he was so happy to know he had been forgiven, and that God loved him, that for a moment he even forgot that he was paralyzed.

"The other men, who were sitting in that room, said angrily, 'Only God can forgive sins!' But Jesus answered, 'I will prove to you that I have the right to forgive sins.' Then he turned to the sick man and said, 'Pick up your bed, and go home.' And instantly this man, who had not left that bed for so many years, stood up, rolled up his bed, and carried it home."

23
Levi, the Tax Collector

Luke 5:27-32

Levi was a tax collector. He sat by the side of the road in his little toll booth. Maybe you have seen such a booth if you have ridden on one of the new superhighways. These roads are wide; there are two lanes of traffic going in each direction, with a strip of grass and trees between them. There are no crossroads and no traffic lights. You can drive very fast. But presently you come to a sign that says SLOW — TOLL STATION AHEAD. There the toll collector sits in his little house. There is a sign on the side that tells you how much the toll is for a car, how much for a truck or a bus, and how much for a trailer.

"Good morning," the collector says as he takes your money and hands you your change. "Have a nice trip." And then you drive on.

But there was no sign about the amount of the toll on Levi's booth. Nor did he greet the passers-by with courteous words. For Levi was a tax collector for the hated Roman conquerors. The Romans did not collect the taxes themselves. They farmed the work out to Jewish contractors, who collected the taxes on shares. No one told Levi how much toll he could collect. The more he collected, the more there was left for his own pocket after he had paid the Romans their share. And though the Romans did not set the tax rate, the Roman army, with the might of its cruel, armed fist, stood behind that little toll booth along the road. Levi did not dare to offend the rich and powerful. But he took advantage of the poor man who had no influential friends to help him. Levi was a rich man, but his money had come out of the pockets of the poor and the unfortunate who passed by his booth. No one — unless it was the Roman rulers themselves — was more hated than Levi and his fellow tax collectors. After all, he was little better than a thief.

And then something strange happened to Levi, something hardly to be believed, something that changed his whole life. As he sat in his little tollhouse, he saw a crowd approaching. He could guess who they were. This must be the new Teacher everyone was talking about, the one who said such startling things and did such almost-unbelievable deeds. It was not likely that Levi would get a close look at Him. The Teacher would not want to dirty Himself by passing near such a sinner as Levi was.

But this Teacher was not like other teachers. He did not seem to be afraid of Levi's bad reputation. He did not seem to hate him as other decent folk did. He stopped right outside the toll booth. He looked at Levi with a look that pierced to his very soul, a look Levi never forgot. There was love in that look, and compassion, and a promise of help. But the words He spoke were very simple.

"Follow me," was all He said. And Levi stood up as if in a spell and followed the Teacher. He left behind the tollhouse and his chance of becoming richer still. He left behind his wicked and thieving way of life. He did not really understand yet, but somehow he knew that this Man could help him. More than anything else in the world, Levi wanted to be near Him, to listen to His words, and to please Him in whatever he did.

Have you seen that look of Jesus that Levi saw, that look of love and understanding and help? Have you heard that call, "Follow me!"? If you have not, it is because your eyes and ears are not really open. For Jesus is looking at you right now with the same look that Levi saw. He is calling you, too, right now. "Follow me," He is saying. If, like Levi, you get up and leave your sinful life and follow Him, you, like Levi, will find that your whole life is changed.

This thing that happened to Levi was so wonderful that he could not keep it to himself. He planned a big party, and he invited all his friends to meet his new Master. Oh, yes, Levi had lots of friends. But they were not the kind of friends most people wanted. They were the bums, the crooks, the riffraff of the town — and other tax collectors. But if Jesus was willing and able to help Levi, perhaps He could help these people too.

The Jewish leaders, the scribes and Pharisees, saw Jesus and His disciples going into Levi's house. They themselves would never have dreamed of entering that house, of going through that door. For the very fact that Levi did business with the heathen Romans made him so filthy in their eyes that he was not fit company for any good Jew.

"How can you lower yourselves," they asked the disciples, "by eating and drinking with people you know are tax collectors and other

sinners?" The scribes and the Pharisees were very proud of their pure way of life. They kept all the commandments carefully, but they had forgotten the heart of God's law, the command to love God and their neighbor.

Jesus answered for His disciples. He knew that the scribes and Pharisees were sinners, just like Levi and his friends. He knew that they needed a Saviour just as much. But while Levi and his friends knew they were sinners and needed help, the scribes and Pharisees thought they were good. They had no use for a Saviour.

"Healthy people don't need a doctor," Jesus said. "Sick people do. I came to save sinners, not good people." And then He gave the scribes and Pharisees something to think about. "God says," He reminded them, "that sacrifices are not enough. He requires mercy and love."

If it sometimes seems to you that you are not such a great sinner after all, that you are really pretty good, it is because, like the scribes and Pharisees, you are looking just at the outside. Sure, you go to church and Sunday school, you say your prayers. But take a good look at your heart. Do you really love God and the people around you? Or are you out first of all for your own advantage? When you really see the selfishness and willfulness of your own heart, then you will feel your desperate need of a Saviour, as Levi did. You cannot change yourself. But if you listen to the call of Jesus, and follow Him, He will change your whole life, as He changed Levi's.

24

The Pool at Bethesda

John 5:2-24

It was the Sabbath day, but that did not mean much to the sick man. He could not go with the crowds to the temple. He could not pray to God while the sacrifice was being offered. He could not stand to receive the blessing of the priest. For a man who lies always on a bed, the Sabbath is much like any other day.

For most people a bed is a place for dreams and pleasant rest. But for him it was a prison. Thirty-eight years he had lain day and night on this hard mattress. It is true, he could crawl a few feet if he had to, but it was slow and painful work. Mostly he just lay there, sunk deep in despair.

Every day someone brought the sick man to this porch beside the pool at Bethesda. There were five porches around the pool, and they were crowded with sick people. Some were blind; some were lame; some, like the man on the mattress, were paralyzed. There was a story about the pool. Every once in a while the waters bubbled and gurgled. Whoever got into the water first would be cured of his illness. Many long hours the paralyzed man had watched for the bubbling. Many times he had struggled to crawl into the water. But someone else, someone who could move faster than he, or someone who had a friend to help him, always got there first. Now he no longer tried. He had lost all hope of ever getting well.

Today there was a visitor walking through the porches around the pool. That was not surprising. It was feast time, and Jerusalem was crowded with visitors. But not many of them ever came to the pool. The crowd of sick and crippled people was not a pretty sight.

Perhaps the stranger had a friend in one of the porches. But no, He did not pause. He came straight to the side of the paralyzed man.

He stood there looking down at his withered body, at the despairing look on his face.

"Do you want to get well again?" He asked him. The man on the mattress felt a wild hope. This man was different from the others. Perhaps He would stay until the water bubbled up again. Perhaps He would help him get into the pool in time.

"I have no one to help me get into the water," the paralyzed man answered. "While I am trying to get there, someone else steps in ahead of me."

The Stranger brushed aside this talk of the pool and the bubbling water. He looked at the man with a strange look, a look of love and pity, and at the same time a look of command.

"Get up," the Stranger said. "Pick up your bed and walk!" At that very moment, wonder of wonders, it happened. The paralyzed man felt new blood, new life, new strength in his half-dead body. Stumbling in amazement, he got to his feet. He rolled up his mattress, lifted it to his shoulder, and set out for home in a daze. He forgot even to ask the Man's name.

He had not gone far before he was stopped by some of the Jewish leaders. They did not praise God that a man who had been sick so long was suddenly well. No, they spoke to him angrily. "Don't you know it is the Sabbath?" they said to him. "It is against the law to carry anything on the Sabbath."

"The man who healed me told me to carry my bed home," he answered.

"Who was it that dared tell you to break the law?" the Jewish leaders asked. The man could not answer this. He did not know who it was.

But you and I know who it was. Only Jesus can heal with a word. He can give life to whomever He wishes, because He is the powerful Son of God.

Later Jesus found the man in the temple.

"You have been made well," Jesus said to him. "Show your gratitude to God by living a life pleasing to Him."

When the Jews found out that it was Jesus who had healed a man on the Sabbath, and had commanded him to carry his bed through the streets, they were angry with Him.

"Men are supposed to rest on the Sabbath," Jesus told the Jews. "But God, who is my Father, works on the Sabbath, and so I work too." This made the Jews even angrier, because now Jesus claimed to be equal to God. This, they thought, was a worse sin than breaking the Sabbath.

But Jesus was not stopped by their anger. He had something to offer them, something to offer you and me too, something the Jewish leaders needed far more than the paralyzed man needed to be able to walk, something much more precious than health and strength.

"I do not do anything by myself," Jesus told the Jews. "I do what my Father tells me to do. Everyone who hears my words, and believes him who sent me, will live forever. As soon as he trusts in me, he has already passed from death to life." Jesus was talking about the new heart, the new life that He gives to all who trust in Him, who walk in His ways.

Even though you are young and strong and well, you cannot know what it is like to be really alive unless you listen to these words of Jesus. You see, God is the only source of life. And He gives this true, this lasting life only to those who trust in the life and death of Jesus. If God gives you this life, even death itself cannot take it away from you. God does not promise that you will have an easy life, that you will never have any trouble or sickness. But He does promise that nothing will ever separate you from the love and fellowship of Jesus, that wonderful fellowship with God Himself, which is what you were created for.

25

We Share the Rest of God

Luke 6:1-11

It was the afternoon of the Sabbath. What do you do on Sunday afternoon? Jesus and His friends were taking a walk. They were walking in the country, through the fields where the ripening grain was growing. This seems simple enough. But it was not so simple as it seems. You see, the Jews had rules about taking walks on the Sabbath. There were hundreds of rules altogether about what you might and might not do on God's day. One of them was about walks. Inside the city limits you could walk as far as you wished. But in the country you must not walk more than half a mile. If you did, you committed a sin. This was not God's law. God had commanded, from the mountain of Sinai, that His people must keep the Sabbath holy. It was the Jewish teachers who had decided it was a sin to walk more than half a mile in the country.

So when Jesus and His friends stepped through the city gates, when they left the crooked, stony streets of the city behind them, they laid themselves open to suspicion. And, what is more, they were noticed. Some of the Pharisees, the Jewish leaders, saw them set out. They followed, not because they wanted to listen to what Jesus had to say, not because they were willing to give Him a fair hearing. They followed because they hated Jesus. They were hoping Jesus would break the Sabbath rules, so that they could bring an accusation against Him.

Jesus paid no attention to the Pharisees who followed them. It was very peaceful and beautiful in the country. He and His friends could talk much better here than on the busy city streets. As they went along the disciples picked some of the ears of the golden wheat. They rubbed out the grains, put them in their mouth, and ate them.

Immediately the Pharisees sprang forward. This was just what they had been hoping for. "It is against the law," they said, "to pick and eat grain on the Sabbath."

"You are quite mistaken," Jesus said, "about the true meaning of the Sabbath. And there is another, even more serious mistake you are making. You do not understand that I am the Lord of the Sabbath."

This made the Pharisees very angry. How could they be mistaken about the true meaning of the Sabbath? Had they not studied the Sabbath law very hard and very long? Had they not set up hundreds and hundreds of rules about the Sabbath? Yes, they had. That was just the trouble. They thought that if they had enough rules, and obeyed them all, they could earn their own salvation. Oh, they thought they were wonderfully good people! They had no idea how far short they fell of really loving God with all their heart, and soul, and mind.

The true meaning of God's day is just the opposite of this. Do you remember the verse in the hymnbook that goes like this:

> *Not what my hands have done*
> *Can save my guilty soul?*

That is the true meaning of the Sabbath. On Sunday we stop our hands from working as a sign that nothing we do ourselves can really help us. On Sunday we remember that God has done it all, that He has paid the price, the very costly price, of our salvation; that He alone has rescued us from the hopeless slavery of sin.

That is what Jesus was talking about when He said that He was Lord of the Sabbath. But the Jews did not understand what He meant. The next Sabbath Jesus gave them an example of His Lordship. This happened on a Sabbath morning. Jesus had gone to the synagogue. There was a man there whose right hand was withered and useless. Once more the Jewish leaders watched Jesus. Once more they hoped He would heal the crippled man — not because they were sorry for the man — but because they wanted the chance to accuse Him of breaking the Sabbath.

"Stand up here," Jesus said to the man. Then He spoke to the watching Pharisees: "Which is allowed on the Sabbath, to do good, or to do harm?" The Pharisees did not answer. Jesus made it even plainer: "Which is allowed on the Sabbath, to save a man, or to destroy him?" Then He said to the crippled man, "Stretch out your hand." And the man stretched out his hand, and in that very instant it was healed, as good as new. The Pharisees were filled with fury. They plotted together how they could get rid of Jesus.

I do not suppose that you were born with a withered hand. But both you and I were born with something much worse, and that is a withered soul. The healing of the man's withered hand on the Sabbath was a sign that Jesus, the Lord of the Sabbath, can heal withered souls as well as withered hands. But the Pharisees could not read this sign.

Can you read the signs God sends you? Sunday is one of those signs. Every week, over and over again, you stop your work and go to church and Sunday school. Every week God is reminding you that you cannot save yourself, but that Jesus can and will save you if you trust in Him.

Perhaps this week has been a bad one for you. You have been disappointed, or worried, or lonely. You have made a mess of things, when you meant to do so well. You have lost your temper, said sharp things, neglected to help at home. Then Sunday is just the day for you.

It was for people just like you that God set up this special day. You can lay all your problems, all your struggles with your own sinful heart, at Jesus' feet.

There is another verse in the hymnbook which says what I am trying to tell you:

> *While we pray for pardoning grace,*
> *Through the dear Redeemer's Name,*
> *Show thy reconciléd face;*
> *Take away our sin and shame;*
> *From our earthly cares set free,*
> *May we rest this day in Thee.*

26
Not Worthy, Lord!

Matthew 8:5-13

*T*here was no one the Jews hated more than their Roman masters. Roman soldiers marched in the streets of Jerusalem. The Jews watched them with hatred in their hearts. Romans made the laws the Jews had to obey. The Romans collected the taxes the poor could hardly pay, and carried the money off to Rome to support the emperor. The Jews submitted, but with bitterness and anger. Yes, there was bitter hatred between the Jews and their Roman conquerors.

But there was one exception. This exception was a centurion in the city of Capernaum. He was an officer in the Roman army, with about a hundred soldiers serving under his command. The centurion was an unusual man. He did not insult and mock the Jews he met, for he had learned to love the Jewish people. He became interested in their worship of the one true God, and he even built a synagogue for them with his own money.

The centurion had a slave; and here was something else that was surprising. For the centurion loved his slave — a slave, mind you, who had no rights at all, whom his master could have tortured or even killed if he had wished, without answering to anyone. He loved this slave. Yes, the centurion was a most unusual man.

One day the slave suddenly became sick. He was dreadfully sick, in great pain, and at the point of death. The centurion was grief-stricken, but he did not despair. For he had heard of the wonderful new Teacher, the one who taught such startling things, and who performed such wonderful miracles of healing. It was plain that this Teacher was sent from God, for only the power of God could perform such miracles. The centurion was convinced of this. But would the Teacher heal a slave — the slave of a hated Roman centurion?

The centurion was determined to try. He knew he was not worthy of a miracle. He was not even worthy, he felt, to appear before the Teacher, the one who had God's power. He asked the Jewish elders of the synagogue to go for him. And they were glad to go. The centurion had done so many kind things for them.

The Jewish elders came to Jesus. They told Him about the centurion, and how he loved the Jewish people and had even built a synagogue for them. They told Jesus about the slave who was so sick, and how much the centurion loved him. Jesus said, "I will come and heal him." And so He set out. But before He got to the centurion's house, another message arrived. It was also from the centurion.

"I am not worthy, Lord," the centurion said, "that You should come into my house. And You do not need to trouble Yourself to come, either. For if You just say the word, my servant will be healed. It is with You as with the emperor in Rome. He does not need to come to Capernaum to see that his orders are obeyed. He just issues his commands, and my soldiers and I obey. You are much more powerful than the emperor. You have only to command, and You will be obeyed."

Jesus was amazed that a Roman soldier, a man who had grown up as a heathen, should show such faith in His power.

"I have not found anyone among the Jews who shows such faith!" He said. These words did not please the Jews. They were proud of being God's chosen people. They thought God's love was only for themselves. But Jesus could see into their hearts. He knew that many of them expected to get into heaven simply because they were Abraham's descendants. They had forgotten that God had promised that *all* nations should be blessed in Abraham.

"I tell you," Jesus said to them, "that many shall come from the north and the south, the east and the west, the far corners of the earth, and shall sit down with Abraham in God's kingdom, because they trust in me. Many of the Jews who ought to be there because they have been brought up in God's way are going to be thrown out because they do not trust in me."

Then He turned to the messengers of the centurion.

"Go home," He said. "As your master has believed, so will it be done unto him." The centurion's slave was healed at that very hour.

Do you ever feel, as that centurion did, that you are not worthy Jesus should come to you, to your house, even to your heart? If this is the way you feel, you have found out the truth. Not one of us is worthy of the love of Jesus. But you must not stop there. Because, you see, Jesus loved us even though we were unworthy. He loved us enough to die for our sins.

It is a great blessing to be brought up in a Christian home, to go to a Christian church. But this will not get you into heaven. To be saved, you must have what the centurion had — you must have faith in the power of Jesus, faith most of all in His death for your sake.

Many Shall Come from the North and the South

Acts 8:26-40

*T*he road from Jerusalem to Egypt runs west at first, crossing a series of low mountain ranges; and then, when it reaches the coastal plain, it turns south, just behind the sand dunes, a mile or two from the shore of the Great Sea. It is a lonely road. There is no inn here where the traveler may spend the night; no, not even a peasant's hut where you could take refuge from one of the sudden, wild Mediterranean storms. Nothing but the great mound of broken stones, once the powerful Philistine city of Gaza, but now the home only of the wild jackals, whose weird laughter chills the traveler's blood at night.

Here, in this forsaken spot, two men met, it seemed by chance. And yet no meeting could have been less accidental than this one. You might say that these two men, who were strangers to each other, had been preparing for this meeting for years. You might even say they had been born for this very purpose, that one day, when they were both well along in years, they should meet each other on this lonely stretch of road.

One of the men was an Ethiopian. He was a man of importance in the kingdom of Candace, Queen of Ethiopia, hundreds of miles south of here, in the heart of the wild continent of Africa. His preparation for this meeting started as far back at least as the family in which he was born, the education his parents gave him, the boys and girls he played with, the faithful way he performed the first small tasks assigned to him, until he rose gradually, task by task, and year by year, to his present position of responsibility as treasurer of all the queen's realm. In all these years of training and preparation, he never dreamed that what he was getting ready for was this unexpected meeting on the road near ruined Gaza.

The country he lived in was a heathen country. The queen he served imagined she was the daughter of the sun. But someone in that heathen country — God alone knows who it was — someone taught this man about the true God. And that precious knowledge was the most important part of all his preparation for this meeting. He was not a Jew, and he could not even become a converted Jew, according to Jewish law. But the Holy Spirit was at work in his heart. He went faithfully to Jerusalem to worship the one true God in the temple there. He was on his way home from such a pilgrimage right now.

The man he met came from the north. He was a Jew by birth, but he, too, was a stranger in Jerusalem. He had been born and had grown up in one of the Jewish colonies in Greece. His father and mother talked Greek at home, and it was Greek he learned to read in school. This, too, was to prepare him for that meeting in the desert. Like the Ethiopian from the south, this Greek Jew from the north came to Jerusalem regularly to worship and to attend the great religious feasts. Perhaps the two men had stood side by side in the temple more than once, but they had never met. They did not dream that God had intertwined their lives.

Philip — for that was the name of the man from the north — was present, I suppose, on the great day of Pentecost when the Holy Spirit came down from heaven with the sound of a rushing wind and with tongues of flaming fire. He may even have been one of the three thousand who were baptized that day. At any rate, he was one of the early converts to the new church, and from the beginning he stood out from the others by his wisdom and his devotion to God.

At present he was preaching the good news about Jesus in Samaria, preaching with great fervor, and hundreds were turning to God. And then, in the very middle of this fruitful ministry, an angel of God said to Philip, "Leave Samaria. Take the road south, to the ruined city of Gaza."

Philip might well have answered, "Lord, these young converts need me. I cannot leave right now. And what good is a preacher on that lonely stretch of road, where there are only wild beasts to listen to his

words?" But Philip did not say this. For he was a man who had yielded his whole life to the guidance of the Holy Spirit. When God spoke to him, he obeyed.

The Ethiopian was sitting in his chariot. In his hands he held a precious possession. It was a scroll of the prophet Isaiah, translated into Greek. Those were not days of printed books so cheap that even a poor man could own a Bible. Only a rich man could own such a scroll. Perhaps the queen's treasurer had bought it just now in Jerusalem. And so eager was he to learn what God had to say to him that he could not wait to get home to read it! As he drove along this lonely road he scanned the letters written laboriously by hand on the parchment, and he spelled out the words aloud, trying to make sense out of what he read.

Philip saw him coming. The Holy Spirit said to Philip, "Go and join this man." So Philip ran up to him. He heard that the man was reading Isaiah. And Greek was Philip's native language! "Do you understand what you are reading?" Philip asked him.

"How can I unless someone explains it to me?" the man answered. "Come up and sit with me in the chariot." So Philip climbed into the chariot. The verse the man was reading was this: "He was led as a sheep to the slaughter; as a lamb before his shearers is dumb, so he opened not his mouth." Yes, in the amazing providence of God, this man had opened his scroll to the very words which describe the death of our Saviour. Philip explained it all to him, teaching him about the free salvation Jesus bought for all who trust in Him. The man drank in the words with hungry ears.

Presently they came to a little stream. "Look," said the Ethiopian, "here is water. Why cannot I be baptized?" So they stopped the chariot, and went down into the stream, and then and there Philip baptized him. He dipped him beneath the water as a sign that this man too, who came from a land far to the south, shared in the death of Jesus. And as the man stood up again, the drops of water dripping from his head and his clothes, he was happy to know that he now also shared in the wonderful, unending life of Jesus.

Immediately after the baptism, the Holy Spirit caught Philip away to Azotus, to preach the gospel there. The queen's treasurer never saw him again, but he was not left alone. The Holy Spirit came into his heart, to teach and to direct him. He went back to Ethiopia, rejoicing all the way. Some say he became a missionary himself in that heathen land. We cannot know for sure, but we can be certain that we will see him some day ourselves at the marriage feast of the Lamb, and then perhaps he will tell us the rest of his story.

28

Jesus Interrupts a Funeral

Luke 7:11-23

*t*he procession wound slowly through the streets of the little town. There was no gay music to keep step to; there were no watching crowds to cheer as the marchers passed by. For this was a funeral procession.

In front walked the mother whose son had died. She had no close relatives to walk beside her and comfort her in her sorrow. Her husband had died some time ago, and now her only child was dead too. She walked alone, and as she walked she shed bitter tears, tears of loneliness and of fear. "What, what will become of me?" she thought, "now that my whole family is gone, and I am left all alone?"

Behind her, her neighbors carried the body of her dead son on a stretcher. Back of them her friends and fellow townsmen followed in respectful silence. And last of all the paid mourners came, wailing and lamenting loudly, as was the custom.

They were approaching the end of their sad journey. Ahead of them was the city gate, and outside, the cemetery.

From the outside another procession approached the city gate. These people were travelers; probably they hoped to spend the night at the town inn. A teacher walked at the head of this procession, and behind him came his students. Following them was a great crowd of interested and curious people.

At the city gate the two processions met. It would have been proper for the Teacher and His followers to stand aside and let the funeral pass first. Even today you and I stop our cars to let a funeral procession pass by. But this Teacher never did what people expected.

Instead He stepped forward. He went up to the weeping mother. "Do not cry any more," He said. The mother stared at Him in as-

tonishment. How could she help crying when there was nothing left to hope for in all the world?

The Teacher did not stop to explain. Instead He turned to the men who were carrying the dead body. He laid His hand on the stretcher. The carriers stood still now, and they, too, stared at the Teacher. No one ever interfered with a funeral! It showed a lack of proper respect for the grieving family.

But the Teacher was not speaking to them. He was speaking to the dead body. "Young man," He said, "get up!" Now the people really had something to stare at. For so powerful was this Teacher's word that the dead body did exactly what He told it to. The dead young man sat up and began to talk. Jesus took him by the hand, helped him off the stretcher, and gave him back to his mother.

You see, Jesus came because He loved us, because He pitied our unhappiness. He came to bring us life.

And what did the crowd do now? At first they did just what you would do if you saw a dead man sit up in his coffin and begin to talk. They shook with fear. And suddenly it dawned on them that this was the power of God Himself speaking to them. They began to praise God.

"God has remembered us," they said to each other. "He has sent us the Saviour He promised."

Many miles to the south there was a man in prison. This was John the Baptist, the one who came to prepare the way for Jesus. King Herod had thrown him into the dungeon because he dared to criticize the way Herod was living. John did not complain because he was bound in the dark cell. He was quite ready and willing to suffer for his convictions. But he was troubled about Jesus. Jesus did not seem to be bringing the judgment of the wicked that John had expected. He began to wonder.

He sent his friends to Jesus. The friends arrived soon after the young man had been raised from the dead. "John the Baptist has sent us," they said to Jesus. "He wants to know, 'Are You the One that was promised? Or must we look for someone else?'"

So often you and I, like John, have our own ideas about how Jesus ought to act, what He ought to do. And then Jesus surprises us. He acts, speaks, teaches quite differently from what we expected. We, too, begin to doubt. Did we make a mistake when we trusted all our lives to this Man? Is He truly what we thought, the Son of God?

Jesus did not answer John's messengers right away. Instead He went on healing the sick, driving devils out of unhappy men who had been seized by Satan, restoring sight to those who were blind. Then he turned to the messengers. "Go back," He said, "and tell John what you have seen. The blind see again, people who are lame walk, those half dead with leprosy find their flesh clean and healthy as it was before they became sick, the persons who live in the dreadful silence of deafness can hear again, and the poor have the Good News preached to them. And God will bless every man who, instead of stumbling over his own ideas of what I ought to do, simply accepts the One whom God has sent."

John's messengers went back. They told John what Jesus had said. And John, I am sure, recognized the words. For these words of Jesus were a quotation from Isaiah. They were the very same words Jesus had read to His boyhood companions in the synagogue of Nazareth.

The people of Nazareth had tried to kill Him because He claimed to be the Saviour sent by God. He was only a carpenter, they said.

But John, and you and I, must accept God's choice of a Saviour. He did not come, first of all, in judgment. He came in love and mercy, to heal our diseases, to undo the tyranny of the devil, to save us from death, to bring us back to God. And it is only those who refuse to listen to His message that He will judge.

29
"Show Us a Sign"

Luke 11:14-36

It was a beautiful October day. I was on my way to town, but I was just as glad to be stopped for a minute by the red traffic light. It gave me a chance to look around me, to take a deep breath of the delicious cool air, to enjoy the cloudless blue sky above me, and the glorious color of the maple leaves. Deep in my heart I said a little prayer: "Thank You, God, for this beautiful world!"

And then I noticed the man standing at the curb. He carried a white cane, so that I knew he must be blind. I do not know how he could tell when the traffic light turned, but as it did he stepped confidently into the street, and tapping his cane ahead of him, crossed to the other side. As he went on down the block, I saw him lift his face to the sky, as if he, too, could see the blue above him and the dazzling colors all around.

As the light turned again, and I shifted gears, a motorcycle roared past me in a cloud of dust and gasoline fumes and noise. That driver certainly was not enjoying the weather. "There is more than one way of being blind," I thought to myself, "and perhaps losing your eyesight is not the worst way."

Jesus often talked about the different kinds of blindness, and when He did, there was usually a deeper meaning to what He said. Just as, so often, there was a hidden lesson in the wonderful things He did.

One day the people brought to Him a man possessed by a demon. This poor man could neither see nor speak. Jesus drove out the demon, and healed the man. The crowds who always followed our Saviour were amazed and delighted. They saw that this miracle was a sign. "This is no ordinary teacher," they said. "This must be the Saviour promised by God; this must be the son of David."

But the Pharisees squeezed their eyes shut tight so that they should not see the sign. "This man," they said, "drives out demons by the power of Satan, the king of the demons."

"How can anyone use the power of Satan to drive out demons?" Jesus asked them. "If a kingdom is divided against itself, how can it stand? If Satan drives out Satan, he is divided against himself. But if I drive out demons by the finger of God, then the kingdom of God has come near to you."

The Pharisees squeezed their eyes shut and thrust *their* fingers in their ears, so that they should neither see nor hear the sign which pointed so clearly, so unmistakably, to the arrival of the kingdom of God.

And then, having turned deaf ears and blind eyes to the sign of the healing of the demon-possessed man, they said hypocritically, "Show us a real sign, a sign from heaven."

"When it is evening," Jesus answered, "you say, 'Tomorrow will be a nice day, for the sky is red.' And in the morning you say, 'Today will be a foul day, for the sky is red and threatening.' How is it you know how to read the sky, but you are unable to read the signs of the times?

"You Pharisees belong to an evil generation. You keep saying you want a sign. I tell you, there will be no sign given to you except the sign of Jonah. Jonah was three days and three nights in the belly of the sea monster. Even so shall I be three days and three nights in the earth."

Jesus was speaking of that greatest miracle of all, that mightiest of all signs, His resurrection from the grave three days after He had been buried.

And then Jesus spoke a warning to the crowds who had understood the healing of the demon-possessed man, to the Pharisees who refused to understand, and even to you and me who have known that great and final sign of the power of God, the defeat of death by our Saviour. "Your eye," Jesus said, "is the lamp of your body. If your eye is clear, your whole body will be full of light. But if your eye is blinded by your wicked thoughts and wishes, then your whole body will be full of darkness."

May God open my eyes, and yours, so that we may see and understand. And may God in His mercy grant that not one of us, at the end of our life, may be found among those who had good eyes, but did not see with them, and had good ears, but never understood what they heard.

30
The Sign of Jonah

Jonah 1, 2

Jonah was a man who had to learn a lesson. The schoolroom where he learned it was the strangest you have ever seen. It was the stomach of a giant fish. God Himself was the teacher.

The lesson Jonah had to learn was the lesson of obedience. Perhaps you think the unpleasant lesson of obedience is only for children. Perhaps you cannot wait till you are grown up, and intend to do then just as you please.

This will be true only if you are not a Christian. For to be a Christian does not merely mean to go to church and Sunday school, to drop your nickels in the offering plate. It does not even mean reading your Bible and saying your prayers. Being a Christian means that you give your whole life to God. You accept His right to decide about your life — even if you do not always like the decision. When God commands, you obey. It is not easy, this learning to obey. You have found this out for yourself, I am sure. It cannot be mastered in one or two easy lessons, either. It will take you a lifetime to learn.

Jonah was a prophet. If he lived today, we would call him a preacher. But though he was a preacher, and though he lived so long ago, he was as much like you and me as if he had been our brother.

Jonah had been a prophet for some time, and he had served God faithfully. But now he received a new, a hard command. "Go to Nineveh, that great city," God ordered, "and cry against it, for their wickedness has come up before me."

Jonah was stunned. The people of Nineveh were the bitterest enemies of God's people. How often the Assyrians had swept down on Israel, pillaging, wrecking, dashing little children to pieces on the city walls, burning men alive, leaving only rubble and smoking ashes behind them! Must he preach to these people? Warn them of God's anger? Perhaps even see them repent, so that God would forgive them in mercy? No, no! Let them die in their sins!

Jonah did not shake his fist at God and say, as disobedient children sometimes do, "I won't do it! Try and make me!" No, Jonah just turned and ran. He ran in the opposite direction from Nineveh, and he ran as fast and as far as he could, until he was stopped by the waters of the Great Sea. There was a ship drawn up on the beach, ready to sail for Tarshish, a town in distant Spain, on the very edge of the known world. Jonah bought a ticket. He got on the ship and went down into the hold. He threw himself on the floor and fell into an exhausted sleep. Running away from God, Jonah found, is hard work! He never even heard when the sailors pulled up the anchor and set sail.

To escape from God is not only hard, it is hopeless. For God had followed Jonah. Not in anger, but in love and mercy, to teach Jonah what Jonah so badly needed to learn. God stirred up a great storm. The wind blew so fiercely and the waves towered so high that the ship was likely to be broken in two. The sailors were terrified. Every one of them prayed frantic prayers, each to his own god.

When the captain found Jonah asleep, he was angry. "What do you think you are doing?" he said. "Get up and pray to your God." By this time the sailors were convinced someone on the boat had angered one of the gods. They cast lots to discover who was guilty. The lot fell on Jonah. "Tell us," they said, "what you have done to bring this dreadful storm upon us."

Jonah did not lie. "I serve the God who made the sea and the dry land," he said. "I am running away from Him." Then the sailors were exceedingly frightened. "What shall we do," they asked, "that the sea may be calm again?"

And Jonah answered, "Throw me into the sea, for it is my fault this storm has come upon you." So the sailors took up Jonah and threw him into the raging waves. Jonah sank beneath the waves, down, down, to the very bottom of the sea. The seaweed wrapped itself around his head. His last thought must have been, "It is all over for me!"

But no, not his last thought. God had not forsaken Jonah, even

though Jonah was running away from God. God commanded a great fish to swallow Jonah. Is it better with Jonah now that he is inside the stomach of the fish? Or is it worse? Would you rather drown than be eaten alive? Who can rescue him from this dreadful living tomb? His situation is hopeless. He will never see the light of day again. But there is One to whom no situation is hopeless, for whom nothing is impossible!

For three days and three nights Jonah lived inside that fish. He had defied God. Now, in utter desperation, he prayed. He prayed, and prayed, and prayed. Helpless and penitent, he threw himself on the mercy of God.

God heard his prayer. He spoke to the fish. The fish threw Jonah back upon dry ground. Jonah lay on the beach motionless, almost as if dead. Indeed he had been as good as dead three days. At last he opened his eyes, stared, puzzled, at the blue sky above him, and squeezed his eyes shut again, as if the light hurt them. After a little he raised a hand, and watched the sand sift back to the ground. At last he sat up.

The waves were breaking almost at his feet. He turned his back on the water, shuddering. For a long time he looked at the sand dunes and the line of blue hills beyond them. Then suddenly he realized. He was not dead! He was alive! This was not the land of the dead! It was God's own earth! Those sprawling sand dunes were, he thought, the most beautiful sight he had ever seen. The little bugs scampered across his feet. The birds soared overhead. A faint odor of fruit trees came to him on the breeze. All these, he thought, God has given back to me! Rescuing me from that horrible living death inside the fish! Answering the prayers I cried to Him from the very pit itself!

He had stood up in the excitement of his discovery. Now he fell to his knees. He prayed, not just idle words, but a prayer from the bottom of his heart, born of his terrible experience. "Thou has brought back my life from the grave, O Jehovah, my God," he prayed. "I will sacrifice to Thee with the voice of thanksgiving!"

God heard the prayer. He looked down on this man whom He was teaching, and answered patiently, "Go to Nineveh, and preach the words I give to you."

This time Jonah obeyed at once.

31
Treasure in Heaven

Luke 16:19-31

If I should ask you what it is that Jesus did when He was on this earth, I suppose you would answer first of all that He was our Saviour, that He came to pay for our sins. And then that He was a teacher, a better teacher than any other the world has ever known. For all our other teachers are sinful and have faults. But Jesus not only taught men how to live, he also showed them how, by His own godly life.

But I wonder if any one of you would say that Jesus was a story-teller? He was, you know, quite the most wonderful storyteller the world has ever known. It is not just that the stories of Jesus are so interesting — though they are that — but also that they have so much meaning. In these stories, as in everything Jesus said, you can find, if you are willing to look, the very secret of life itself. And if you know this secret, you need never have a dissatisfied heart again.

Often when somebody asked Jesus a question He answered with a story. He told a story to teach His followers something important about God. But especially He used stories to reveal to those who listened the secrets hidden within their own hearts. We call these stories parables, because they not only delight and interest us; they also teach us the things we most need to know.

This story is one He told the Pharisees, who dearly loved their money.

Once there was a rich man. He had more money than his heart could desire, and he spent it all on himself. His coat was made of costly purple cloth, that royal color usually worn only by kings. Under the coat his other clothes were of the softest and finest linen. He had a party every day, and spent all his time laughing and amusing himself.

But when he went out of doors, there at the gate of his beautiful mansion lay a beggar. Lazarus was a hideous sight. His body was covered with loathsome sores, and he was so weak from hunger and sickness that he could not walk at all. Every morning someone else brought him there, and laid him down at the rich man's gate. He hoped that someone going in or out would take pity on him and offer him a few pennies, or perhaps that the rich man would let him eat the crumbs left from the table after the big evening banquet. But the rich man did not offer him anything. When he had to pass him at the gate he turned his head the other way. Only the dogs took pity on poor Lazarus. They came and licked his sores.

After a while the poor beggar died. The angels carried his soul up to heaven, and they put him beside his great ancestor Abraham. The rich man died too, and had a funeral such as was fitting for his important rank. But he did not go to heaven. No, he found himself in hell. And as he was suffering the torments of hell, he looked up and

there, far off,
whom should he
see but poor Lazarus
sitting near Abraham.

"Father Abraham!" he
cried out, "have pity on me and
send Lazarus that he may dip the tip of
his finger in water and cool my tongue, for I am
burning up!"

But Abraham said, "Remember, you had nothing but good things while you were alive, and Lazarus had nothing but trouble. Now that life is over, Lazarus is comforted, but you are in torment. Besides, there is a great precipice between us, so steep that no one can cross over from one side to the other."

Then the rich man said, "Send Lazarus, then, to my five brothers who are still alive, that he may at least save them from this place."

"Your brothers have the writings of Moses and the prophets," Abraham answered. "If they listen to them, they will know how to live."

"Yes," the rich man said, "but if someone comes back to them from the dead, then they will really listen."

But Abraham answered, "If they do not listen to the teachings of the Bible, they will not listen either even if someone comes back to them from the dead."

This was a solemn story, indeed. But it is also an important story for us to know. You see, life itself is serious. And that is because death is not the end of things. And nobody, after he has died, gets a second chance.

When that day of judgment comes, it will not matter whether you were rich or whether you were poor. It will not matter whether you were popular and admired, or whether you were lonely and friendless, as poor Lazarus was. It will not even be enough that you went to church and Sunday school, and read your Bible and said your prayers, and gave your pennies to the missionaries. I do not mean that you should not do these things. You should, of course. But the question

God is going to ask is *why* you did these things. The Pharisees did all these things, yet God was not pleased with them. He was not pleased because they did them only on the outside; their heart was filled with the love of money. And God looks not at the outside, but at your heart.

The question God is going to ask is, Did you trust in Jesus? Did you ask God to forgive your sins for the sake of your Saviour's death? Did you love God enough to try to live in a way that was pleasing to Him? Did you use the talents and the money God gave you, not for your own selfish pleasure, but to serve Him? Did you reach out a helping hand to whoever was in trouble? Did you offer a smile and a friendly word to someone who was lonely?

If you try to do these things because you love God, some day you, too, are going to see the King Himself. God is going to wipe away every tear from your face. And you will know a life so wonderful that this life here on earth will fade away into nothingness.

32
Take Heed How You Hear!

Mark 4:1-25

Close your eyes just for a minute and think. When I say *farm,* what is it that you see? I see large rolling fields, stretching off into the distance, fenced with a single strand of electric wire. I see big barns, and complicated machines that can open a furrow, spread fertilizer, sow the seed, and cover up the furrow, all in one operation.

The farm I wish to tell you about is not like that at all. This is a small, rocky farm, on a sloping hillside. Through the middle of the farm fields runs the road — no shoulders, no fence, just a ribbon of dirt packed hard by hundreds of passing feet, a road on which people walk, or, at the most luxurious, ride a little donkey.

The farmer has no fancy machines to help him grow his crops. A wooden plow, perhaps, and a sickle to cut down the grain when it is ripe. And now that it is planting time, he sows his seed by hand. Hanging at his side is a big bag of grain. He dips his hand into the bag. With a skill acquired from many years of practice, he scatters the grain ahead of him as he walks across the field.

What kind of a crop can he expect? Well; some of his seed falls on the road itself. Passers-by stamp it down into the hardpan roadway. Or, if it is not a busy day on the road, the birds snatch the grain up and eat it.

Some of his seed falls on parts of the field where there is only a thin layer of soil barely covering the rock. This seed is the first to sprout, for the thin soil warms up quickly. But its roots cannot sink down to where there is moisture. When the hot summer sun blazes down upon the seedlings, they wither and die.

Some seed falls on spots that look fertile enough, but there last summer's thistles have already dropped their seeds. Wheat and thistles grow up together, but the thistles are more vigorous than the grain. Soon the wheat is choked out of space and sun and moisture by the rank weeds.

But the farmer is not discouraged by these crop failures. For he knows that some of his seed will fall on good ground. And here he will get a harvest, sometimes thirty times what he sowed, sometimes sixty times, sometimes even a hundred times as much.

This is a sermon preached by Jesus, and it is as different from the sermons you and I are used to as the farm is different from our farms. And it is perhaps even more different from the sermons Jesus' friends usually heard. "Never did any man speak like this man!" the listeners used to say after they had heard Him preach. And others said, "He is so different from our regular preachers! He speaks with authority, as if His words come direct from God Himself!"

Yes, this sermon, which falls strangely on our ears, fell even more strangely on theirs. His closest followers, even those whom He had chosen to carry on His work after He had returned to God, His Father, were puzzled by it. The farm, the farmer, the road, the thistles, the rocks, the harvest — all these were part of their everyday world. But what about them? What was Jesus talking about?

Later, when the crowd had left and they were alone together, they asked Him, "What does the story about the farmer sowing his seed mean?" And Jesus explained it to them.

"The seed," He said, "is the Word of God. The roadway is like the heart of those persons who hear the Word, but do not understand what it is all about. At once Satan snatches it out of their hearts. The thin, rocky ground is like the heart of those who, as soon as they hear the Word, receive it with gladness. But as soon as trouble or temptation or suffering comes, they are offended. 'It costs too much to be a Christian,' they say. 'I am not going to give all these things up.' The thistle-covered places are like the heart of those who hear the Word, but are just too busy, or too worried about something, or too absorbed in the pleasures of this life to grow a good crop. The Word is smothered by their cares, their money, their fun. The good ground is like the heart of those who receive the Word, understand it, gladly pay the cost, and patiently bear fruit, some of them thirtyfold, some sixtyfold, some a hundredfold."

And then Jesus added a terrible warning: "If anyone of you has ears to hear, let him hear! And take heed how you hear!"

And now I would like to say something to all of you, yes, and to myself as well. We ought indeed to take heed how we hear. For this business of hearing right is a matter of life and death. Nothing less.

Unless the farmer plants seeds, he will have no crop. The life is in the seed. And unless you and I understand and live by God's Word, we will never come alive either.

Do not for one moment suppose Jesus spoke these words only to heathen people who had never before heard the life-giving Word of God. He spoke them to God's own people.

Perhaps, then, you and I ought to look carefully at our own hearts. Do we really study to understand God's Word? Are we willing to change whatever in our lives is not according to God's will? Do we accept trouble and suffering when God sends it? Are we willing to pay the cost? And what about the thorns and thistles in our lives?

If this is what you see when you look into your heart (and I must admit it is what I see in my heart!), then there is just one thing you can do. Tonight, when you are alone, pray to your Father in heaven to change your heart, to forgive your sins, to make you a fruitful member of His kingdom. If you ask earnestly, and in faith, He will surely grant your prayer.

33

A Small Boat and a Big Storm

Mark 4:1, 2, 21, 35-41

The lake was a good fishing lake, and the beach was used mostly by men who earned their living in this way. The actual fishing was done at night, but during the day you would see the men sitting beside their boats, untangling and mending their big nets.

That is the way it usually was. But today the beach was crowded with people. Some had come out of idle curiosity, to see for themselves

112

whether the stories about this Man were true. Others could not have told you why they came. An emptiness in their heart, perhaps, an unspoken longing for something more satisfying, drew them. The ones who stood out most in that crowd were the sick and the crippled. There were so many of them. Their faces were pale, lined with years of suffering. But in their eyes there was a new gleam of flickering hope. For they had heard the stories too.

A big crowd is a contagious thing. Men busy at their work, seeing strangers hurry past, dropped their tools to join them.

"Where are you going?" they asked. "What has happened?"

"He has come," the hurrying people answered. "The One who heals the sick by a word or a touch."

"Who is He? Where does He come from?"

"His name is Jesus. He grew up in Nazareth. They say Joseph, the carpenter, is His father."

The new arrivals pushed through the crowd on the beach to get near enough to hear, or perhaps even to touch. There was nothing in the appearance of the Man who stood at the water's edge to explain the crowd. He looked like other men. Except, perhaps, that He was so very tired. And there was reason for this. The crowd gave Him no rest. He could not even sit down to eat a bite of food, so constantly they pressed upon Him. He could have sent them home, of course. But, tired as He was, He could not bring Himself to do this. There were still so many in need.

New people constantly arriving pushed their way through the crowd. Those nearest the Teacher were not willing to step back. It looked for a moment as if the eager listeners would push the Teacher right into the lake itself. But see! He steps into one of the little boats drawn up on the beach, and His friends row Him out a little way. Now everone can both hear and see.

"When you have lighted a lamp," the Teacher told them, "you do

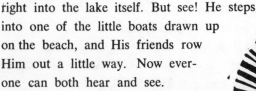

not put it underneath the bed, or under a bushel basket. No, you set it on the lamp stand, so that everyone who comes into the house can see. Even so, let your light shine before men, so that they may see your good deeds, and glorify your Father in heaven." The people listened with hungry hearts. No one had ever talked to them like this before.

By now it was growing dark. At last Jesus turned to His friends who were with Him in the boat. "Let us go to the other side of the lake," He said. His friends picked up the oars, and Jesus Himself went to the end of the boat and lay down to rest. At once He fell fast asleep. He was worn out from all His helping those in need.

It was about seven miles across the lake. Jesus' friends took turns rowing, and always they kept an anxious eye on the sky. This lake was well known for its sudden, violent storms.

It was not long before the night sky began to darken with heavy, black clouds. A wind sprang up, and at once the water around them was choppy; the little boat rose and fell on the swells. The wind became more violent, and now there were whitecaps breaking over the bow of the boat. No matter how hard they rowed, or how fast they bailed, the boat began to fill with water.

These men were not cowards. They were fishermen, who made their living on this lake. They had seen many such storms and had heard of others, from which men never came back. Were they to drown just now — now that life seemed more worth living than ever before, now that they had found the Teacher? They looked at one another with troubled eyes.

Jesus still slept peacefully at the end of the pitching boat. One of them shook Him to wake Him up. "Teacher," he asked, "do you not care that we are drowning?"

Jesus got up at once. He did not take a hand with the oars or the bailing pail. He spoke quietly to the wild water around them.

"Peace," He said. "Be still!" Immediately the wind stopped, and the water was as calm as on a quiet afternoon. Then the Teacher turned to His friends.

"Why are you afraid?" He asked them. "Do you not trust in God?"

The men stared at Him in amazement. A new fear now filled their hearts. "Who is this man?" they whispered to one another, "that even the wind and the sea obey Him?"

And, if you stop to think, you will see for yourself that it is not surprising they were troubled. For there never was another person like Jesus. He was not the son of Joseph, as some supposed, but the very Son of God. That is why He had only to speak, and the wind stopped and the sea was quiet. But He was also a real man. That is why He was tired, and needed sleep, just as you and I do. And though He used His wonderful power to help many who were sick or troubled, and still uses that power to protect every single person who trusts in Him, He never once used this power to make His own life easy or pleasant. He bore all the troubles you and I bear, and many besides, and by His perfect life and His self-sacrificing death, He purchased our salvation.

34
The Hem of His Garment

Mark 5:21-34

*T*wo people met Jesus on the road outside Capernaum that one morning, and neither of them was ever the same again.

Jairus was the first to find Him. Jairus was an important man. He was the ruler of the synagogue. You might call him the chief elder, the man in charge of all the services, for the synagogue had no regular pastor, as our churches do. The ruler supervised all the synagogue business, and when a service was held the ruler chose those from the congregation who should read the Old Testament and explain it.

Almost certainly Jairus had seen Jesus before. Very likely he had chosen Him to preach in his own synagogue. And surely he had heard about the amazing miracles Jesus worked. But Jairus, as I said, was an important man. Not many people of importance paid any attention to this new, wandering Preacher. The rulers of the Jewish synagogue, most of them, feared and hated Jesus. They saw in Him a threat to their traditions, to their way of life, even to their jobs. What made Jairus different? What drove this important man to seek out our Saviour on the road outside the city?

There is something strange about the answer to this question. It was trouble, serious trouble in Jairus' family, that brought him to Jesus. Yes, trouble was the means the Holy Spirit used to bring Jairus to our Lord.

Jairus had a happy family. There were only three of them, Jairus himself, his wife, and their darling daughter, a girl just twelve years old. As in many families that have only one child, this girl was the very center of the lives of her father and her mother.

And then one day she became very sick. Her parents were worried. When she did not improve, no matter what they tried, but only got worse, they became alarmed. They saw that their daughter was dying. And then, in his terrible despair, Jairus remembered Jesus.

What was Jesus doing on the road outside the city? The night before He had crossed the lake with His few close friends in a little boat. When they landed on the beach outside Capernaum in the early morning, there was a great crowd waiting to hear and see Jesus.

I don't know if you have ever been in a crowd like this. The people in front refuse to move; they have not waited that long just to go away again. Those on the outside of the crowd keep pushing in to see. Others, noticing the crowd of people, come running to see what is happening. And so the crowd gets worse and worse, until it is almost impossible to move, until those in the center are in danger of being crushed.

This is what Jairus found when he arrived at the beach. But a man who is desperate can perform feats of strength impossible for ordinary people. And Jairus was desperate. Otherwise he would never have been here at all. Somehow, frantically, he clawed and pushed his way through that crowd. He had to see Jesus, and he had to see Him at once! And so he came at last to Jesus. He threw himself at His feet. He cried out pitifully, "My little daughter is at the point of death. I beg you, come and lay your hands on her, so that she may live, and not die!"

Jesus looked at him, and He understood. It was no accident that He had been there on that beach just when Jairus needed Him! He set out at once for Jairus' house. But the crowd was so big that they could scarcely move. Their progress was agonizingly slow, and Jairus was in a fever of anxiety.

And just then the second person who desperately needed Jesus' help arrived. This was a woman who had been sick for twelve years. She had gone from doctor to doctor in hope of a cure, but she only got worse and worse instead of better. Now all her money was gone. She was poor, she was exhausted by the drain of her disease, she had almost lost all hope.

How did she hear of Jesus? God has not told us, but I want you to notice something especially. Just as God's Holy Spirit used Jairus' terrible trouble to drive him to Jesus, so the same Holy Spirit used this woman's hopeless condition to draw her to her Saviour. She could not, I am sure, have told you how she knew, but somehow she did know that Jesus could help her. "If I can only touch the hem of His garment," she said to herself, "I shall be healed." So she was in that great crowd too, and she, like Jairus, was struggling to get to the front where Jesus was.

This woman was ashamed of her sickness. So she did not speak to anyone in the crowd. She worked her way slowly to the front. She reached out her hand, and touched just the edge of Jesus' robe. Instantly she felt that she was well and strong again.

Jesus stopped right where He was.

He knew that healing power had gone out from Him. "Who touched me?" He asked. (Jairus was in a new agony at this new delay!)

The disciples thought Jesus' question was absurd. "You see all this crowd around You," they said, "and then You ask, 'Who touched me?'" But Jesus just stood still, and looked around to see who it was. Then the woman, afraid and trembling, came slowly forward and threw herself at His feet. She told Him just what had happened. And Jesus — I think He must have smiled at her, lovingly, though the Bible does not tell us this — Jesus said to her, "Daughter, your faith has made you well again. Go in peace; you are healed of your disease."

And then Jesus set out again, and Jairus followed, half sick at heart, because it might already be too late. Do not be afraid, Jairus! God has prepared something better for you than what you asked for.

35
Never Too Late

Mark 5:35-43

Perhaps it has happened to you — I know it has happened to me. You pray for something you want very much, something you feel you need desperately. You pray and pray, but no answer comes from God. And then you wonder to yourself: "Why is He so slow? If He does not answer soon, it will be too late!"

Why is God sometimes slow in answering our prayers? The Bible gives us many answers to this question, not vague answers that hang in the air, but real answers, as we see how God has led His children long ago. Abraham, you remember, waited years and years and years, until at last he and Sarah said to each other, "It is too late! We will never have a baby boy any more." And then God answered after all, and the answer was better than what Abraham had hoped and prayed for.

Why is He slow in answering our prayers? There is always a reason. God is *never* late with His answer to our prayers. Jairus learned this lesson that morning, along the road to Capernaum. It was no accident that Jesus stopped to talk to a sick woman. Nor was it an accident that Jairus' little daughter was sick, to begin with. There are no accidents in the lives of those God loves. And one reason God has set down the story of Jairus for us to read is so that you and I can learn this lesson too!

The woman whose disease had been healed went away with peace in her heart, even as Jesus had told her. And the crowd, with Jesus and Jairus in the middle of it, moved forward slowly, and with some difficulty.

Jairus was in an agony of fear — and of impatience. He did not dare to think how things must be at home. But he had a dreadful feeling in his heart that they would get there too late. Jesus was in no hurry at all. He knew what Jairus did not know, what Jairus had to learn that very day: It is never too late for God! God's timing is always exactly right!

Suddenly there was a new commotion at the edge of the crowd. Someone else was pushing forward. I am sure that when Jairus saw this he must have felt despair. Were they to be delayed again? And when the newcomer actually got to the front, when Jairus saw and recognized who it was, then his heart seemed almost to stop beating. For this was his own servant.

"Do not bother the Master further," the servant said to Jairus. "Your little daughter is dead." *Dead* — that dreadful word. For this is the end of hope. No doctor, however skillful, can call people back from the dead. But Jesus was not troubled. He said to Jairus, "Do not be afraid. Only believe." And then Jesus sent the crowd away. There must have been authority in His voice, for, as He commanded them to go, the people melted away. Jesus took with Him only His three closest friends, Peter, and James, and John.

Now that the crowd was gone, they could walk more quickly. They came at last to Jairus' house. A crowd of friends and neighbors were already there, come to comfort the saddened father and mother. And, as was the custom in that country, paid mourners had arrived too. They played sad music on their flutes, and they wailed loudly to express their grief.

Jesus came into the house. "Why are you making such a commotion?" He said to the people. "The little girl is not dead, but only sleeping." The friends and the paid mourners laughed out loud. Who had ever heard such nonsense as this? they thought. Jesus did not stop to argue with them. He simply put them all out of the house. And then, taking her father and mother and His three friends with Him, He went to the room where the girl's lifeless body was stretched out. He took the child's hand in His and said simply, "Little girl, get up!"

And, wonder of wonders, she did just that. She got up and walked around the room. She was not dead, not even sick any more. She was alive and well. And everybody — Jesus' own friends, and Jairus, who had believed Jesus could heal his sick daughter, but had never dreamed Jesus was powerful enough to bring her back from the dead, and the neighbors, and the paid mourners who had laughed at Jesus — everybody was astonished.

Then Jesus showed again His tender love. Though He was such a busy person, He was not too busy to think about how a little girl felt. This child had been very sick, too sick to eat anything. Now she was alive and well again. She was hungry. Jesus thought of this too. "Give her something to eat," He told her mother. Her mother had been so overcome with surprise that she had never thought of this. She hurried to get her little daughter some food.

And so, if you are sick, or afraid, or in trouble, remember Jairus. Jairus had to wait for an answer to his prayer, but when the answer came it was far beyond what he had asked for. Not only was his little daughter healthy and well again, but Jairus had discovered that Jesus is stronger even than death itself.

To you, as to Jairus, Jesus says, "Fear not; only believe." And if your faith trembles and falters (as mine often does), and if you are still afraid in spite of Jesus' reassurance (as I often am), then there is a prayer especially for you, and for me. It is this: *Lord Jesus, I believe. Help Thou my unbelief!* If you pray this from you heart, God will surely answer. And you, too, even though you may have to wait for it, you, too, will see the marvels of God.

36

A Brave Man Dies for Jesus

Mark 6:14-29

far to the south on the desolate cliffs overhanging the Dead Sea, stands the fortress of Machaerus. It is a forbidding structure, its stone walls towering high above the surrounding countryside, a symbol of the brutal might of the Roman rulers. The building is at once fortress, prison, and palace, but the palace is not a favorite of King Herod. Machaerus looks out to the west over the lead-colored waters of the Dead Sea, lowest spot on our earth, and to the east on the trackless desert. The heat is oppressive, and the desert wind whips the sharp sand into travelers' ears and eyes and nose. Indeed, it is only because this is a convenient overnight stop on trips to Mesopotamia that the place is ever occupied at all.

Most of the time Machaerus stands empty except for its garrison of soldiers. And except for the dungeons, cut deep into the rock beneath the palace floor. Its very remoteness makes Machaerus a safe prison for important prisoners, who, if jailed in the busy cities of Galilee, might cause riots and street demonstrations.

Tonight, however, the palace was ablaze with lights. King Herod had arrived, and with him a great crowd of nobles, officials, and officers. And even with his wife Herodias — if it is right to call her his wife. Herodias was Herod's niece, daughter of one of his half brothers. For Herod's father had had ten different wives at one time or another. Herodias was also Herod's sister-in-law, married to his older brother (and her uncle) Philip. But when she and Herod "fell" for each other (and "fell" I think is exactly the right word for what happened!), Herod promptly discarded his first wife, like a worn-out shoe, and Herodias simply left her first husband without even the bother of divorcing him. She took her daughter Salome with her, and moved into Herod's palace.

It is this wicked arrangement that explains the most famous prisoner at Machaerus. John the Baptist, that fearless prophet who came to prepare the way for Jesus, had denounced the sins of all the "little" people, the common folk who came to hear him preach at the River Jordan. But he was not afraid to denounce also the sin of King Herod himself. "It is wrong for you to take your brother's wife," he said to Herod. Herod's conscience was troubled. But Herodias did not know what shame was. She never forgave John for these words. From that day forward she schemed and plotted to kill him.

Partly to please her, but partly also to protect John from her cruel schemes, Herod had imprisoned him at Machaerus. John the Baptist had spent more than thirty years preparing himself for his life's work. He had spent five months preaching. And now he had been in prison for ten months. God's timetable is different from our timetable. But John did not despair. He allowed God to do the deciding, and he followed wherever God led. He was willing to be less than nothing in God's kingdom, so that Jesus could be all in all. "He must increase," he said of Jesus, "and I must decrease."

Whenever Herod stopped at Machaerus, he had John brought out from his dungeon so that he could talk to him. Herod was not entirely without conscience. He was a weak man, torn between his desire to walk the path of God and his guilty love for Herodias.

But on this visit Herod did not send for John. It was Herod's birthday, and a great feast was being prepared. In that country, and at that time, only men attended such a party. The guests ate and drank until all of them, including Herod himself, were half-drunk.

This was the very chance Herodias had been waiting for. She sent her daughter, Salome, to dance for the guests. The guests applauded uproariously. And their approval delighted Herod.

"Ask whatever reward you want," Herod solemnly swore to Salome, "even if it is half of my kingdom, and I will give it to you." Salome went out. "What shall I ask for?" she said to her mother. And Herodias answered without hesitation, "The head of John the Baptist."

It was nothing either way to Salome. She had grown up in a family where murder was commonplace. Her great-grandfather murdered her great-grandmother (the favorite of his ten wives), and then went on to murder her grandfather, and several of her uncles and aunts. She came back into the banquet hall and said to Herod: "I want the head of John the Baptist on a platter, right away!"

If Herod was half-drunk, this request shocked him cold sober. But he was too proud to go back on his solemn oath in the presence of all his guests. He called the executioner and sent him down to the dungeon cell. The executioner beheaded John and brought his head to Salome on a platter, and she gave it to her mother. John's friends took his body away and buried it.

But if Herodias thought she was rid of John, she was mistaken. For Herod was a superstitious man. For the rest of his life he was haunted by John's "ghost." When he heard of the miracles Jesus was performing, he said in terror, "I know who He is! He is John the Baptist, whom I beheaded, come back from the dead!" Later Herod was badly defeated in battle by the father of his first wife, the one he had cast off like a worn-out shoe. He lost his kingdom and spent his last years in exile.

And John — what about John? Shall we feel sorry for him who served Jesus so faithfully, and died so horrible a death? No, I do not think we should. For John was one of the great heroes of faith, one of those who are looking for a better country than our troubled world, of whom it is said that God Himself is not ashamed to be called their God.

Jesus Feeds the Hungry

John 6:1-14

It is the first pleasant Saturday in spring. "Today," you say to Mother as you finish your breakfast, "I am going to walk around the lake. Do you think you could pack a lunch for me?" Mother smiles at you. "Have a good time," she says. "Perhaps you could pick me a bunch of violets." And so you set out, carrying the sandwiches Mother has made.

Long ago there was another boy who set out to walk along the lake. It was early spring. The hills were covered with fresh green grass, and there were wild flowers blooming at his feet. He carried a lunch — five little buns and two salted fish to put on them. Was he looking for wild flowers for his mother? Or was he just enjoying the soft, warm air, the fresh green look of spring? I do not know. But whatever he looked for, he could hardly have found a lovelier place to find it.

The lake was calm. Its deep blue waters mirrored the snow-clad peak of Mt. Hermon to the north. Here and there a fishing boat moved slowly from place to place. But there was little else to disturb the quiet. For this was the east shore of the lake. The west shore was a busy, crowded place. There were towns nestled at the water's edge, fishermen sorting their catch and drying their nets, farmers on their way to market, traders selling goods from distant places. But this eastern shore was deserted except for a tiny fishing village. No one

climbed these hills which rose almost from the lake itself. Not enough rain fell here to farm the land. And where there are no farms, there are no little market towns.

Someone else was looking for a quiet place this beautiful spring morning. A little boat appeared in the distance. Instead of moving slowly from place to place, as the fishing boats did, it came towards the shore. The boy saw nothing strange about that little boat. He did not dream he was about to meet his Saviour face to face.

And then his attention was distracted by another sound, far stranger in this lonely spot. It was a soft murmur of many voices, which gradually grew louder. Around the bend in the shore a great crowd of people burst into sight.

And so, when Jesus stepped onto the shore, He did not find the quiet spot where He had hoped to rest. The crowd was there ahead of Him. Have you ever been so tired that you did not want to see any of your friends, so tired that you said to them, "Go away! I am too tired to play with you today"? Jesus was much more tired than you have ever been. The crowd did not even allow Him time to eat, much less to rest! But He did not say, "Go away! I need to rest. I am human too!" (He *was* human, you know.) No, Jesus never says, "Go away!" to anyone who really comes to find Him. He looked at those people, and pitied them. He climbed up the hill by the water's edge, and sat down on the grass.

And sitting there on that beautiful spring morning, He talked to the people (to the boy who brought his lunch, too) about God, about the things they needed most, and about how God planned to help them. There were many sick people in that crowd, but they must have come up after the others, I suppose, because they could not run so fast. One by one, as they were brought forward, Jesus healed them all. The blind people saw again; the lame, who had to be helped forward, began to walk and run. Those who had been wasted from suffering, at Jesus' word were strong and well.

The sun rose straight up above their heads, and then gradually it sank down again, turning the water of the lake to gold and scarlet.

His friends, who had come with Him in the boat, now dared to interrupt their Master. They were tired too, and by this time hungry as well.

"Send the crowd home," they said. "Let them go down to the village there and buy something to eat."

"You give them something to eat," Jesus answered. They stared at Him.

"Half a year's earnings would not be enough to feed so many," Philip answered. Philip came from the little fishing town there at the water's edge.

"How much food do we have?" Jesus asked.

"There is a boy here, who has a lunch of five small buns and two fish," someone answered, "but what good is that among so many?" But Jesus said, "Make the people sit down." So they went through the crowd, and got everyone sitting on the grass, divided up into groups of fifty or a hundred. Then Jesus took the five buns and the two little fish in His hands and, looking up to heaven, He thanked God for the gift of food. Then He handed the buns and the fish to His disciples, and they began to hand them out to the people. And, wonder of wonders, there was enough, and more than enough, for everyone to eat his fill.

"Pick up the pieces left over," Jesus said, "so that nothing is wasted." The disciples picked up what was left, and the pieces filled twelve baskets. How many people did Jesus feed that day? About five thousand.

This, of course, was a miracle. And you know as well as I do that Jesus does not work a miracle every day. But can you guess why He worked this miracle of feeding five thousand people with five buns and two fish? I think one reason was to show us (you and me, I mean) that He cares very much when we are tired or hungry or in any kind of trouble. He not only cares, but He provides us with everything we need — food and clothes and homes, and doctors and medicines too, to heal us when we are sick. Never forget that all these things are gifts from God.

38

Walking on the Water

Matthew 14:22-36

Jesus had been very busy. He was always surrounded by crowds of people. There were so many people who wanted to hear what He had to say, and to get His help, that He did not have time enough left to teach His disciples, who were going to carry on His work after He had gone back to live with God, His Father.

And so, after He had taught the people, and healed the sick, and fed the five thousand hungry men and women with a boy's picnic lunch, He sent the crowds away. He sent His close friends away too. He wanted to talk to His closest Friend of all, His Father. So He went up into the hills, where, all alone, in the quiet and the dark, He could pray.

You know, of course, that you can pray any time, anywhere, and God will hear you. But you can talk to God best when you are alone, when it is quiet, and there are no distracting sights and sounds to interrupt you. That is one reason Jesus tells us to go into our own room and close the door when we pray.

The crowd went back to their homes and their everyday affairs. The disciples took a large rowboat, and started across the Lake of Galilee. On a calm night this would have been a beautiful trip. But this was not a calm night. There was a fierce wind blowing against them, and no matter how hard they rowed, they didn't seem to make any progress. They rowed and rowed. They were beginning to get discouraged. Perhaps they were a little afraid too. You could never be sure just how bad the storms on the lake would turn out to be.

All this time Jesus was alone on the mountain, talking to God. But He had not forgotten His disciples. He saw what a hard time they were having. He knew they were discouraged, and even afraid.

The wind howled. The waves tossed the little boat to and fro.

The disciples rowed on and on. Suddenly they saw the figure of a man walking on the top of the waves. "It is a ghost!" they cried. The disciples were strong men, but they were terrified.

Jesus did not want to frighten them. Immediately He spoke to them. "Do not be afraid," He said; "it is I!"

Still the disciples did not understand. These men were fishermen. They had lived and worked on the sea all their lives. They had a healthy fear of the dangers of a storm. They had seen all too often what could happen. But they had not yet realized how powerful Jesus was. They had seen Him do many wonderful things. But they did not understand that the same Lord who can multiply five little buns and two salted fish into food for five thousand hungry people can also walk on the top of the waves of the sea.

As the disciples cowered in the boat, not knowing whether to be more afraid of the storm or of this strange figure coming towards them on the water, Peter spoke up.

"Lord," he said, "if it is really You, tell me to come to You on the water."

And Jesus said simply, "Come!"

Peter climbed out of the boat. He did not look at the wild waves beneath his feet. He did not hear any longer the wind which howled around his head. He looked straight at Jesus in simple faith. He walked on the top of the stormy water towards Jesus.

But after a moment, Peter looked down. He saw the water beneath his feet. He heard the wind. He was afraid. And the very moment that he stopped trusting Jesus he began to sink.

"Lord, save me!" he cried to Jesus. Immediately Jesus stretched out His hand and took hold of Peter.

"How little your faith is!" Jesus said to him. "Why did you doubt my power to care for you?"

Together, Jesus holding firmly to Peter's hand, the two of them came to the boat and climbed in. At that very moment the wind stopped blowing; the storm was over.

Now the rowers made better progress. Soon they drew up on the shore. As soon as Jesus got out of the boat the people on the beach recognized Him. They ran all around the neighborhood to tell that the wonder-worker had come. From all sides people brought the sick and the crippled to Jesus to be healed. Those who couldn't walk were carried by their friends on stretchers.

Did Jesus heal them all? Yes, He was so powerful that the sick had only to touch Him, and they became well again.

Perhaps you have never been in a boat when a storm blew up, and the whitecaps broke against your boat, and you were afraid you could not get safely back to land. Certainly you have never looked up in such a moment to see the figure of Jesus walking on the water.

I am sure, though, there have been times in your life when it seemed as if everything was against you, when you could not seem to get anywhere no matter how hard you tried. Maybe at such times you have even wondered, as the disciples did, whether Jesus had forgotten you, or perhaps was too busy with more important things to attend to your troubles.

The next time you feel this way, remember this story. While the disciples thought they were fighting the storm alone, Jesus was thinking about them. He saw they were in trouble and He came walking on the water to bring them help.

He sees you when you are in trouble also. He will come to your aid too. He is still the amazing, the loving, the powerful Lord. He can solve your worst problems, and save you in your most desperate troubles.

39
Jesus Tests a Woman's Faith

Mark 7:24-30

Once upon a time there was a woman who had a little daughter who was very sick. This happened long, long ago. But you must not think this mother and her daughter were different from you, just because they lived so long ago. They were quite like you. The mother loved her daughter, just as your mother loves you. And because the little girl was so hopelessly sick, and there was nothing she could do to help her except to take care of her as best she could, the mother's heart was dark and hopeless too.

Every single night, long after you are sound asleep, your mother kneels beside her own bed and prays for you. But if you should become very sick, your mother would not wait till night to pray for you. Many, many times during the day, as she went about her work, she would close her eyes for just a moment, and ask God to make you better. Your minister would pray for you, and lots of people from your church, some of them people that you hardly know by name. Perhaps you yourself have sometimes prayed for a friend who was sick.

But this unhappy mother could not pray for her daughter. She lived in a heathen country, where only idols were worshiped. She may have heard a little about Jesus, for she lived at the same time as He did. But she did not live in the same place. Her home was fifty miles north of Galilee, where Jesus preached and healed the sick. In those days ordinary folk who traveled had to walk. And fifty miles is a long way to walk — much too long a way for a sick girl.

There was another, even bigger, reason why this mother could not take her little girl to Jesus. Jesus was a Jew. And this woman was not a Jew. The Jews had nothing to do with people who were not Jews. Nothing at all. They would not even come into their houses.

This mother knew a little bit about the Jews. There were some of them who lived where she did. She knew they worshiped one God, instead of the many idols of the people all around them. She knew they were hoping and praying for a Saviour God had promised to send them, a descendant of their great King David who had lived so long ago. But the one thing she knew best was that the Jews hated and scorned all other peoples. "Dog of an unbeliever" was the name they called them.

Meanwhile, far to the south — only fifty miles, but as far as this mother was concerned it might as well have been five hundred miles — Jesus went about His work on the shores of the lake.

Everywhere He went the crowds followed Him. When He crossed the lake at night, He found a crowd waiting for Him on the other side. When He went to a lonely, deserted spot to rest, the crowd came running too. It was important that He get away from the crowd for a little while. Not only to rest — though He needed rest too — but even more to get a chance to tell His closest friends what they would need to know when He left them. For He was going to leave them. He had come down from heaven into the world not just to preach and to heal the sick, but most of all to die. He had come to pay for my sins and yours, so that God would forgive us, and we could once again become His dearly loved children.

He called His friends together. "We are going to the north," He said, "to the land of Tyre and Sidon." Was there a reason why He chose this place? Perhaps there was. Certainly He knew about the little girl who was so desperately sick and about her grieving mother. He knows all things, even what is going to happen in the future, because He is the very Son of God.

Tyre and Sidon were large and busy cities. Jesus did not stay there. Instead He chose a place out in the country, the home, perhaps, of some friendly Jewish farmer. "Do not tell anyone I am here," He warned His friends.

One of the strange things about Jesus was how hard it was to hide Him. He had not been there long when there came a knocking on the door. Who was it that pounded so on the door of that quiet farmhouse? Can you guess? It was the mother of the sick little girl. Somehow she had heard that Jesus had come. Somehow she had found the courage to seek him out — even though she knew how the Jews felt about heathen people. Somehow she was certain in her heart that Jesus could help her daughter.

The woman threw herself on the floor at Jesus' feet. "Have mercy on me, Lord, Thou Son of David," she said. "My daughter is grievously sick."

Jesus did not answer her at once. He did not answer because He wanted to test her faith, to show whether it was really firm and strong; just as sometimes He does not answer us at once when we pray, so that our faith may grow stronger and surer.

"The children must eat first," He said at last. "It is not proper to give the children's food to the dogs."

"That is true, Lord," the woman answered humbly. She knew that she was not a Jew, not one of God's chosen people. "But even the dogs under the table eat the crumbs the children spill."

"O woman," Jesus answered (He was pleased with what she said), "you have great faith. Go home. Your daughter is well again."

And the woman went home. Her feet, which had faltered as she came to knock at Jesus' door, now ran; they almost flew for joy. And the little girl, what did she say as she threw her arms around her mother? I think perhaps that both of them cried just a little, because they were so happy.

40

Thou Shalt Love Thy Neighbor

Matthew 15:29-39

Sometimes when your father comes home at night he is tired. He takes off his coat, sits down in his special chair, and puts his feet up on the footstool. You run to get his slippers, and Mother brings a cup of coffee. When your older brothers come in from play, your mother says to them, "Be a little quiet now. Your father has had a hard day."

It is wonderful to have a comfortable home to come back to when you have worked hard and are tired. Jesus never had a home like that. As He traveled from city to city, bringing the good news of God's salvation, He had to sleep where He could. Sometimes He could stay with friends. Sometimes He must have spent the night at an inn along the road. Sometimes, I am sure, He lay down under the open sky, with only a stone for a pillow, like Jacob so long ago. Sometimes He did not sleep at all, but spent all night talking to His Father in heaven.

He was often very tired. The crowds especially wore Him out. Everywhere He went people crowded around to see and hear Him. When He preached on the seashore, the crowd became so big, and pushed so hard to get near Him, that He was almost pushed into the water. He had to get into a boat and row out a little way before He could finish what He wanted to say. When He crossed the lake to get a few hours of rest and quiet, He found another crowd waiting for Him on the other side.

One day He took His disciples and climbed up into a high mountain. This was a desert place where almost nothing grew, and no one lived. Perhaps here He could get a chance to rest, a chance to pray, and time to tell His disciples the many things He must teach them while He was still here on earth.

But it was very strange how quickly the news spread that He had come. Hardly had He sat down on the mountainside, when little groups of people began to appear in the distance. The groups grew larger and larger, till soon there were hundreds, and then thousands, of people. Many of them led or carried members of their family who were sick, or blind, or crippled.

Jesus did not say, "I am tired. Come back tomorrow. I cannot help you any more tonight." No, He looked at the sick, the crippled, the unhappy, the troubled, and He felt pity for them. He forgot that He was Himself worn out. He walked through those crowds and He touched the mouths of those who could not speak, and they spoke praises to God. He opened the eyes of the blind, and He gave back to the lame the strong, straight legs they had once had. He spent three whole days healing the sick people in that great crowd. And the people who had come, all four thousand of them, stared in amazement as they saw what was happening. And after they had recovered from the shock of what they saw, they began all together to thank God for the wonderful way He had come to the help of His people.

Now Jesus had healed them all, every single one. Did He say, "Now please go home, and let me get a little rest"? No, He never stopped to think how exhausted He Himself was. He was still thinking about others. He said to His disciples, "These people have been here three days, and have had nothing to eat. I don't want to send them home hungry for fear they faint on the way." Jesus Himself had had nothing to eat either, of course, but He did not mention that. The disciples said, "How ever in the world could we find food for a crowd as big as this, here in the desert?"

"How much bread do we have?" Jesus asked.

"Seven loaves, and a few small fish," they answered. Those were not big loaves of bread, such as we buy in the store, but little loaves, about the size of a hamburg bun. This was the food the disciples had brought along for Jesus and for themselves.

"Tell the people to sit down," Jesus said. Then Jesus took the

seven buns and the little fish, lifted up His eyes to heaven, and thanked God for food to eat. Then He broke them into pieces and handed the pieces to His disciples to give to that great crowd of people. And, wonder of wonders, there was plenty for every single one of the four thousand men and women and children. After they had all eaten till they were full, the disciples picked up the broken pieces and they had seven baskets full.

That was how Jesus fed four thousand people with seven small buns and a few small fish. There is something special I want you to remember about this story. It is this: Jesus did this for you and for me. O, I know, we were not there on the mountainside that day so long ago. But He was thinking of us just the same. You see, this was the way Jesus obeyed God's command, *Thou shalt love thy neighbor as thyself.* Jesus loved those sick and hungry people there in that desert place. He loved them so much that He forgot how tired and hungry He Himself was. And this wonderful love was part of the perfect obedience He offered God in our place. If you belong to Jesus, then God accepts His obedience as if it were your very own.

And there is one thing more you must never forget. Jesus loves you too, just as He loved the four thousand there on that mountainside. He sees you when you are sick. He knows when you are tired or hungry. He is concerned whenever you need something, or are in any trouble. And He will do something about it, just as He did that day on the mountain. You can trust all your needs to Him, and He will provide you with every good thing.

41
Peter Makes a Great Discovery

Matthew 16:13-25

a new baby is expected. Perhaps at your house, perhaps at the home of one of your friends. The new clothes lie all folded ready, so very tiny, so very soft and white. Mother and Father pick out a name (with your help). And Grandmother has come to help take care of the baby.

"Will it be a boy or a girl?" you ask. Mother smiles.

"God decides that," she says.

"Will it have brown eyes or blue?" You have brown eyes, like Father, but Mother's eyes are blue.

"God decides that too," Mother answers. "He even decides ahead of time what kind of a person the baby will be."

"You mean, whether he will be good at arithmetic, like me, or good at spelling, like Peter?" Peter is your best friend.

"Yes," Mother says, "God has special work for this baby to do in His world, and He matches each baby to his own work."

"Does He have special work for me to do too?"

"Yes," Mother says, "that is just what I mean." This is something new to think about. It is all very strange, and all very exciting.

In Bible times, when a new baby was born, it was even more exciting. For God had promised to send some Jewish mother a very special baby. This baby would be the Saviour, sent by God to help His people.

The Jewish people did not live in a free country, as you and I do. They had been conquered by the Romans. They had to obey Roman laws and pay Roman taxes. They hated their Roman masters. They expected that the Saviour, when He came, would be a great general and drive out the Roman armies, and a powerful king who would make every other nation afraid of the Jews. They hoped and prayed and waited for God's promise. Every mother wondered whether her baby might perhaps be the longed-for Saviour.

But when the Baby came at last, He was not born in a king's palace but, instead, quietly in a cave. And when He grew up, He did not wear a crown and purple robes, and ride on a white horse, so that everyone could see He was a king. He looked just like ordinary people, and at first He was just a carpenter.

For a while great crowds followed Him everywhere He went. But some of them became angry because He said such strange things, talking about giving His flesh and blood to feed His followers. Others were offended when He healed a sick man on the Sabbath. And many did not like it when He told them to pray for their enemies, and to turn the other cheek. There were twelve, His closest friends, who stuck to Him even when the others turned away. They did not always understand what He said, but they were more and more certain who He was.

One day, as they were walking along the road, Jesus asked these friends a question: "Who do people say I am?" Jesus knew the answer before He asked the question. Because He was the Son of God as well as the son of Mary, He knew all things. He asked the question to help His friends, not to help Himself.

"Some say You are John the Baptist come back to life again," they answered. "And some people think You must be Elijah come back to earth, or Jeremiah, or some other prophet."

"But who do you say I am?" Jesus asked.

Peter was the one who always spoke up first. "You are the Saviour sent by God," Peter answered. "You are the Son of the living God."

Jesus was pleased with this answer. "You are blessed, Peter," He said. "You did not discover this by yourself. My Father showed it to you. But do not tell anyone that I am the Saviour."

Do you wonder why Jesus did not want His friends to tell people He was the long-promised Saviour? It was because even these twelve closest friends, who had been with Him from the beginning, did not understand yet what kind of a Saviour He was. They were looking for a conquering hero, a powerful king. That was not the way God planned to save His people, not the way at all.

These twelve friends, whom we sometimes call apostles, were going to carry on Jesus' work after He had gone back to heaven. And so He must teach them carefully what kind of a Saviour He was.

"I must go to Jerusalem," He said. "I must suffer many things at the hands of the religious leaders there. They will kill me, and after three days I will rise again from the grave." His friends were shocked. They were almost speechless. Their conquering Saviour, their mighty King! How could He possibly suffer and die?

Peter drew Jesus to one side: "This must never happen to You, Lord," he said.

"Get behind me, Satan," Jesus answered sharply. "You are talking about man's plans, not God's plans." Peter meant well, but what he was doing was tempting Jesus to refuse to follow God's plan. It was not easy for Jesus to walk the path of suffering and death, but still He said, "I *must* go; I *must* suffer; I *must* die." Why must He? Have you ever wondered?

He *must*, because of the love of God. God loved us so much that His Son came willingly to this earth to suffer and die in our place, to pay for our sins. You cannot love anybody unless you are willing to sacrifice for their sake. We know this for sure because we have seen how terrible a sacrifice Jesus was willing to make for those He loved. And you and I, if we love our Saviour in return, must be willing to walk in His footsteps and make sacrifices for Him.

"If any man wishes to follow me," Jesus said to His twelve friends, and to you and me as well, "he must deny himself, and make sacrifices for my sake." This is not always easy. But it is not nearly as hard as what Jesus did for us.

42

The Glory That Belonged to Jesus

Luke 9:28-36

Peter and his friends were all mixed up. When Jesus asked them, "Who do you say that I am?" they answered with sure and happy conviction, "You are the Saviour sent by God, and the Son of the living God Himself." And Jesus answered, "It was God Himself that showed this to you."

Their hearts swelled with joy and anticipation. For if Jesus was God's own Son, surely their troubles were over. Soon He would drive out the hated Roman rulers, and He Himself would be their king.

But even as they were thinking these things, Jesus dashed their hopes to the ground. "I am going to suffer many things," He said. "I will be arrested and killed. But after three days, I will rise again."

Can you imagine what a shock these words were to the disciples? How could the Son of God be killed? Who would save the Jewish people, if Jesus was going to die?

"This must never happen to You," Peter said. And Jesus answered sharply, "You speak the words of Satan!"

Yes, Peter and his friends were all mixed up. They no longer knew what to think. For the things that Jesus said were going to happen were quite unthinkable. Perhaps in their hearts there was even a moment's doubt. Had they been, could they be, mistaken as to who Jesus really was?

Jesus could read their hearts. He saw how confused and troubled they were. He knew they needed help and encouragement.

"Come," He said to the three who were His closest companions, Peter, and James, and John, "Come up into the mountain, and we will pray."

So they started up the mountain. It was evening. Soon it became

dark. Alone on the mountaintop with God, they knelt in prayer. They prayed a long time.

Finally the three disciples could stay awake no longer. They wrapped themselves in their blankets and fell asleep. Jesus still talked to His Father.

Suddenly they were awakened, but they did not know by what. Still dazed with sleep, they were half-blinded by a dazzling light. Then they saw the light clearly, and suddenly they were wide awake.

It was their Master who shone with this unearthly, dazzling light. His clothes were whiter than any garment they had ever seen, so white it hurt to look at them. Even His face had changed; it shone with brilliance and glory.

And He was not alone. Two men talked with Him. The disciples had never seen them before, but they knew at once who they were. On one side stood Moses, the great lawgiver, the man known as the friend of God. On the other side was Elijah, the famous prophet, the one who had been carried to heaven in a chariot of fire.

Why had these men come back from the dead? What were they saying to Jesus? They were talking about the very same thing Jesus had been telling His disciples, about Jesus' death at Jerusalem.

The disciples listened to this talk with burning ears. They were struck with terror at the sight of Jesus' glory. But Peter, as he so often did, spoke out, hardly knowing what he said:

"We will make three booths out of branches," he said to Jesus, "one for each of you." Jesus did not answer.

And then a cloud came over them, and out of the cloud they heard the voice of God Himself.

"This is my beloved Son," God said. "Hear ye Him."

The disciples were so afraid they fell to the ground on their faces. And then Jesus came and touched them on the shoulder.

"Get up," He said. "Do not be frightened." When they dared to look up, they saw Jesus only, their dear Lord and Master.

This wonderful glimpse of the heavenly glory of Jesus had lasted only a few minutes. But the disciples did not forget what they had seen. During the dark days of Jesus' suffering and death they were strengthened by the memory of the glory that belonged to Jesus.

What Peter and James and John saw that night was only a little glimpse of the glory Jesus has right now, seated at the right hand of God. Some day, if you love Him and follow Him, you are going to see this marvelous sight yourself. And more than this. The sight of His beauty is so marvelous, so powerful, that you yourself are going to be changed just by looking at Him. You are going to have a share in that wonderful glory which Jesus bought for you when He died in your place on the cross. "We know that . . . we shall be like him," John tells us, "for we shall see him even as he is."

43
Face to Face with God

Exodus 33:17-34:8

Moses come back from the dead to see for himself the heavenly glory of Jesus! Moses talking to Jesus about His approaching death in Jerusalem! What was Moses doing on that mountaintop in Palestine? Why was it that the death of Jesus interested him most of all?

142

And God talked to Moses face to face, as a man talks to his friend.

So the Old Testament tells us. There is only one other person in the whole Bible who is called the "friend of God." God spoke to Moses face to face, but Moses did not see the face of God. And Moses longed to see God's face — not because he doubted God, as did the Israelites, who found it easier to trust in a golden calf than in the unseen God. No, Moses wanted to see God's face because he loved God so much. And the more you love someone, the greater your longing is to know him through and through, to find out everything there is to know about him.

It is only a little more than a year ago that God spoke to Moses for the first time. This Moses, who now so longs to see God's face, is the same man who hung his head and dragged his feet, and made excuse after excuse after excuse, when God first spoke to him out of the burning bush. The presence of God is so delightful, His friendship is so sweet, that once a person has tasted it, all other joys seem to grow pale by comparison.

But now Moses has a special reason for longing to see God's face. God's people have sinned a terrible sin. They have made a golden calf and worshiped it. And Moses hopes to read in the face of God whether there is any hope at all for such rebellious people. Next to God, Moses loves the people of Israel most of all. And Moses wants to search God's face, to see whether there is any hope of forgiveness for this undeserving people.

All this Moses has told to God, as a man tells his dear friend the deepest longings of his heart. And God has answered Moses, as a man answers the questions of his dear friend.

"You cannot see my face," God says, "for no man can look into my face and live. But see, here is a rock, and there is a deep crack in the rock. I will hide you in the crack of the rock, and I will cover you with my hand while my glory passes by. And then I will take away my hand, and you shall see my back. But you cannot see my face."

So Moses went up the mountain to God. And God came down and stood beside Moses. And God held his hand over Moses, so that Moses

would not be blinded by the glory of God. And there God revealed Himself to His friend, saying, as He passed by: "I am the Lord, a God merciful and gracious, slow to anger, and overflowing with steadfast love and faithfulness, a God who forgives sinners, though I will also punish those who do not trust in me."

And Moses, quite overcome by this revelation of God's goodness and love, bowed his face to the ground and worshiped God. He did not understand how a just God could forgive His sinful people. He did not know why. He would have to wait for the answer to these questions. Long afterwards, on another mountaintop, he talked to his Saviour, and ours, about God's wonderful plan. For now he was content to trust in the promise that God would somehow provide a way so that at last even sinful men might see His glorious face.

44

The Treasure That Cannot Be Lost

Luke 12:13-21; Mark 12:41-44

It takes a miracle of God to get a rich man into heaven," Jesus said once; "but God is so powerful that He can do even this."

A miracle to save one rich man! What kind of a miracle? Is it that the rich man is so fat that it takes a miracle to squeeze him past that narrow gate Jesus sometimes talked about? No, not that kind of miracle. But it takes a miracle of the Holy Spirit working in the rich man's heart to prevent him from trusting in his money instead of trusting God. And when we put our trust not in God, but in what our money can do for us, then we are making an idol of our money. For that is exactly what an idol is — something or someone we trust instead of God.

Sometimes the only way for a rich man to escape is for God to snatch out of his life the money that endangers his soul. That, you remember, was how God rescued Lot from the wicked city of Sodom, taking away his home, his money, his property, and even his worldly wife, in order to save Lot, as it were, by fire.

One day a man in the crowd said to Jesus, "My parents died recently. Make my brother give me half the money they left."

"Man," Jesus answered, "I did not come into this world to divide up money." Then He turned to His disciples. "Be very careful," He warned them, "that you do not become greedy for money. There is much more to life than the things you own." Then, as He so often did, Jesus told a little story to make His meaning clear.

Once there was a farmer. He was a rich man. He did not have a big farm, but what land he did have was very fertile. His plants stood tall and straight; as they got ripe, the heavy ears of grain bent the stalks down. When the harvest came, the farmer did not have room to store all his crop.

"What shall I do with all this grain?" the farmer said to himself.

"My barns are not big enough to hold it all. But I have an idea. I will pull down my barns, and build bigger ones. Then I will say to myself, 'Soul, you have a lot of things stored up in your barns, enough to last for many years to come. You don't need to worry about the future; you don't even have to work any longer. You can just eat, and drink, and enjoy yourself all day long.'"

Do you see what it was he trusted in?

But that very night God said to him, "You fool! This very night you are going to die. Whose then will all those things be that you have stored up?"

"So," Jesus said, "is every one who lays up treasure for himself, but is not rich toward God."

I do not want you to think that Jesus meant it is wicked to be rich. It is just that money, like all the other gifts of God, is a trust from God. And a trust is always a dangerous thing. A man is held responsible for how he uses what is entrusted to his care. When God entrusts us with money, He expects us to use it, not for our selfish pleasure, but in His service.

"If you want to be truly secure and safe for the future," Jesus said, "then sell your property, and give the money to the poor. And you will have a treasure in heaven that can never be lost."

Perhaps you think, "Well, this is one problem I do not have. There is no danger I will trust in my riches, because, you see, I don't have any. And I haven't any property I can sell, either, in order to lay up treasure in heaven."

But this wonderful treasure that cannot be lost is available even to the poorest of the poor. There was a poor widow in Jerusalem. Either she had no family to look after her, or else her family did not care what happened to her. She was so poor that all the money she had in the world was two mites — and those two mites together would be worth about one quarter of a cent. When that was spent, she did not know how she could live. There was no way for her to get any more money.

Jesus was teaching in the temple. Many rich men came into the court, and they dropped large, generous, gifts into the boxes set out there for offerings to God. And then the poor widow came. She gave her two mites to God. Jesus said to His disciples, "This poor widow gave more than all those rich men. For they gave God what they had left over, what they did not need for themselves. She gave God everything she had, even all her living."

The poor widow recognized that it was God who had given her the two mites. And she trusted God to continue to supply her needs after she had used her one quarter of a cent for the heavenly treasure that can never be lost. Are you and I as poor as she was? Are we as rich?

45

Seventy Times Seven

Matthew 19:21-35

Once there was a king. His kingdom was big and it was rich, so big and so rich that he could not begin to tend to everything himself. So he chose deputies to help him. To collect taxes he chose especially men whom he could trust.

One day he called these men in, to look over their accounts. And then the king made a shocking discovery. One of these men, one of those the king had trusted, was short in his accounts. He was not just a little bit short. It was a dreadful shortage. He owed the king ten million dollars. I do not know whether he had stolen the money himself, and wasted it on wild living, or whether he had just been careless and allowed others to make away with it. At any rate, he could not pay any of this tremendous debt.

The king was saddened by this discovery.

"I will have to sell you as a slave," he told his deputy, "and your wife and children too. That way I will get back some of the money you owe me, though it will not begin to settle all your debt."

The deputy was terrified. Would he have to spend all the rest of his life in slavery? And his wife, and his precious children too? He threw himself on the ground at the king's feet.

"Have patience, and I will pay back everything," he promised. Of course, no matter how long he lived or how hard he worked, he could never have really paid back so big a debt. But the king took pity on him.

"I will forgive you your whole debt," he said. "You do not have to pay anything back at all. You can go now, a free man."

So the man went out from the king's presence. A terrible load was lifted from his shoulders; he felt like a new man. But as he was walking away he saw one of his own servants, and he suddenly remembered that this servant owed him seventeen dollars. The deputy flew into a terrible rage. He seized the servant by the throat, almost choking the breath out of him.

"Pay me what you owe!" he shouted at the servant.

The servant was terrified. He fell down at the deputy's feet.

"Have patience, and I will pay you everything," he said. Did the deputy remember how just a minute before he had spoken these very same words? (And this man could have paid him back this small amount!) Did he remember how frightened he had been? Did he remember the gracious forgiveness of the king? No, he did not. He dragged the servant off to prison. As the gate clanged shut on him, he shouted, "You shall not get out till you have paid back the very last cent."

This cruel deed did not go unnoticed. Those who were standing nearby went and told the king what had happened. The king was very angry. He called the deputy back.

"You wicked servant," he said to him. "I forgave you all your debt. Don't you think you ought to have had mercy on your servant, just as I had mercy on you?"

Then the king called the police and had the deputy put in prison.

"You shall not get out," he told him, "till you have paid back the very last cent."

It was Jesus who told this story. He told it to answer a question Peter had asked. Jesus had been talking to His disciples about what they ought to do when someone treated them badly.

What do *you* do when someone is mean to you? When he tells lies about you, or cheats you, or snatches what is yours and breaks it, or makes fun of you? Is your first thought, "How can I get even? How can I pay him back?"

Jesus said we ought to love the person who is mean to us. We ought to pray for him. We ought to forgive him.

"How often ought I to forgive him?" Peter asked. "Is seven times often enough?"

"No," Jesus answered, "seven times is not often enough. You are to forgive the person who has wronged you seventy times seven times."

That seems like a lot of times. After all, you are not the one who is in the wrong. It is the other person who has been mean to you. Why must you forgive him over and over and over again? He does not deserve such treatment.

No, he does not deserve it. And so Jesus told this story to explain why we must give our brother forgiveness he does not deserve.

You see, God Himself is the great king. And you and I are His deputies. He has trusted us with His possessions. But when the day of reckoning arrives, you and I, yes, every single one of us, find that we are hopelessly in debt. We have sinned against God over and over and over. We could never possibly pay back what we owe. Does God try to get even with us? You know the answer. God forgives all our debt. He does it "for free." He forgives us because Jesus, His own Son, has paid our debt for us. He freely gives us forgiveness and love that we do not deserve.

And you and I must copy the wonderful mercy of God. We must remember that we were scared, and despairing, and facing a hopeless future. We must remember the day we fell on our knees before God and begged for help and forgiveness. We must remember how God forgave all our debt, every single last sin, for the sake of our blessed Saviour Jesus. That is why we must forgive our brother when he sins against us.

46
Good News

Luke 10:1-6, 17-24

I've got good news for you," Teacher said as she closed her book. "Our class won the paper drive. You are going to have a day off next week."

"Good news!" Mary shouted as she ran into the house, waving her report card. "I went up in arithmetic."

"The news is good," the doctor said, smiling at Tommie as he limped into the office on his crutches. "We are going to take off your cast today."

"Listen to my news," Father said at the supper table. "We are all going to Washington, D.C., for our vacation this summer."

Good news! What fun it is to hear it! Perhaps the only thing that is more fun is to tell it! And if for some reason you don't get a chance to tell it right away, sometimes it seems as if you will almost burst before you get it out!

Have you ever stopped to ask yourself what would be the very best news that you could hear? What would be better than hearing that you had been elected class president? Or that someone had given your family a million dollars? Or that Dad had promised you a car as soon as you finished Drivers' Training?

The very best news of all is news about a person. It is better than money, or honors, or vacation trips. If you have ever known a boy or girl whose parents could not get along with each other, you know that this is so. Nothing else really seems to matter if your father and your mother are always fighting.

The very best news is about someone even more important in your life than your father and your mother. It is the news that the great God of heaven and earth loves you, that He is willing to become your friend, your daily companion. Even more exciting than this, it is the news that everything that stood between you and your God has been wiped out. The hopeless struggle to live a life pleasing to Him is all over, because Jesus has already lived this life for you. Of course, you will still want to please Him in every way you can. But now you will do it out of a heart overflowing with love, not because you are afraid.

This was the news that was burning in the hearts of Jesus' friends. They, too, just as you sometimes do, felt that they would burst if they did not tell someone soon, if they did not tell everyone they met. And Jesus understood how they felt. He knew that good news can hardly be called good news unless we share this news with others.

Once before Jesus had sent His twelve closest friends out to tell the news. Now He sent a much larger group, seventy of them altogether. "Heal the sick," He said to them, "and tell everyone you meet that the rule of God is near at hand. Do not stop even to greet people who pass you on the road. There is a plentiful harvest waiting, but not enough workers to gather it in."

Perhaps you think these are strange words. The harvest Jesus was talking about was not the fields of ripe grain along the road. No, Jesus was thinking of the men and women — and the children too — who were hungry for the news about His coming, who would actually starve unless they heard that God's promised Saviour had come at last. Not in their bodies. They had bread enough to eat. It was their souls that were starving, starving for the love and the friendship of God.

152

And so the seventy set out, going in pairs, two by two, traveling from one little town to another, carrying the precious news. What kind of people were these seventy news-bearers? They were not learned preachers who had studied for years to learn how best to bring God's message. They were just plain folk, like you and me. Most of them had never gotten very far in school. And I am sure that most of them were shaking in their boots that first time they got up to tell about Jesus. Just as you and I are scared if we have to speak about Jesus to others, or perhaps pray in front of others.

But every single one of the seventy had met Jesus face to face, and every single one of them had been a changed person since that meeting. And so, though they were scared, they went out gladly, to share with others the wonderful news that had changed their own lives.

After a time they came back again, still two by two, just as they had gone out. They came back, the Bible tells us, with great joy.

"Lord," they said to Jesus in surprised delight, "even the devils went away when we spoke to them in Your name."

"Yes," Jesus answered, "because you carry God's message, nothing can hurt you, not even the devil himself. But this is not what you should be happiest about. The fact that should make you happiest of all is that God has written down your names in His book in heaven."

When Jesus said that nothing can hurt us when we are busy about His work, He did not mean that God was going to take out of our lives every problem, every trouble, every disappointment. No, He meant that even those things that seem hard to us will never really hurt us. For all these things will be used by God to change us into the kind of person God always meant us to be.

Well, you say, that was long ago. Yes, you are right. And yet things have not changed much since that day when Jesus sent out His seventy friends to spread the good news. The church of God still grows in this very same way — those whose lives have been changed tell the wonderful news to others. Even you, though you are not yet grown up, can have a share in this exciting work.

47

Who Is My Neighbor?

Luke 10:25-37

As he entered the mountain pass, the traveler looked up fearfully at the wild, overhanging rocks. They called this trail "The Road of Blood," because so many travelers had lost their lives along it. Over and over the governor had sent troops into the mountains to clear out the bandits that infested them. But always they had failed — so inaccessible were the rocky slopes, so numerous the hideout caves.

The traveler had hoped to avoid this dangerous journey altogether, or at least to find a traveling companion, someone to encourage him and share the dangers of the road. But here he was, alone. He wondered, as the path wound further and further into the narrow, shadowy valley — for here the sun hardly ever reached — whether this could be his last day on earth.

There was not a minute's warning. As he came around a bend in the road, the bandits dropped on top of him from the rocks above his head. They beat him savagely with sticks. For a moment the rocky walls echoed to his screams. Then there was silence again. The robbers melted back beyond the rocks from which they had come.

The traveler lay in a heap by the side of the path, bleeding from half a dozen wounds. The bandits had not only taken his money, they had even torn the clothes off his back.

Presently a priest came around the turn. He stopped, frozen in his tracks, when he saw the bloody heap by the side of the road. If there was a fleeting thought in his mind that he, God's priest, ought to show God's love to this wounded man, he quickly thrust it away. This was plainly a dangerous spot. He crossed the road, to get as far away as he could from this repulsive sight, turned his head away, and went on.

A little later a Levite came along. The wounded man groaned. He was in a state of shock, and scarcely conscious. The Levite drew his robes more closely around him and went hurriedly on. He was to serve in the temple that day and did not wish to soil his hands with this stranger's blood.

Was there no one to take pity on this poor dying man? No one to stand by him as he breathed his last breath? No one to comfort him by reminding him of the promises of our faithful God? It is dreadful to die, but even worse to die all alone.

The next sound was the soft plop-plop of a donkey's feet. The man who rode the donkey was a Samaritan merchant. This man certainly would not stop. He was not a fellow countryman of the wounded traveler. He was his bitter enemy. All his life he had endured insults and injuries from Jews. This was his chance to pay them back.

But no! This man knew God only very imperfectly. Yet in his heart he had felt the love of God. Because God loved him, a Samaritan, he also pitied this poor traveler, his enemy. He climbed off his donkey's back. He examined the wounded man. He took oil and wine from his pack and poured them over the traveler's wounds — oil to soften the pain and heal the wounds, and wine to disinfect them. He took some of his cloth — the cloth he had hoped to sell in Jerusalem. He tore the cloth into strips and bandaged the bleeding wounds. Then he lifted the man onto the donkey's back, and, walking beside him, half supporting him as they went, he brought him to the nearest inn.

That night the Samaritan stayed up all night to nurse the wounded man. The next morning his patient showed improvement. He left him in the care of the innkeeper.

"Here is money," he said to the innkeeper. "Take care of him, and when I stop on my way back from Jerusalem, I will pay you back if you have spent more than this."

* * * * *

When Jesus had something important to teach His followers, He often told them a story. Today they were on the way to Bethany. Perhaps they were walking along the very road our story tells about. There was a stranger with them, a student of the law of Moses, who had caught up with them as they walked. They were talking about what God's law actually means in our everyday lives. You know the law I mean: *Thou shalt love the Lord thy God with all thy heart, and with all thy soul, and with all thy mind; and thy neighbor as thyself.* How far does God expect us to go in this loving other people? You love your father and your mother, your brothers and sisters, your friends. Even this is not always easy. How many other people are included? Who is your neighbor?

This story was Jesus' answer to that question. You are to love every man who needs your help. *Every single one.* No matter whether or not he belongs to your church. No matter whether he is of the same race or not. No matter, even, whether he is your enemy, and has been mean to you.

Perhaps you say, "This is all very well, but love cannot be commanded. If I don't love you, there is nothing I can do about it."

You are thinking about the wrong kind of love. The love Jesus spoke about means that you do everything you can to help those who are in trouble, even if they are not lovable. You do this for just one reason. You are trying to walk in the footsteps of your Saviour, who loved you when you were unlovable. Unlovable? Your soul was hideous and deformed with sin. You were not dying, as was the man along that mountain road. You were already dead. And Jesus, who hates sin, so loved you in the degradation of your sin, that He gave His life for you. That is why your heart overflows with love to Him, and this love cannot help spilling over towards all the people you meet who are in need of help.

48
How Much More!

Luke 11:1-13

Johnnie is your best friend. You like to do things together, and you like to talk things over. If you get into any trouble, or even into a fight (though I certainly hope not!), Johnnie takes your side. If Johnnie is sick and cannot go to the class picnic, you would almost as soon stay home yourself. And if something exciting happens to you when he is not along, you do not really enjoy the excitement until you get a chance to tell your friend about it.

Our story today is about friends and praying. I am sure that if Johnnie was very sick, or in great danger, you would pray for him. But there is more than that to this business about friends and praying.

Praying is not always easy. Probably you have found this out for yourself. It is hard to know just what to pray for; hardest of all to keep on praying when God does not seem to answer you.

Often Jesus used to spend all night alone on the mountaintop talking to God. His friends envied Him those wonderful night-long talks. Like us, they found praying hard. "Lord," they said to Jesus, "teach us how to pray." And so Jesus taught them that short, beautiful prayer that we call the Lord's Prayer, the one that begins, "Our Father, who art in heaven."

This prayer teaches us what we ought to pray for. But Jesus knew that you and I need to know much more than that. And so He went on to tell His followers *how* to pray. You and I, when we talk to God, often stumble. We are tongue-tied, or we fall into a sort of mechanical repetition, saying the same thing over each time in identical words. And this, Jesus said, is partly because we do not see the connection between praying and being friends.

Praying, He said, is like talking to your best friend. You can ask Him for whatever you need, because He is your Friend and He loves you. You can ask Him at any time of the day or night. You never need to think, "This might be an inconvenient moment for Him to listen to me," or "Probably He is too busy to bother with my little problems." A friend who loves you is never too busy! And if He does not answer when you ask for something, you can go on asking over and over again. You can plead with Him to help you. You can throw yourself on His love. God is not angry — no, quite the opposite, He is pleased — when we come to Him over and over, when we remind Him of His promises, when we refuse to go away just because He has not at once answered our request.

Then Jesus told His followers a little story, to make all this clear. In the story it is late at night. The door is locked. The children — all of you — are ready for bed. Just as your father puts out the light, there is a knock. "Now who on earth could that be, at this hour of the night?" Mother asks. Father goes to the door and peers out into the darkness. And there on the step stands an old friend you have not seen for years. The door is thrown open. The lamp is lighted. All thought of going to bed is forgotten in this delightful, unexpected visit. Even you children are allowed to stay up and listen.

But Mother is uneasy. She calls Father to one side. "We have no food in the house, to give our guest for supper," she says, "not even a single piece of bread." Father says, "I will slip next door and borrow some from our friends there."

So now it is Father who is knocking at the door of a darkened house. At first there is no answer. Finally a man's gruff voice calls out, "Who is it?" And Father answers, "It is I, your friend. We have unexpected company, and have nothing to give him to eat. Please lend us three loaves of bread." But the neighbor answers, "Don't bother me! The door is already locked. I and all my children are in bed. I can't get up to give you some bread."

But Father does not stop knocking. He has a right to ask, because the neighbor is his friend. At last, because Father refuses to go away, the neighbor does get up. He lights the lamp, unlocks the door, and gives Father the bread.

Jesus does not mean to say by this story that we should expect from God just what we expect from our friends here on earth. We are not to decide what God is like by comparing Him to the people we know. No, it is just the other way around. What Jesus is telling us is that God is the *great* Friend, the *first* Friend. You might even say that was one big reason God made you and me in the first place, so that He might be our Friend — that we might talk to Him, bring Him all our problems, ask Him for whatever we need, and go together with Him everywhere.

And whatever of friendship you and I find in our troubled world is a poor, faint reflection of that true, never-failing friendship of God Himself. The man in the story, you see, got up in the end not out of friendship, but simply because he wished to sleep in peace. But where human friendship falters and fails, God's friendship is always faithful.

First of all, of course, you must be sure you are talking to your

Friend. Your very first prayer — and you will need to pray it over and over — must be, *Forgive me all my sins, for Jesus' sake.* But as soon as you have done this, as soon as you have gained back that lost friendship with God who is both your Master and your Saviour, then you are not just *allowed* to ask, and seek, and knock. You are *commanded* to do all these things. For Jesus said, "If you, being evil, know how to give good gifts to your children, how much more shall your Father who is in heaven give good things to them that ask Him?"

49

We Sit at Jesus' Feet

Luke 10:38-42

The road from Jerusalem to Jericho first dips down to cross a little stream, and then it climbs up and up, through groves of olive trees and date palms, to cross the Mount of Olives. On the further side of the mountain it passes a tiny village called Bethany. There is nothing about this little settlement to make it stand out. No one who lived there would ever have dreamed that the dusty street, the white-walled houses, yes, and even the quiet cemetery would some day be famous. Still that was the way it happened. For in Bethany, along that dusty street, in one of those white-walled houses, lived two sisters and a brother — Mary and Martha, and Lazarus.

To neither of these women had God sent a husband, and He had given no wife to their brother. And so there were no happy children's shouts in this house. But, as if to take the place of the children God had denied them, there was plenty of love. Lazarus loved Mary and Martha, and each of the sisters loved her brother and her sister dearly.

This was the more surprising because the two sisters were so different. Martha was the manager. She ran the house, planned the meals, took the responsibility. Mary was a dreamer. It was not that she meant to shirk her share of the work. It was just that her thoughts ran away with her, so that, while she was in the middle of sweeping the floor, she would stand staring into the distance, her thoughts, it seemed, a thousand miles away, and the broom motionless in her hands.

I am sure the sisters had longed and even prayed for a husband and children. And at last God answered their prayers in His own loving way. He sent them a gift far better than the husband and children He had denied them. God sent them a friend. The Preacher from the north country, yes, the very one everyone was talking about, stopped one day at their house. He stayed for dinner, and He spent the night. They listened eagerly to the strange, wonderful words He spoke. They begged Him to come again. They welcomed His friends also. They gave Him the best food they had. It was nothing fancy — for they were ordinary folk — but it was their best, and it was served with love.

And so there grew up a strange and beautiful friendship between Mary and Martha and Lazarus and Jesus. Jesus filled to overflowing the empty places in their hearts, and they, in turn, welcomed Jesus into the warm, loving circle of their little home.

Of course, much as they loved each other, Mary and Martha were not perfect. They did not always agree. They had sinful hearts, just as you and I do. Martha was a very particular housekeeper. For a special guest like Jesus, she wanted everything to be just so. When Jesus arrived, she rushed about, almost distracted; there were so many things she thought she ought to do, and not enough time to do them. She could not spare a moment to talk to Jesus. Mary, quite differently, was so happy to see Jesus she quite forgot that there was work to do. She seated herself quietly at His feet, and listened to every word He said.

As she rushed from one task to another, all hot and bothered, Martha noticed her sister sitting with folded hands at Jesus' feet.

"Lord," she said to Jesus, "don't You care that my sister has left all the work to me? Tell her to come and help."

And Jesus answered gently, "Martha, Martha, you are fretting and fussing about so many things! There is only one thing that is really necessary. The place Mary has chosen is the best place, and it shall not be taken away from her."

I am sure Martha found this hard to understand. After all, what she was doing was all for Jesus, wasn't it? And people do have to eat! Houses must be kept clean and in order!

But there is something I want you to notice about Martha. She did not talk back to Jesus. She did not say, "That is all very nice, but someone has to do the work." No, I think that as she finished her tasks, she thought about what Jesus had said. And that is just what Jesus wanted her to do, and what He wants you and me to do too.

Your cousins live a long way off, perhaps in California. For the first time in many years they have come to visit. They have traveled all those long miles to see you, to become better acquainted, to be friends. You are excited about this visit. You rearrange your room. You finish the model plane you are making. You set up all your planes so they make a fine display. When at last your cousins arrive, you open the door and invite them in, and then you say, "Excuse me, please. I am fixing something I want to show you. I will be back later. Sit down and make yourself at home."

Would you do this? You smile. "Of course not," you say. "It would not be polite. They did not come to see my model planes. They came to see me." Yes, that is just the point. The important thing about any friendship is being with your friend, sharing talk with him, yes, and sharing even your inmost thoughts. It is quite impossible to be a friend if you are too busy to sit down, and listen, and answer what your friend says.

Do you mean, you ask, that Jesus is my Friend? Yes, that is what I mean. Of course, He is much more to you than any other friend. He is your Maker, who called you into being out of nothing. He is your Saviour, who gave His own life to pay for your sins. He is your

162

Teacher, who will show you how to climb out of the dark pit of sin into which you have fallen, and to find your way back into the sunlight of God's favor. But, besides all these things, He is your Friend. Everyone who trusts in His death, and tries to walk in His way, is His friend. He has said so Himself.

And that is just why, like Mary so long ago, you will want to sit at His feet. To listen to what He tells you, and to tell Him in return how much you thank and love Him, and how desperately you need Him every day. There are many other things you want to do, even things you want to do for Him. But nothing else is as important, as absolutely necessary to your life, as this.

50
Jesus, the Life-Giver

John 11:1-44

Jesus cradled in a manger
For us facing every danger
Living as a homeless stranger.

He came, John tells us, to His own people, and they would not let Him in — not into their homes, not into their hearts!

Mary and Martha and their brother Lazarus were exceptions. They invited Him to stay with them — in their home, and in their hearts as well.

Have you ever been homesick? Alone, and among strangers? So that you thought back with longing to the love and shelter and peace of your home? If you have, perhaps you can understand a little bit of what it must have meant to Jesus to be welcomed into that home in Bethany.

But it was only for a few days. Mary and Martha and Lazarus would have liked Him to stay with them always. But that could not be. Even they could see that every day it was getting more dangerous for Jesus to be seen on the streets. The Jewish leaders hated Him with a bitter hatred. Twice in the last few days they had tried to kill Him.

Jesus knew what you and I ought to know, but so often forget. He knew that God had planned His life. And that plan included the day when He was going to die. His day, the day when Jesus would lay down His life for His friends, had not yet come. It was close now, but there was still work for Jesus to finish.

And so He left that home He loved, and went away to a safer place. He took with Him the twelve disciples whom He was training to carry on His work after He left this earth and returned to heaven. They went eastward to the Jordan River. The people there listened eagerly to Jesus, and many of them believed He was the Saviour sent by God.

Meanwhile, back in Bethany, the family Jesus loved went about their daily work. One day, not so long after Jesus had left, Lazarus became sick. It was a serious sickness; his two sisters were very worried. They remembered how many sick people Jesus had healed. "If only He were here," one of the sisters said to the other. They knew it was not really safe for Jesus to come back; still, they thought, surely He would want to know. And so they sent a message. The messenger reached Jesus at Bethabara, on the further side of the Jordan River.

"Lord," the message said, "he whom You love is sick."

"This sickness," Jesus told His disciples, "is for the glory of God." Still, He did not leave. He went on with His teaching for two more days. Then He said to His followers, "We will go back now to Bethany." The disciples tried to persuade Him not to go. "When we left there," they said, "the Jews were trying to kill you. Are we to go back there?"

"Lazarus," Jesus answered, "has fallen asleep. I am going to wake him up."

"If he is sleeping, he will get better," they said. Then Jesus told them plainly, "Lazarus is dead. And I am glad, for your sakes, that I was not there, so that you may see and believe." What was it the disciples would see? And you and I also? Jesus did not say.

By the time they reached Bethany, Lazarus had already been buried for four days. Mary sat at home, weeping. Martha met Jesus outside the village. "If You had only been here," she said to Jesus sadly, "my brother would not have died."

"Your brother will rise again," Jesus answered.

"I know that he will rise at the last day," Martha said.

"I am the resurrection and the life," Jesus said. "The person who believes in me, even if he dies, will nevertheless live. And whoever is alive and believes in me will never die. Do you believe this?"

"Yes, Lord," Martha answered, "I believe that You are the Son of God and the Saviour sent by God into the world." Then she went to call her sister.

"The Teacher is here," she said to Mary. "He is asking for you." Mary got up at once to go to meet Jesus. The friends who were sitting with her in the house, who had come to comfort her, followed her. They thought, "She is going to the grave, to weep there." Mary fell down at Jesus' feet.

"Lord," she said, as the tears streamed down her face, "if only You had been here, my brother would not have died!" Jesus' heart was torn with love and pity when He saw her grief.

"If you only believe," He said to her (and there were tears in His eyes also, tears of love), "you shall see the glory of God. Where have you laid him?"

They said, "Come and see." When the Jews saw Jesus weeping,

they said, "See how much He loved him!" So they all came to the grave. Lazarus was buried in a cave on the hillside, with a stone rolled before the entrance.

"Take away the stone," Jesus said.

"Lord," Martha answered, "he has been dead four days already. The body will be decayed!" But Jesus said,

"Did I not tell you that if you believed you would see the glory of God?" So they rolled away the stone. Then Jesus, looking up to heaven, prayed, "Father, I thank Thee for hearing my prayer." Then He cried out with a loud voice, "Lazarus, come forth!" And then there was seen such a sight as no man had ever seen before. For the dead man came walking out of his grave, still wrapped in the grave clothes. Jesus said, "Loosen the clothes, and let him go."

Was this the greatest miracle Jesus ever did? No, there was a greater miracle. That greatest miracle of all was the one which made the bringing of Lazarus back to life possible. The greatest miracle was that our Lord conquered the power of death, and Himself rose from the grave.

51
Sightless Eyes

John 9:1-41

In the city of Jerusalem, at the gate of the temple, there sits a ragged man who stares up at you with sightless eyes. He has been blind since the day he was born. He has never seen the sky, the trees, the birds; he has never seen the beauty of God's temple. He still lives at home with his parents, so he is at least assured of a roof over his head for as long as they live. But there is no work he can do to support himself. And so he is reduced to that most hopeless of all occupations — he has become a beggar.

As he sits on the pavement, the crowds push past him. Many of them are well dressed. Some are rich. Some occupy seats of honor, as judges, priests, or teachers. A few pause to drop a thin coin in the beggar's hand, and then hurry on. But the interesting thing about this crowd — and you will need seeing eyes to notice this — is that many of them are more hopelessly blind than the poor beggar who sits outside the gate. And that is what this story is about.

It is the Sabbath morning. Jesus is coming out of the temple. "Master," His friends ask Him, "did this beggar sin, or was it his parents, that he should be born blind?" And Jesus answers, "Neither this man, nor his parents. He was born blind in order to show clearly the wonderful works of God." And then Jesus stoops down. He spits on the ground, and makes a little mud. He plasters the mud on the blind man's eyes. "Go," He says to the blind man, "and wash your eyes in the pool of Siloam." And then Jesus and His friends go on their way.

The blind man gropes his way to the pool, which lies below the temple wall. He washes the mud off his eyes, and, marvel of marvels, he can see clearly. For a while he stands still, staring at those things

he had never seen before — the water, the trees, the temple towering above him. But at last he turns and goes home.

The neighbors crowd around him in amazement. "Is not this the man that sat and begged?" one asks. And another remarks, "It looks like the same man, but it cannot be." But the man himself says simply, "I am the one." Now there is a chorus of questions. "How were your eyes opened?" And the man answers, "The man called Jesus made clay, and put it on my eyes, and said, 'Go, wash in the pool of Siloam,' and I went, and washed, and now I can see." Then they ask, "Where is he?" But the man can only answer, "I do not know."

Someone brings the man to the Pharisees, those religious officials who make all the rules, and take such pride in their way of living. The Pharisees ask the same questions as the neighbors did. "How is it you can now see?" And the man answers again, "He made clay, and put it on my eyes, and I washed it off, and now I see."

At once some of the Pharisees say, "You see! This Jesus cannot come from God, for He breaks the Sabbath." To make clay, even such a little dab of clay, and to heal a blind man in whatever way, both break the Pharisees' rules about the Sabbath. Others among them object, "How can a sinner do such wonders?" So they begin to argue with each other.

At last, to settle the matter, they call the blind man's parents. "Is this your son?" they ask. "You say he was born blind? How is it he can now see?" The parents are afraid to answer. They know the Pharisees have decided to throw out of the synagogue any person who dares to say that Jesus is the Saviour. "We know this is our son," they answer, "and we know that he was born blind. But we do not know how he is now able to see. Ask him. He is grown up. He can speak for himself."

The Pharisees call the blind man in again. "Tell us the truth now," they order him. "We know that this man Jesus is a sinner." And the man answers, "Whether He is a sinner I do not know. One thing I know. I was blind, and now I can see." This makes the Pharisees angry. They will never admit they themselves are blind; the truth is they do not want to see. "How did he open your eyes?" they ask again. "I told you once," the man says, "and you did not listen. Why do you keep asking me? Do you also want to become His followers?" Now the Pharisees are furious. "You are his follower!" they shout at the man. "We are followers of Moses. We know God spoke to Moses, but we do not know who this man is." And the man says, "This is truly a wonder! Since the world began it has never happened that anyone has been able to open the eyes of a man born blind. If this man were not from God He could not do this." And the Pharisees retort, "You, who were born in sin, do you dare to try to teach us?" And they throw him out of the synagogue.

Jesus hears what has happened. He looks for the man. "Do you believe on the Son of God?" He asks him. And the man who had been blind asks, "Who is He, that I may believe on Him?" And Jesus answers, "I who speak to you am He." Then the man says, "Lord, I believe!" And he bows down and worships Jesus.

Now Jesus says, "I came into this world for judgment, that those who are blind may see, and that those who think they see may become blind." The Pharisees ask Him, "Are we also blind?" And Jesus answers, "If you were blind, you would have no sin. But now you say, 'We can see'; you remain in your sin."

And so, you see, there is more than one way of being blind. The poor beggar knew he was blind, and Jesus opened the eyes of his body and also the eyes of his soul. But all those who will not admit they are in darkness, who are certain they do not need a Saviour, for them, alas, there is no hope.

52
Please Excuse Me!

Luke 14:15-24

*t*he mailman has come, and there is a small, square envelope addressed to you. *You are invited,* the little card says, *to a beach party at Susan R's cottage.* You run to show Mother. "I never hoped to be invited," you say excitedly. "Why, she is the most popular girl in our class."

The day before the party you meet Susan in the hall at school. "Be sure to bring a warm sweater," she says. Some evil spirit seems to have caught your tongue. "You'll have to count me out," you answer before you can stop the words; "I've got some other things I'd rather do tomorrow." Susan stares at you in disbelief. Then she says, "I'll never ask you to a party again."

"But I thought you wanted to go to that party," Mother says when you get home. "I did," you say sadly. "I don't know what got into me."

Is it possible to want to go to a party — to want to go desperately — to be invited, to plan on going, and then in the end to be left out? Yes, it is possible.

God also gives parties — and the invitations are much sought after. Some people are very sure they are on the invitation list. They have attended church so faithfully, prayed so loudly and so often, dropped such large gifts in the collection plate! They are, so they think, on such good terms with God. A lot of these people are going to be surprised. Some people have no hope of getting an invitation. They are not important enough, not successful enough; they don't know enough; their lives are stained with sin. Many of them are going to be surprised too.

Jesus often talked about these parties God gives. And He always came back to the surprised guests. One day He was invited to have dinner at the home of one of the rulers of the Pharisees. All the other guests were important people. And, like all Pharisees, they took great pride in their "good" lives. They obeyed meticulously the hundreds on hundreds of rules which they themselves had added to the simple commandments of God. They never ate with less "holy" people, nor went into their houses; and if they passed ordinary folk on the street, they pulled their coats tight around them for fear they might brush against a sinner and catch his wickedness by contagion.

As they sat around the Pharisees' table that noonday, one of the guests piously exclaimed, "How happy it will be to sit at God's table feasting when He comes in His kingdom!" It was quite evident that the speaker expected to be one of the first to be invited to that feast. And that all his friends, his Pharisee friends, would be at the party too. They were the leaders of God's people, weren't they? Jesus answered, as He loved to do, by a little story:

A certain man once made a great feast. He sent out invitations ahead of time, so that his guests could figure on the date. Then he prepared his party. Sheep and cattle were roasted, elaborate sweet-meats were baked, wine was brought up and tasted, the table was set with the best of everything. When all was ready, the man sent his servant out to remind the invited guests. "Come," the servant said to each one, "the banquet is all ready."

Immediately they began to think of excuses. The first guest said, "I have just bought a piece of land. I have to go and look it over. Please excuse me." The second guest said, "I have just bought ten oxen, and I want to try them out. Please excuse me." The third guest said, "I have just been married. You can't expect me to leave my new wife to come to your banquet."

When the master heard these excuses, he was angry. "Go quickly," he said to his servant, "into the streets and alleys of the city, and bring to my party the poor, the crippled, the lame, and the blind." When the servant came back, he said, "I have done as you commanded, but still there are empty seats at the banquet table." And his master said, "Go out to the country roads and the fields, and urge whomever you meet to come to my banquet. For I tell you, not one of those people who scorned my first invitation shall even taste of my supper!"

What did Jesus mean by this story? Perhaps you yourself can guess. The Man who gave the wonderful banquet was God Himself. And the first people to be invited were people who had known God since they were children, who went to the synagogue or the temple faithfully and observed all the outward forms of religion. Jesus was the servant who went out to tell the guests that everything was ready, and the party about to begin. One by one they turned their backs on Him. "I have something else I'd rather do today," they said in effect.

What does God do when people like ourselves, people on whom He has showered so many blessings, reject His invitations? He does a terrible thing, a thing that should make every one of us tremble. He simply scratches our names off His invitation list. And then He invites others to take our place at His table, people who have never known the blessedness of being God's friends, strangers from outside the church, sinners with whom respectable church folk would not want to be seen. For only those who truly trust God and appreciate His love will ever taste of His supper.

53

The Wanderer

Luke 15:3-7

We laughed when we first saw this sign. OPEN RANGE — STOCK ON HIGHWAY. "Now who," said I, "would allow a valuable cow to wander onto a busy road?" Back in Michigan, where we came from, cattle were pastured in neat fenced-in fields during the summer, and in the barnyard within easy reach of shelter during the winter. Here in South Dakota we could see no fences, no barns, not even any houses. Only the endless prairies stretching to the horizon, broken here and there by small groups of cattle.

"Who takes care of those animals?" my husband wondered. "Where do they get water? Or food and protection when blizzards strike? Who looks after them when they are sick, or calving?" I didn't know. There was no sign anywhere that people lived in this lonely country.

Later, sitting on a beach near our campground, we learned some of the answers from a Montana rancher who sat next to us. He smiled at our puzzled questions. "Those cows are wild," he said. "They don't see a man from one year's end to the next. If they are really sick, or need help in calving, we have to rope them up before we can do anything for them."

I asked, "How do you ever find all your cows when it is time to market them? Don't you lose a lot of them?"

"They carry our brand, of course," he said. "But we do lose many of them. If we keep an average of ninety out of a hundred, we feel we have had a good year. In my father's day, seventy out of a hundred was usual. Improved breeding has made the difference."

The sheep of whom Jesus talked so often, like the cows in South Dakota, were not fenced in. Large flocks of them roamed at will over the countryside, looking for pasture and water. But they were not wild. Each flock had its own shepherd, and this shepherd was not like the cowboys you and I know. He was more like a father to his sheep. He lived with them twenty-four hours a day. He found the greenest grass and the freshest water for them. He protected them from the hyenas and jackals and wolves who always lurked around the edges of the flock, looking for the weak or the old to pick off. The sheep knew him so well that they recognized his voice, and came when he called them. And he in turn knew each sheep by name.

These sheep did not have to be tied down when they were sick or in trouble and needed help. They trusted the shepherd. And the shepherd loved his sheep — loved them so much that he was willing to risk his life to protect them. The shepherd was not a businessman counting the odds, saying, "If I save ninety out of a hundred, it will be a good year." No, the relationship between shepherd and sheep was loving, personal, intimate.

Sometimes, even with the best of care, a sheep wandered away from the flock. The shepherd did not shrug his shoulders and say, "Well, you can't win them all! I have ninety-nine left. I will forget the one that has wandered, and take care of these others." No, he left the ninety-nine in the care of a helper, and he set out, over gully and rocks and briar patch, searching without rest, till he found the one sheep that was lost. For this was not a matter of percentage of profit. This was a matter of love.

And when at last he found the one lost sheep, he picked the frightened animal up, and carried it home on his shoulders. And then he called out to all his friends and neighbors, "Share my joy! For I have found my sheep that was lost!"

Perhaps you say, "It is a nice story, but what does it have to do with me? It is all so long ago, so far away!" Well, if this is only a nice story to you, then you have missed the point entirely.

In an earthly kingdom those who are rebels or traitors pay for it with their lives. In the kingdom of Jesus, every single loyal subject was once a rebel or a traitor. Every one of us starts out as a lost sheep, wandering far away from the Shepherd of our souls.

And our Shepherd risked His life to find us and bring us back. Not because He needed one more sheep to send to market in the fall, so that this would be a profitable year. No, He risked His life to find *you* because He loved you, because He knew you by name, because you — wandering rebel though you were — were very precious and dear to Him. So precious, and so beloved, that He chose of His own free will to die for you. He said to His Father, "I will pay the price for this child's rebellion and treachery. I will take the punishment he deserves, so that he may go free."

Was there ever such a shepherd?

I do not know your name. Nor do I know how badly you are lost, or even how you came to wander so far away from home in the first place. But there is a Shepherd who knows you by name, who searches for you wherever you are, who does not even ask why you wandered away, or how soiled and ruined your life may be out there in the wilderness. For this is why He came — to search for and find the lost ones like you.

Tonight, when you are alone, pray to the Good Shepherd: "Lord Jesus, find me too, and bring me home!" He will answer that prayer. And when He carries you back in His loving arms, then even the angels in heaven will sing for very joy that you, His lost sheep, have been found.

54

The Runaway Son

Luke 15:11-32

Once, several years ago, the queen of the Netherlands visited Grand Rapids. Because my husband had served on one of the committees which arranged her visit, I was invited to have lunch with the queen. Juliana and Prince Bernhard sat on a raised platform at one end of the big ballroom in a downtown hotel. Important people — the governor of Michigan, the city mayor, the Netherlands ambassador to the United States — sat on the platform with her. The rest of the guests sat at small tables below and some distance from the queen.

Who gets to have lunch with the queen? The two hundred gathered in that crowded room, all wearing their best clothes, and most of the women new hats, were a carefully selected group. The president of Calvin College was there, and the professor of the Dutch language. There were ministers from the large downtown · churches. And there were Michigan senators and representatives who had come all the way from Washington for the occasion, and the official city greeter, who was to give the queen the key to the city.

It was interesting to look around and see who had been invited. But it was just as interesting to notice who had not been asked. There were no professional gamblers there, no drunkards, no pickpockets, no hoodlums, no delinquent teen-agers who had committed crimes and been put on probation by a judge who hoped to win them back to an honest life, no ex-convicts, none of the bums who stumbled, dirty and half-starved, along our city's skid row. Only the good, respectable, hard-working, successful, well-dressed people had been asked to have lunch with the queen.

A man is known, says the old proverb, by the company he keeps. The queen is a symbol of what is fine and noble and rich. If she ate

lunch with the riffraff of our world, the symbol would grow tarnished and soiled.

This is just what the Pharisees said about Jesus. "This man claims," they said, "to be a prophet. But just look at the kind of people he associates with! If he were really a prophet, he would see that these people are sinners. They are no fit company for a leader in our synagogue. Why, he even goes into their houses, and sits down and eats with them!"

The Pharisees themselves were very careful about whom they ate with. They took great pride in their "holy" lives. They not only obeyed all the laws God had given His people, but they even obeyed the hundreds of rules that someone had thought up later. But they never once remembered what God had said about loving God and your neighbor. And though they sometimes prayed for forgiveness, they did not really mean it. They were quite sure they did not need to be forgiven. Indeed, they thought God must be well pleased with such fine people as they were.

And this Jesus preferred the company of bums and crooks, the dregs of society! It was not — I hope you understand this — that Jesus did not care whether or not a man was honest, whether he obeyed God's law. He cared so much that He gave His own life to pay for all our dishonest, wicked acts. But Jesus saw that before a man can be saved he must know he *needs* to be saved, must know that he is a sinner. Then, if that man is sorry for his sins, and asks God to forgive him, there is hope for that man, no matter how wicked, how dreadful his past life has been. There is hope just because of the suffering and death of our Saviour.

No matter how wicked? Yes, no matter how wicked. Jesus once told a story which proved this very point. Once there was a prosperous farmer who had two sons. The older one was obedient, respectful, hard-working. The younger son hated life on the farm. He was rebellious and lazy. "Give me my share of your property," he said to his father. So his father gave him what would rightfully have been his share after his father died. The younger son took the money and left home, going as far away from that hated farm and his father's advice as he could get. Here he wasted his money on wild parties, and wild women. It was not long before all his inheritance had disappeared.

Just about then there was a famine in this country. The companions who had helped him spend his money had no use for him now that he was poor. Desperate for something to eat, he finally got a job looking after a herd of pigs. He was so hungry that he would have liked to fill his stomach with the garbage given to the pigs.

How often it happens that dreadful trouble is the means God uses to call us back to Him! One day the younger son remembered how even his father's servants had plenty to eat. "I will go home," he said to himself. "I will say to my father, 'I have sinned against God and against you. I am not worthy to be called your son. Treat me as one of your servants.' "

His father saw him coming far off. He ran to meet him, and threw his arms around him, and kissed him. The son started to confess his wrongdoing: "I have sinned," he said; "I am not worthy to be called your son." But the father called the servants. "Bring out the best robe and put it on him," he said, "and put a ring on his finger, and new shoes on his feet. Kill and roast the best calf, for we must have a celebration. My son was dead, but is alive again. He was lost, and is found."

Soon the older boy came back from his work in the fields. When he heard what had happened, he was angry. "I have always obeyed you," he said to his father. "But this fellow has thrown away your money on wild living. It is not fair for you to celebrate his return." His father looked at him sadly. "How can we help being glad?" the father asked his oldest son. "Your brother was dead, and now he is alive. He was lost, and he is found."

55

Unclean! Unclean!

Luke 17:11-19

"*U*nclean! Unclean!" the despairing voice cried out from the hills beside the road. "Unclean! Unclean!" the hills beyond echoed back the cry. The little group of travelers walking along the road instinctively drew closer together. Instinctively they shrank from any contact, even at a distance, with this disgusting disease. "Unclean! Unclean!" the cry came again.

This was not the main road to Jericho and Jerusalem. The main road ran through Samaria. This was a side road, used mainly by travelers who wished to avoid the towns. It ran along the border between Samaria and Galilee, and thus passed through a sort of "no man's land."

That was how the travelers met the lepers. For lepers are not allowed to live among other people. They must leave their home, their family, their friends, and live as best they can in the lonely countryside. Here in this desolate "no man's land" a group of them had banded together to ease their desperate loneliness. Nine of them were Jews. One was a Samaritan. Ordinarily Jews would have nothing to do with the Samaritans. But the dreadful affliction these men shared had done away with all such distinctions.

The disease itself was terrible enough. The deformities it produced — the loss of fingers and toes, of hair and teeth — were hard to bear. But perhaps even worse was being separated from those you loved and having to live as an outcast. And if anyone came near you, you had to warn them away. You had to cry, "Unclean! Unclean!"

But there was one of the little group of travelers on this lonely road who did not shrink away from the lepers. And somehow the lepers recognized Him. How did these outcast men who lived by themselves know about Jesus? How did they, who had no contacts with ordinary men, hear of His healing power? I do not know. But somehow they had heard.

The news spread quickly among the ten lepers. This was the new Teacher, the One who did such amazing things. And as they stood off to the side — for they did not dare to go near Him; it was against the law — they all called out in a longing voice, a voice that, for the first time in many years, had some hope in it: "Jesus, Master, have mercy on us!"

"Go and show yourselves to the priest," Jesus answered.

There was something about the person of Jesus that inspired their trust. Something in His words that awoke hope within their hearts. And so they obeyed His command. All ten of them turned at once and set out, as fast as they could walk, to find the priest. And as they went, suddenly, miraculously, by the power and mercy of our Lord, they were healed. Their terrible deformities disappeared. They felt like new people. They *were* new people.

What was their first thought when they discovered that they were healed? Nine of them hurried to find their friends and family. They could not wait to get back to their everyday lives, which they had had to give up. But one of them had something else he wanted to do more. That one was the Samaritan.

The Samaritan hurried back along the road where he had met

Jesus. He no longer had to walk by himself, crying, "Unclean! Unclean!" Now he walked along with other travelers, and as he walked he told them all about the wonderful thing God had done for him. At last he saw Jesus in the distance. He ran up to Him and fell down on his face at Jesus' feet. He poured out all the thanks of his heart, all the love and trust he now felt for his Lord.

Jesus looked at him sadly.

"There were ten lepers healed," He said. "Where are the other nine? Did not a single one of God's chosen people, the Jews, return to give thanks, but only this Samaritan?" Then Jesus said to the Samaritan:

"Get up and go home. Your faith has saved you."

And so the Samaritan got up and went to look for his family. But I am quite sure he never forgot what Jesus had done for him. I am sure that as long as he lived he told others about what had happened there on that lonely road. I am sure that from that day on he trusted in Jesus, and tried to show his thanks in the way he lived.

And now I would like to say something personal, if you will let me. You and I are unclean, too. No, we do not suffer from leprosy. Our disease is something worse, something far worse. Leprosy is only a disease of the body. You and I suffer from a disease of the heart. Our hearts are desperately wicked; they are deformed and made filthy by sin.

Is there no hope for us? Yes, there is hope. If we cry out to Jesus, "Jesus, Master, have mercy on us," He will hear our cry. He will heal our sin-sick hearts just as He healed the broken, deformed bodies of the ten lepers. He will do this if we ask Him, and if we trust in His death on the cross.

And if Jesus does this for you, what are you going to do? Are you going to be like the nine lepers who hurried away and forgot the gift they had received? Or will you be like the one who came back, the one who poured out his love and praise and thanks at Jesus' feet? Jesus gave His life for you. Will you give your life back to Him in trust and service?

56

A Cry for Mercy

Luke 18:9-14

Marlene followed her father and mother down the aisle and sat down in her seat. There were not many girls her age in church this morning. Most of the gang had decided to stay at the house party over Sunday, and go to church in the little chapel near the beach. Marlene had talked this over with her father. Together they had decided she should be present in her own church on Sunday. "I'm proud of you, Marlene," her father had said. Well, she was pretty proud of herself, too. Not many girls her age would give up a house party at the beach just to go to church. After all, she went to church twice every Sunday, didn't she?

She settled down and looked around her. Over there sat the Weirdy. They called her that because of her queer clothes. None of the girls ever had anything to do with her. She wouldn't have had enough money for things like house parties, anyway. When they had to sit beside her in school or Sunday school, they pulled faces and held their noses when the teacher's back was turned. It was not that she really smelled. It was just — well, just that she was so different.

A middle-aged couple filed in and sat down in the same row as Marlene. Marlene smiled to herself. She liked to watch them when the sermon was dull. The man's eyes would begin to glaze, then his eyelids would droop, finally his head would nod. Then his wife would nudge him with her elbow; he would sit up straight again with a start. After a few minutes the whole thing would start all over again. Disgusting, Marlene called it. Why didn't he go to bed earlier on Saturday night?

A family with several small children came next. The father carried the smallest; the mother led one only a little older by the hand. Marlene looked at the mother critically. Her hair was really a mess. It looked like a bird's nest. Was that any way to come to church? Sure, she was busy, but anyone could find the time to fix her hair decently. Marlene touched her own naturally curly hair with satisfaction.

And then Marlene almost laughed out loud. For that was Sally's boy friend coming down the aisle, sitting down next to Marlene herself. She edged a little closer to him, and smiled at him shyly out of the corner of her eyes. Before the service was over she would have him hooked for a date. Sure, Sally was her best friend. But when it came to dates, it was every girl for herself.

The organist played softly, and everyone bowed his head. Marlene prayed silently: "O God, I thank You that I have such nice clothes (not like the Weirdy over there). I thank You that I know how to behave properly in church, and that my hair is naturally curly. And most of all I thank You for Paul sitting beside me, as my reward for having come to church, and not staying at the house party. For Jesus' sake, Amen."

Perhaps you say I am exaggerating. I would like to think I am. But can you honestly say no such thoughts ever run through your mind before (or even during) church? There are some people who come to church not to worship God, but to show other folk how much better they are than the other worshipers. Jesus Himself said so. Listen to the story He tells:

Once there were two men who went up to the temple to pray. One of them was a Pharisee. This man was very strict about his religion. He obeyed all the laws of God, and all the rules the priests had set up too. The other man was a tax collector, a man who, for the sake of money, had betrayed his own people and sold out to the hated Roman conquerors. Besides being a traitor to his country, this man was a thief, collecting more taxes than were due, and lining his own pockets with the extra.

The Pharisee prayed to God. "God, I thank You," he said, "that I am better than other men, and especially better than that tax collector over there. I do not steal, I am fair to everyone, I do not break up

other men's homes and families. Besides all this, I fast two days a week, and give a tenth of everything I get to the priests."

The tax collector hardly dared to come into the temple. He stood far off, not daring even to raise his eyes to heaven, and beating his breast in his agony of soul. "O God," he prayed, "have mercy on me, a sinner!"

God heard the tax collector's prayer, and He forgave him. But He did not forgive the Pharisee. Why not? What was wrong with the Pharisee? What was wrong with the way Marlene came to church? Both of them offered God only an outward obedience, only an empty shell, obeying God only where other people could see what they did. They forgot that God can read the heart, and that it is your heart, your love, that God wants first of all.

The things the Pharisee did were good and right. It was right for Marlene to give up the house party to go to church too. But it was not enough. Because Marlene and the Pharisee thought of obedience as only an outward thing, they did not see how far short they came, how badly they needed God's forgiveness. The things the tax collector did were wrong. But he came to God for mercy; he trusted in God's salvation. And God forgave his sins because Jesus paid the price of those sins when He died on the cross.

You and I are sinners too. God grant us the grace to know this first of all. I do not know what you have done that is wrong; you do not know my sins. God knows. But whatever we have done, if we are truly sorry, if we cry out to God, as the tax collector did, "God have mercy on me, a sinner!" if we trust in our Saviour, Jesus, God will surely forgive. "For He has laid on Him the iniquity of us all."

57
Like Little Children

Mark 10:13-16

All of this time we have been talking about grown-up people. Does Jesus also have a message for you? Does He look at you with that same look of love and understanding with which He looked at Levi, that look which pierces to your very soul? Does He say to you too, "Follow me!"? Does He have time to talk to you, busy as He is? Will He listen if you talk to Him?

Does He care what happens to you? Yes, Jesus has a special love for children. Sometimes we who are grown-up forget that this is true. Sometimes we seem to think Jesus should not be bothered with a child's "small" problems. And Jesus, who knows us better than we know ourselves, understood that this was so. He took special pains to show us how mistaken we are.

Once there were some mothers with little children who tried to get into the house where Jesus was staying. They wanted Jesus to talk to their children, and to lay His hands on their heads and bless them. As soon as the disciples saw them, they started to shoo them away.

"Whatever are you thinking of?" they said. "The Master is much too busy to talk to children. He has important work to do. How dare you interrupt Him with your children?"

Jesus heard the commotion, and He was angry. "Do not send the children away," He said to His disciples. "My kingdom belongs especially to children. Do you suppose these children have to grow up before they can become followers of mine? You could not be more mistaken! Just the opposite is true. You will have to become like these children, or you yourselves will never get into my kingdom."

Then one by one Jesus took the children onto His lap. He put His arms around them in love, and talked to them. He blessed them.

What did Jesus mean when He said that only people who become like children can get into His kingdom? Did He mean that you are a better person than your father and mother are? That you are less sinful? That you *deserve* a place in heaven, but they will first have to be sorry for their wrongdoing, and ask for forgiveness, before they can be admitted?

No, that is not what Jesus meant. Jesus had no use at all for people who thought they deserved a place in heaven, that they could earn God's love. A doctor does not call at a house where everybody thinks he is in good health. He goes to see those who are sick, and who know that they are sick. Jesus did not come to help those who think they are so good that they do not need a Saviour. He came to help those who are sinners, and who know it all too well.

No, you are not a better person than your father and your mother are. We are all of us sinners who desperately need God's mercy.

In the morning when the alarm clock rings, your father does not turn it off and say, "I think today I will sleep another hour or two." No, he gets up, and eats his breakfast, and goes off to work. He works all day, day after day, to earn the money which will buy clothes and food and shelter and even toys and vacations for you. And your mother works all day every day, cooking your meals, making the bed you have slept in, washing and ironing your clothes, cleaning the rooms you have messed up. Your father and your mother do not send you a bill once a week for the things they have done for you. They know you could never pay for all this, and they do not expect you to pay for it. They give it to you as a free gift, because they love you.

Jesus told us we should speak to God as "our Father in heaven." Does He mean that God is like our earthly fathers? No, He means just the opposite. Our earthly fathers and mothers are like God. Their love for us is a faint reflection of the much greater love of God. And the many things they do for us which we do not deserve, which we do not have to pay for, and could never pay for, no matter how long we worked or how hard we tried — these gifts of love are intended to remind us of how many more, how much richer gifts God gives us. For day by day He showers unnumbered blessings down on our undeserving heads.

God does not send us a bill for all these blessings. He does not expect us to pay for them. He knows we could never pay for them. He gives them to us free, as a gift of His love.

And you and I — do we understand that it would be quite impossible for us ever to buy such love? Have we given up even wanting to pay for it? Do we accept it as a little child accepts the loving care of his parents? Do we reach out our empty hands, and wait expectantly, confidently, for God to fill them? Then we have taken the first step towards God's wonderful kingdom. The first step along the only road there is to get there. Then we can sing the prayer of the child:

> *Nothing in my hand I bring,*
> *Simply to Thy cross I cling;*
> *Naked, come to Thee for dress;*
> *Helpless, look to Thee for grace.*
> *Foul, I to the fountain fly;*
> *Wash me, Saviour, or I die.*

58

The Rich Young Man

Mark 10:17-25

Jesus never stayed long in one place. Even if you knew when He was going to pass through your village, it was not easy to see Him. Some people fought their way through crowds just to touch the hem of His clothing. One man climbed a tree to catch a glimpse of Him as He came past. Another, who could not walk, was let down, bed and all, through a hole in the roof to the room where Jesus was.

The man in our story came running to Jesus. Why was he in such a hurry? He had a serious problem, about which he was deeply concerned. He hoped Jesus could solve it for him.

He ran up to Jesus and knelt at His feet. As soon as he could catch his breath, he asked this question:

"Good Teacher, how can I obtain life that never ends?"

Jesus answered him with a question of His own: "Why do you call me good? Don't you know that only God is good?" Jesus wanted the young man to realize right away that, to obtain eternal life, he needed much more than the help of a good man. He needed God's help.

Since the young man still did not understand, Jesus added, "You know the Ten Commandments." The Ten Commandments are the law God gave to the Israelites when He spoke to them from the mountain of Sinai. Every Jewish boy and girl learned them when still young. The young man answered confidently, "I have always kept them, since I was a child."

He was mistaken about this, of course. He may have kept the outward form of the Ten Commandments. But the spirit of the Ten Commandments, as Jesus Himself taught us, is to love God with all your heart and soul and mind, and to love your neighbor as much as you love yourself. No man can do this by himself. He needs God's help even to begin doing it. This young man had tried hard. He was eager to learn and had the enthusiasm of youth. Jesus looked at the young man, and He loved him. He said to him, "There is one more thing you must do. Go and sell everything you own. Give the money to the poor, and come and follow me."

The young man's face fell. He turned sadly away, dragging the feet that had carried him so eagerly to Jesus. Jesus had asked him to do something too hard for him. You see, this young man was very rich. He wanted to go to heaven, and he wanted to do what is right. But he did not love God enough to make this sacrifice. He did not love God as much as he loved his money.

After he had gone, Jesus said to His disciples, "It is very hard for a rich man to get to heaven." The disciples were very much surprised by this remark. They thought of riches as a great blessing. The man who had a lot of money, enough to satisfy his every wish, must, they thought, be specially favored by God.

Jesus said again, "Children, it is very hard for a rich man to get to heaven, because a rich man is likely to trust in his riches, instead of trusting God. It is easier for a camel to go through the eye of a needle than for a rich man to get into heaven." Now the disciples were so amazed, they were almost speechless. At last one of them spoke: "If it is as hard as that to get to heaven, how can anyone be saved?"

"With men it is impossible," Jesus answered, "but for God all things are possible. God can do anything."

Peter was the impulsive one of the disciples. He often spoke before he stopped to think. He spoke up now. "Lord, *we* have left everything to follow You." And Jesus answered him, "Whoever sacrifices anything for love of me, if he leaves his home, or his family, or his money, that man will receive back in this life a hundred times as much as he gave up, though he will still have troubles, and in the world to come he will have eternal life."

Why did Jesus ask the rich young man to sell all his possessions? Why did He say that it is especially hard for a rich man to get to heaven? Is it wrong to be rich? No, it is not wrong to be rich. Money is a gift of God. The disciples were right about that. But it is wrong to love the things God gives you more than you love the God who gives them to you. It is wrong to love God's gifts so much that you are not willing to sacrifice them if God asks you to.

Because, you see, Jesus does sometimes ask us to give back to Him the things He has given us. He asks us to do this in order to test us, to see whether we really love Him. He may ask you to give up your money for His sake, or He may ask you to leave your home or your family or your job. He may turn to you, as He turned to the rich young man, and say, "Do you love me enough to give up this thing for my sake?"

Jesus has a right to ask us to sacrifice for His sake. You see, He showed us the way by sacrificing for our sake. He loved us so much that He gave up His home in heaven to live and die for us here on earth. When we make a sacrifice because we love Him, we are following in His footsteps.

Does this seem too hard for you? Are you afraid that, like the young man in our story, you might turn sadly away? You do not need to be afraid. The rich young man turned away because he was trying to do it all in his own strength. That was where he made his mistake. If you turn to God for help, you will find that it is just as Jesus said. Nothing is impossible for God. Not even to change your hard heart. Not even to fill you with such love for your Saviour that you will go gladly wherever He sends you, and give back to Him willingly whatever He asks.

59

God Gives Us Presents Instead of Wages

Matthew 20:1-15

*t*he owner of the vineyard arrived at the market early in the morning, shortly after sunrise. It was the time of harvest. He needed men to pick his fruit while it was at the peak of its flavor, to carry the baskets to the wine vats, and to tread out the juice. He came early, but there were already men waiting there, hoping to find work.

"My grapes are ready for picking," the farmer said to the men. "I will pay one denarius for each day's work." The men were eager to work, and they were satisfied with the wage. A denarius was enough to buy food for their family, and even to leave a little over for extras such as clothing, or perhaps a gift to the temple. Soon they were busy in the vineyard, cutting the bunches of grapes and filling the baskets with the fragrant fruit.

The vineyard was large, and the owner needed still more workers. In the middle of the morning he returned to the market place. There were other men waiting there now, also hoping to find work.

"Go into my vineyard," he said to them. "Tonight I will pay you what is right." And they joined those who had been working since sunrise.

At noon, when the sun was high overhead, the farmer visited the market place again. Again he hired those who were standing waiting; again he promised to pay them a fair wage. In mid-afternoon he came once more.

"Come with me," he said to the unemployed men standing there. "I need workers, and I pay a fair wage." Just before sunset he made one last trip. The market was nearly deserted now, but still there were some who had found no work, who were reluctant to return home without having earned what their families needed.

"Why do you stand here all day idle?" the farmer asked them.

"Because no man has hired us," they answered.

"Come and work for me," the farmer said. And these, too, joined the others in the vineyard.

When the sun sets in Palestine, darkness follows quickly; the rest of the picking would have to wait till morning. The farmer's steward set up a little table, and the men filed past to receive their wages. Those who had been hired last came first. The steward paid each one of them a denarius, a full day's wage, even though they had worked only one hour. Then came those who had been hired in mid-afternoon. They, too, received a denarius. Those who started work at noon were paid the same, and so also those who began in mid-morning. Last of all came the men who had worked all day. Each of them received one denarius. It was what they had agreed to work for, but now, strange to say, the men were angry.

"We have worked all day," they complained. "We have borne the scorching heat, and the heavy loads. And now you have given the same wages to those fellows who have worked only one hour!"

"One denarius is what we agreed on," the farmer answered. "Take your money and get on home. It is my business if I wish to give these last workers the same as I have given you. It is my money, isn't it? Can't I do with it as I wish?"

The men picked up their money. But as they walked away, I have an idea that they muttered to themselves, "That's not fair!" And the disciples — to whom Jesus told this story which I have told you — I rather think they, too, were troubled, and asked each other, "Is that fair?" Perhaps you wonder about this also. The men who worked one hour were paid one denarius. Then the men who worked twelve hours should have received twelve times as much, shouldn't they? They worked twelve times as long. Surely they earned twelve denarii. Wouldn't that be the fair thing, what they deserved?

That is exactly the question Jesus intended you to ask, just the very thing He wanted you to think about. How much do you and I deserve? What have we earned? How should God treat us if He is to be fair?

Perhaps you have never thought about it really. The truth is, nobody in this world gets what is fair. Every single person born into God's world gets much, much more. If there is a tiny baby in your family, then you know how much work a baby is. All that he can do at first is cry, and kick, and drink. Every other single thing has to be done for him. He has to be washed and dressed and fed and carried about. He does not earn any of this. His parents give it to him as a gift, out of love. Once your parents did all this for you. And then, as you grew older, and could walk and talk and dress yourself, what then? What of the nights your mother went without her own sleep to watch by your bed when you were sick? Of the days when your father, tired though he was, worked overtime so you could have the bicycle you wanted for your birthday? What of all the times (which you perhaps do not even know about) when your father and mother lay awake at night praying for you, bringing your needs and problems to the throne of God? Did you deserve all this? Did you earn it?

But there are much greater gifts than those your parents have given you. There is the greatest gift of all, the Christmas gift, when God gave us His own Son to be our Saviour. There is the gift of the Holy Spirit, God Almighty coming down to earth to live in our undeserving hearts, to give us courage and patience and love. We deserved God's anger; He has given us love instead. We deserved death; God has bought life for us, at the cost of His own death on the cross. We deserve hell; God has offered us heaven. Every single day of our lives we ought to be thankful that God is not fair. Instead, He is merciful, loving, generous, giving us far more than we even know how to ask Him for.

60
A Blind Man Meets His Saviour

Mark 10:46-52

Some cities are known for their buildings; some, for the people who live in them. Jericho was famous for its flowers and its fruit trees. Imagine yourself a weary traveler who has walked all day through the sweltering heat and the stinging dust of the desert. (Only the Roman soldiers ride horseback, and only the very rich or the very old have a donkey to ease the journey.) There suddenly before your eyes, on a little height of ground, you see the famous date palms of Jericho, lush and dark green, waving luxuriantly in the evening breeze. The air is sweet with the fragrance of the balsams and the delicate pink of the almond blossoms. Everywhere there are roses, red and pink and yellow, seas of roses to perfume the air and to delight the eye. And among the trees and the flowers your weary eyes rest delightedly on fountains and pools of water. A lovely city, set in the middle of the desert, a city where the rich and the powerful — Cleopatra was one of them, and King Herod another — come to rest, building luxurious summer palaces with water gardens attached, and, in Herod's palace, you could even find a swimming pool.

But all of this meant nothing to Bartimaeus. Bartimaeus could not see the waving date palms, the early flowers of the almond trees, the exquisite shapes and colors of the roses, the flowing fountains and pools of water. For Bartimaeus was blind.

How does a blind man earn his living? Even in a city as rich as Jericho, what work is there a blind man can do? Will a farmer hire him to weed his fields or tend his flocks? Can he become a merchant in the market place, a carpenter, a fisherman? No, it seems that in all of Jericho, or in all God's world, for that matter, there is no place, no hope, for the man who is blind.

And so Bartimaeus has been reduced to that most hopeless of all occupations. Bartimaeus has become a beggar.

The best time for begging is just before the great religious festivals. Then thousands of pilgrims from the north pass through Jericho on their way to Jerusalem to worship God. And then men's hearts are more tender than at other times. Then they remember that God has commanded us to show mercy to the poor and the afflicted. And so, as Passover approaches, and the pilgrims stream through the city in great crowds, perhaps even in a blind beggar's heart there is a momentary gleam of hope. Not hope that he might become like other men who can work and earn what they need, and even marry and support a wife and children. That would be too much to hope. But hope at least that God will touch the hearts of the pilgrims, so that Bartimaeus may have enough to eat for a few days again.

This Passover was not quite like other Passovers. There was a strange ferment in the air. A blind man has no eyes, but he has ears, better ears, perhaps, than those who can see. He had heard of the marvelous Wonder-worker who healed the sick and the lame, and even brought back to life those who had been dead for days. He had heard the whispered questions: "Is it possible this could be the Saviour God promised so long ago?" And in the mind of Bartimaeus there was a persistent echo. He thought of the promise of the prophet Isaiah:

"Then shall the eyes of the blind be opened." Almost without Bartimaeus himself being aware of what was happening, something changed within his heart. The Holy Spirit was working in Bartimaeus. Silently, as He always works, but with power, as He always works. Silently and with power as He works in your heart, and in mine. Teaching us who our Saviour is, creating within our hearts the faith to trust in Him.

The road was crowded today. Many were on their way to the feast. It was a happy crowd, but they were in a hurry too. Some of them had never seen God's beautiful temple in Jerusalem before. They could hardly wait to get there. Others had made the pilgrimage often; they, too, were eager to arrive.

"Yes, the Wonder-worker is coming," one said. "He is right behind us."

"I wonder that He dares to appear in Jerusalem," another answered. "They say the priests have sworn to kill Him." Suddenly something swelled up in Bartimaeus' heart — all his past despair, all his longing to be like other men, all the new faith he scarcely knew he had. He called out as loud as he could,

"Jesus, thou Son of David, have mercy on me!"

"Be quiet!" the crowd said. "He is on His way to the feast. He has no time to listen to the likes of you." But Bartimaeus would not be quiet. He could think of nothing but the greatness of his need, and the nearness of his Saviour. He cried out again and again, "Jesus, thou Son of David, have mercy on me."

Jesus heard him. He did not say, "I cannot stop to help you now. I myself must die within the week." No, He stopped, and He said to the crowd, "Call him." And the people said to Bartimaeus, "Cheer up. He is calling you. Come!" Bartimaeus jumped up from where he sat, and groped his way to Jesus.

"What do you want?" Jesus asked.

"I want to see again," Bartimaeus answered.

"Your faith has made you whole," Jesus answered. And, even as He spoke, Bartimaeus' eyes were opened. He could see the blue sky, the golden sunshine, the waving palms, the roses. But most of all, he could see his Saviour's face. Can you guess what was the first thing he did with his newfound sight? He used it to follow Jesus.

Lord Jesus, may thy Holy Spirit open our eyes too, that we may recognize and trust our Saviour. And teach us, too, to use our new-found sight to follow wherever He leads us.

61
We Share the Work of God

Luke 19:11-27

It was the first day of spring vacation, and for once the weather was lovely. All the children were out. Some were riding their bikes around and around in figure-eights, from sheer delight in the freedom and the warmth of the sun. A group of little girls sat on a porch, busy with their dolls. The older boys were playing softball in the street.

All the children were out except Betsie. Betsie was in the kitchen drying the dishes. Her usually happy face was black with a scowl, and as she dried each dish she banged it down on the pile of clean ones. Mother was washing.

"Be careful, Betsie," she said. And then, as Betsie banged the last plate into the cupboard, Mother went on, "Now I want you to clean your room. Make the bed, straighten the bureau drawers and clean up the closet. Then you may go out and play." Betsie could hear the other children laughing and shouting outdoors as she climbed the stairs.

"Why do I have to work when no one else does?" she muttered. "This is vacation. Vacation is for having fun, not for work."

Perhaps you feel the same way that Betsie did. You would rather have vacation than school, rather play than work. And if I should tell you that someday you will change your mind about this, you probably would not believe me. But, believe it or not, one of the biggest surprises of growing up is the discovery that work is fun. More fun even than play. And this is because the work you and I have to do is of earth-shaking importance, and the Person for whom we do it is no one else than the King of kings.

The friends of Jesus felt as you do. They, too, were more interested in the fun than in the work. As they walked along the road from Jericho to Jerusalem, Jesus talked to them again about what was going to happen.

"I am going to be arrested," He said. "They will make fun of me, spit at me, beat me, and then kill me. But, after three days, I will rise again." These dreadful words about the Saviour they loved so dearly fell on deaf ears. Jesus' friends were thinking, each one of them, his own selfish thoughts. "Will it be tomorrow, His glorious kingdom?" they wondered in their hearts. Some even dared to ask the question aloud: "Will I get to sit on Your right hand when You are seated on Your throne in power and majesty?" If not tomorrow, then surely next week!

No, not tomorrow! Not next week, either! The royal throne on which Jesus was going to sit was in their hearts, not in a palace at Jerusalem. The enemy He was going to drive out was their own sin and selfishness, not the Roman conquerors. It is true that someday He was going to come in such glory and power that every eye would see Him, and every knee would bow. But before that day arrived there was much work to do. And Jesus, looking in love at His selfish friends, planned a precious gift for them. He was going to give each one of them a share in His work; to each one He was going to trust part of His Father's wealth, taken from His treasure house, gifts that could be used in His service.

"Once upon a time," Jesus said to His disciples as they walked along that wilderness road from Jericho to Jerusalem, "there was a nobleman. He was going to receive a kingdom, but he had to go to a far-off country to obtain it. He left his friends and servants behind.

To each one he gave a large sum of money, as much as he could have earned in many months of work. 'While I am away,' he said, 'use this money in my service. Trade with it, make it grow and bear fruit.' Then he left them. He was gone a long time.

"At last he returned. He called his servants to find out what each had done with the money entrusted to him. The first one said, 'Lord, your gift has increased ten times.' And the nobleman, who was now a king, said to his servant, 'Well done! You have been faithful in a small trust. You shall rule over ten of my cities.'

"Next came a servant who said, 'Your Majesty, the money you entrusted to me has grown five times over.' And the king said to him, 'You shall rule over five of my cities.'

"At last there came a servant who said, 'Lord, here is the money you entrusted to me. I hid it away in a napkin. I was afraid of you, for I know you are a severe master, who expects to get back more than you have given out.' The king was angry.

" 'I will condemn you by your own words,' he replied. 'Why didn't you at least put my money in the bank, so that when I returned I should have gotten it back with interest?' And, turning to the officials who stood beside the throne, he said, 'Take away his money. Give it to the servant who increased his trust ten times.' The officials were puzzled. 'My Lord,' they answered, 'he already has ten cities.'

" 'Even so,' the king replied. 'The servant who is faithful in his trust shall receive a greater trust, a more important job. The one who is faithless will lose his chance to serve in his Lord's kingdom.' "

Our God is above all a Giver. He does not hoard His vast wealth in underground storage houses. No, He pours it out on us, His children. The greatest gift He has given us is certainly His own Son, our Saviour. But if we should try to arrange His other gifts in the order of their importance, I think the second greatest would be God's gift of a chance to share in His work. And with this second gift He also gives us whatever we need to do the task He has entrusted to us, whatever that task may be. And the promise, too, that whoever does one little thing for Jesus faithfully will be given new and ever greater opportunities to serve.

62
Jesus, Our King

Matthew 21:1-11, 15-17

As usual at this time of year, the city was crowded. Everyone who could possibly get away, came to Jerusalem for the Passover celebration. If you have ever visited a city where there was a blossom festival going on, or a home-coming celebration, or a water carnival, you can imagine the traffic jam. The streets, which were narrow and crooked to begin with, were choked with people going to and from the temple, with merchants shouting their wares, with cattle being brought in from the country for the feast. Everyone who could spare a room in his house rented it out to the visitors. Many pilgrims simply spread their bedrolls on the flat roofs of the homes of friends or relatives. Many others had to find lodging in the villages outside the city walls.

It was like this every year. But this year there was something special about it. There was an extra excitement in the crowd, an air of breathless anticipation. For nearly everyone in that crowd had heard of the wonder-working Teacher. And now, to all His earlier marvels, the Teacher had added this quite unbelievable marvel that He had brought back to life a man already four days dead and buried. Altogether unbelievable — and yet trustworthy men said that it was so!

"Will He come, do you think?" the visitors asked one another. And others answered, "I doubt it. They say the Jewish authorities have a warrant out for His arrest."

And then another spoke up: "He is coming! He left Bethany this morning. Even now He is coming around the Mount of Olives." The news spread like lightning through the crowd. The people rushed out through the city gates and up the hillside road to meet Him, to see for themselves this man who spoke as no other man had ever spoken, and who performed impossible miracles.

And what did they see? A great king, dressed in scarlet and cloth of gold, riding a white horse, preceded by his heralds, and followed by his soldiers? This was the sort of king they were looking for, were hoping for — a king who would lead them into battle, would drive out the hated Roman conquerors, and would restore the Jewish people to power.

Oh, they saw a king all right, but it was not the kind of king they had expected. This was a king such as no other king had ever been in all the world's history. For this King commanded not just the hands of His subjects; He commanded their hearts. He ruled not by the sword, but by the conquering power of love. And He won His kingdom not by fighting battles, but by giving, and loving, and serving, and in the end by dying for His people.

Jesus was not riding a white horse with a saddle of the finest tooled leather and a golden bridle. He was riding a donkey, the animal a poor man used to take a journey or to plough his fields. Even the donkey did not belong to the King. He was so poor He had to borrow this humble beast for His royal entry into His capital city. And He

had not been able to borrow a saddle to sit on; His friends took off their coats and laid them on the donkey's back to soften the King's ride.

The people must have been very surprised, even disappointed. But their disappointment did not stop them for long. If their king did not look like a king yet, He soon would. They themselves would be the first to acclaim His arrival. They took off their coats and laid them on the ground to provide a royal carpet. Others cut palm branches and spread them on the ground in front of Jesus.

"Praise God!" they shouted as they walked beside Him. "Blessed is the king who comes in the name of the Lord. Blessed is the Son of our father David."

The procession grew larger and larger as they drew near the city. The noise of their shouts was so great that all the city came to the gates to see them arrive.

"Who is this man?" the people asked one another.

And the crowds who accompanied Jesus stopped their shouting just long enough to answer: "This is the prophet, Jesus, who comes from up north, in Galilee." And so they all came in, through the gate that is called the Golden Gate, and they went, all of them together, to the temple.

Because the festival was so close at hand, the temple was crowded. There were not only many grown-ups there, but there were children also. Perhaps for many of them this was their first visit to Jerusalem.

When Jesus and the accompanying crowd poured into the temple, something amazing happened. The Holy Spirit Himself came into the hearts of these children, and they, too, began to praise their Saviour.

"Praise God," they said over and over. "Praise God for the Son of David!"

The high temple officials, the very ones who planned to arrest Jesus the first chance they got, saw all this with horror. They spoke angrily to Jesus. "Do you not hear what the children are saying?" they demanded. They knew that "Son of David" was the name of the Saviour whom God had promised. They were furious the people should give this name to Jesus.

"Yes, I hear it," Jesus answered. "Have you never read the psalm which says, 'God has brought praise out of the mouths of little children'?"

And so our Saviour was proclaimed king, and surely no person ever deserved a royal throne more than He did. But there was not one person in all that crowd, not even His closest friends, who dreamed how He was going to win His kingdom. Are your eyes keener than the eyes of that shouting crowd on that Sunday morning so long ago? Are you ready to welcome Him as King into your life? Then you, too, can cry with those children so long ago, "Praise God for our King, the Son of David!"

63
Jonathan Visits the Temple

Matthew 21:10-17

The year that Jonathan was thirteen Father said: "You are almost grown up now. You are too big to stay home with Mother and the little ones. This year you must come along to Jerusalem, to celebrate the Passover feast." Jonathan's face lighted up. At last he was going to see the capital city, and the temple where God dwelt. But he never guessed — and Father did not either — that this was going to be a very special Passover, a celebration neither one of them would ever forget.

The trip to Jerusalem was long, and they had no way to get there except to walk. Jonathan did not think this was a hardship. He was used to walking, and there were so many exciting new places, so many different people to see. And at the end there would be the temple. Jonathan had heard about the temple since he was a baby: the beautiful courts rising one above the other, each one more beautiful than the one before, and each one nearer to that dreadful and yet happy place where God lived. The Holy of Holies they called it, and no one but the high priest could go in there, and he only once a year.

Jonathan and Father started out with a group of friends and relatives from their own town. Soon they met other pilgrims, men from distant places, wearing strange clothing such as Jonathan had never seen, long black robes, or coats made of goats' hair, or silk suits embroidered in silver and golden threads. Strange, foreign-looking men, and yet, Father said, they were their brothers, traveling just as he and Father were, to worship their faithful God. Some were very old, and yet this was their first pilgrimage. They had saved and scrimped for a lifetime so that just once before they died they might see the house of God at Jerusalem.

Someone started to sing, and all the pilgrims picked up the song, until the hills echoed back their hymn: "I was glad when they said unto me, Let us go up to the house of Jehovah." More and more joined the group, until the road was crowded with singing pilgrims as far as the eye could see. Sometimes at night, if the weather was stormy, they slept on the porch of an inn. More often they rolled themselves up in their blankets and lay down to sleep beneath the stars, just as Jacob had done so long ago. Jonathan fell asleep dreaming of the wonderful golden temple.

The most exciting moment of all was when they came around the slope of the Mount of Olives. There stood the holy city, set on the top of the hill, surrounded by deep ravines, glowing in the sun's light. And towering over the city was the temple, built of shining white marble, with golden spires reaching, it seemed, almost to the sky. The whole procession stopped, awe-struck, to stare silently at the house where the invisible God of heaven and earth lived among His people. And then they started on again, down the mountainside, singing as they went: "My soul longeth, yea even fainteth, for the courts of Jehovah."

And yet, after all his waiting and hoping and dreaming, Jonathan was disappointed when he finally saw the temple. Oh, it was beautiful — that is, what you could see of it for the crowd. The shining white marble Father had told him about, the heavy bronze gates, the embroidered curtains, the gorgeous robes of the priests, the golden altar for the incense — they were all there. But Jonathan had expected something more. This was God's house. He had expected silence, eyes scarcely daring to look up to the Holy of Holies, heads bowed in sor-

row for sin, lips moving in silent prayer. Instead it seemed he had stumbled into a market place. All around the walls there were booths offering animals for sale, and wine, oil, salt; and other booths where the money you had brought from home could be changed for coins the priests said were the proper ones to offer God. The animals squealed and bleated, the customers argued noisily, and many people who were not interested in God's house at all hurried through the court on their way to work or to the market, carrying packages or a bag of tools.

"What are all these people doing here?" he asked Father. "Why don't they do their business outside, instead of in God's house?" Father did not hear his question. He was staring at the gate. Another procession of pilgrims had arrived, and a man rode at its head, sitting on a donkey. There was a great crowd with Him. They ran ahead as He came into the temple, crying out, "Blessed is the King who comes in God's name. Praise God! Praise God!"

A sudden hush fell on all that noisy crowd as this man came up the steps. Father spoke softly to Jonathan: "It must be the Teacher we have heard so much about. Some say He is the Saviour promised by God." The Teacher looked around the temple court. He strode angrily across to the booths of the money changers. With one hand He tipped over their tables. The coins rolled in all directions across the marble floor. He upset the chairs of the merchants who sold the animals. He drove out of the temple everyone who had not come to worship God.

"My Father's house," He said, "is a house of prayer. You have made it a den of thieves." The priests, who got a percentage of the merchants' profits, muttered angrily in the background. But the common folk flocked around the Teacher, listening eagerly to His words. And the young boys — those who, like Jonathan, had come this year to the temple for the first time — felt an excited stirring in their hearts. It was God's Holy Spirit who was speaking to them. "Praise God," they shouted, "for the promised Son of David!" And all the pilgrims picked up the cry, "Praise God!"

64

The Crooked Farmhands

Matthew 21:33-45

*t*he vineyard was a patch of bright green set on the hillside among the grey-greens of the olive trees and the darker greens of the figs. You can usually tell, as you pass by a farm, whether or not the man who owns the place likes to farm. Some places have ramshackle buildings, broken tools lying around rusting, fields full of weeds. Other farms look neat and well cared for.

This vineyard plainly belonged to a man who liked to farm. Everywhere you saw signs of loving care. The owner had picked a spot especially suited to growing grapes, a fertile hillside sloping to the southern sun. All the stones in these fields had been picked up and carried to the edge of the vineyard, and there built into a wall to protect the grapes from thieves — whether they had two legs or four. There was a watchtower set in the middle of the vines. From its flat top you could see a long way in all directions, and usually, as harvest approached, there was a man stationed here to guard the ripening fruit. The tower was so designed also that the workers could find shelter in it during the harvest season, when they usually spent both day and night among the vines.

There was even a winepress built in the middle. This was unusual. Most of the farmers carried their fruit to the village press, and had to wait their turn to tread out the juice. But here a pit had been dug in the vineyard itself, and carefully lined with stone; and a little down the hill another pit into which the juice could drain. The workers dumped the grapes fresh from the vines into this pit, and then, holding on to a rope above their heads to keep their balance, they stamped out the juice with their bare feet, singing as they worked. Yes, it was plain that no expense and no trouble had been spared to make this the finest vineyard possible.

From such a vineyard you would surely expect rich returns. And yet something had gone wrong. Not long after the owner had finished planting the grapes, he had had to go away for a time. He rented his vineyard to servants he had chosen for their skill and their trustworthiness. He arranged with them about their share of the profits, and he left careful directions about the cultivation of the grapes.

But alas! there are many men who can be trusted when the boss's eye is on them, but few who will work with equal faithfulness when he is far away. Perhaps you have found this out for yourself. It is much easier to be good when Mother is in the room, or when Teacher stands beside your desk.

When harvest time came, the owner sent a servant to collect his share of the profits. By this time the workers had quite forgotten how glad they had been to get such a good job, had quite forgotten who it was that bought and cleared the land, planted the vines, built the wall and the watchtower. They looked on the vineyard as their own private property. They made short work of the servant their master had sent. They simply picked up the sticks that lay on the ground and drove him violently out of the vineyard.

The owner could hardly believe what had happened. He sent another servant. This one was greeted with stones. Still other servants received even rougher treatment.

"There is only one thing left to do," the owner said to himself. "I will send them my son. When they see my only, my dearly loved son, they will surely honor him. They will not dare to treat him so."

When the worker who manned the watchtower told the others that the owner's son was coming down the road, then those wicked workers put their heads together.

"He is the heir," they said to each other. "If we get rid of him, the vineyard will belong to us." And so, in anger and greed, in rebellion against the owner who had never done them anything but good, they killed his only son, and threw his body outside the vineyard wall.

Here Jesus, who was telling this story, turned to the priests who were listening. "And what do you think the owner will do to these workers when he himself comes back to his vineyard?"

The priests shifted uneasily from foot to foot. They had an uncomfortable suspicion that Jesus was talking about them.

"He will destroy those wicked servants," they said, "and rent out his vineyard to other workers who will give him his due share of the fruit."

But even as they spoke, the priests, like the workers in the story, were plotting in their ungrateful, rebellious hearts how to get rid of Jesus, God's only, beloved Son. Jesus looked at them in sorrow. They would not recognize the one Person who could save them. They would not admit they needed to be saved at all.

"Do you not know the verse," He said, " 'God has made the very stone which the builders discarded into the cornerstone of His house; the man who stumbles over this stone will be broken in pieces'?"

The priests did not answer. They only stared at Jesus with a cold, bitter hatred. Yes, they stumbled over Jesus, who was God's cornerstone. And they would be utterly destroyed, even as they had themselves said the crooked vineyard workers should be.

And you — you are one of those other workers whom God has taken into his vineyard. And in other places Jesus speaks of you even as a vine. Perhaps it seems strange to you to think of yourself as a vine planted in a vineyard, surrounded on all sides by God's loving care. But is not your life filled to overflowing with His special mercies and His daily love? If you should count your blessings, do you think you would ever be done?

Yes, you have been placed in God's vineyard. Take care then, my friend, that you do not rob God of the fruit He has a right to expect from this vine He has cultivated with such care. For the plant that does not bring forth fruit will be cut down and thrown into the fire.

65
Not Dressed for the Wedding

Matthew 22:1-14

the whole palace was buzzing with excitement. For the prince was going to get married, and the king planned a great wedding feast to celebrate the happy occasion.

The servants had swept and cleaned the whole palace. They had washed and polished the best dishes, and set up the long tables. The royal taylor had measured the prince for a new wedding suit, and the royal jeweler had made a wedding crown for him to wear when he went to fetch his bride — as was the custom in those days. The king

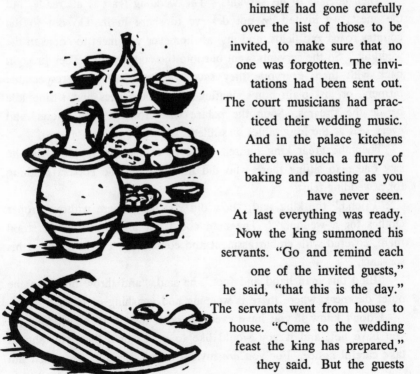

himself had gone carefully over the list of those to be invited, to make sure that no one was forgotten. The invitations had been sent out. The court musicians had practiced their wedding music. And in the palace kitchens there was such a flurry of baking and roasting as you have never seen.

At last everything was ready. Now the king summoned his servants. "Go and remind each one of the invited guests," he said, "that this is the day." The servants went from house to house. "Come to the wedding feast the king has prepared," they said. But the guests had made other plans. They shrugged their shoulders and said, "Just count me out. I find that I will be busy." If you receive an invitation to an audience with the queen, or to dinner at the White House, you do not turn it down lightly. And in those days to refuse an invitation to a royal wedding feast was a deadly insult. Even so, the king did not grow angry. He sent other servants to repeat the invitation: "I have made everything ready," he said. "Come now to the wedding feast." But the invited guests treated it all as a joke. One of them left town for his farm. Another went instead to the market place, to buy and sell. And still others ganged up on the king's servants, and beat them. When the fight was over, the servants lay bloody and dead on the ground.

Now the king was angry indeed. He called his soldiers. "Go and kill those murderers," he said, "and burn down their houses."

Then he said to his servants, "The wedding feast is all ready, but the guests we invited do not deserve to share in it. Go out to the country roads and fields, and invite whomever you meet to come to the wedding." So the servants went out into the countryside. They brought back with them everyone they saw, whether they were respectable farmers, or just plain bums, loafing along the fences and sitting idle beside the streams. Soon the palace was crowded with guests, and every seat at the long tables was filled.

Then the great king himself came in to see his guests. And he saw one man sitting there who did not have on the correct clothing for a wedding feast.

"Friend," the king said, "how did you get in here without proper clothes for a wedding?" The man could not answer. He just stood there, covered with embarrassment and confusion. The king called his servants.

"Bind this man hand and foot," he said, "and throw him into the outer darkness, where there is weeping and gnashing of teeth."

I don't know if you have ever yet been invited to a wedding. If you have not, and if you would like to go to one, then you should take careful notice. For you *are* invited to this wedding. I myself am one of the king's servants, and I have been sent to give you the royal invitation.

For this great king is God Himself. And at that wedding feast that He has prepared, all those who love Him will be present.

There are some of us who have known about this amazing invitation as far back as we can remember. We could hardly tell you the day we first heard about God, and His Son Jesus, and His invitation to each one of us to come to the great feast. But, my friends, let us be very careful, let us be very careful indeed, that familiarity does not make us careless or indifferent.

God is not an impatient God. He invites us over, and over, and over. But not forever. If we spurn all His invitations, if we laugh at His call, then at last we, too, will be rejected. "Those people whom I have invited," our great God will say, "do not deserve to share my wedding feast. I will invite someone else instead, to take their places."

Some of you are perhaps hearing about this invitation for the first time. Accept it with gladness, for there is nothing more wonderful that could happen to you than to be present at that great wedding feast. Do not allow any self-doubts, any sense of unworthiness to keep you from coming. Do not say, "I would never know how to behave at a king's party. I am not good enough! He can't mean to invite me!"

For the bitter truth is that not a single one of us deserves to be invited. Not one of us belongs by right in His palace. Not one of us is fit to sit at His table, or to share in His love and care. But He *has* invited you — and that is enough.

But perhaps you think, "I do not have the right clothes for such a grand party. I would be like the ragged beggar who is thrown into the outer darkness." Then let me whisper my secret in your ear. The king gives a spotless wedding garment to everyone at that feast. You have only to put it on — for He has already provided it. No one has to come in the rags of his own sinful life. The King's own Son shed His blood to wash you white as snow. If you are truly sorry for your sinful life, and if you put your trust in Jesus' death on the cross, then you, too, will be a welcome guest at that marvelous feast.

66
The Seed That Dies

John 12:20-32

t ommy was helping Mother plant the vegetable garden. Two weeks ago they had made a first planting of peas. Now it was time, Mother said, to make a second planting. "These will be ready to pick when the first planting is finished." They fastened a string to get a straight line, and made a little ditch with the tip of the hoe. "Put the seeds close together," Mother said. "We can always thin them later if they all come up." They covered the seed with dirt, and stepped it down to make a firm seedbed. Tommy marked the end of the row with a little stick run through the package the peas had come in.

"Now," Mother said, "we must thin the ones we planted earlier. We will pull up every other one, so that those that are left will have plenty of sun and air. Take a good hold of the stem, and pull gently, so you get roots and all."

The earliest peas were already little green plants. Tommy pulled one up very carefully. There was the green stem, the fresh, new green leaves, and the white roots reaching out to find food and water for the plant underneath the ground. "I don't see the pea I planted," Tommy said. "What happened to the seed?"

"The seed is gone," Mother said. "It died to give life to the plant. Soon there will be many new seeds on each of these plants. That is God's way of feeding us."

Tommy stared at the plant in his hand. It was already beginning to wilt in the hot sun. "Did the seed want to die?" he asked.

Mother smiled. "A seed is not like a person," she said. "It cannot talk and feel."

"But if it could," Tommy insisted, "would it want to die so we could have peas to eat?"

Mother looked thoughtful. "I suppose," she said at last, "that if a seed could feel and talk like a person, perhaps the seed would say, just as many persons do, 'I do not want to die. I do not care whether you have peas to eat or not.' But that would be foolish. Because, you see, at last the seed would decay and die anyway, and then there would be nothing left to show that it had ever lived at all."

Tommy's eyes opened wide. "Do people have to die too, if they want to have something to show for their lives?" he asked.

"In a sense they do," Mother said. "You see, Tommy, Jesus had to die for you and me. He did not really want to die either. He wanted to live. But because He loved us so much, He was willing to die so that you and I and all His children could live. He gave up what He wanted for our sake, and if you and I want to be His followers, we will have to give up what we want for His sake. All the selfish thoughts you have, all the mean things you sometimes say to little sister, all the times you talk back to Mother and Father — all these have to die in your heart. Only when you are willing to see them die can you begin to be fruitful, as God intends you to be — just as the pea can grow into a beautiful green vine, with many peas hanging from its branches, only if we first bury it in the ground so that it dies."

There was one forgotten pea seed lying on the ground. Tommy picked it up. He stared at the wrinkled green skin, and then at the row of growing plants.

That night, after supper, Father opened the Bible storybook. "I will read you," he said to Tommy and little sister, "what Jesus said about planting seeds."

Jesus had come to Jerusalem to die. There were many other people who had come for another reason. They came to celebrate the great

Passover feast. Some of them had come from far away. But even these strangers had heard about Jesus and the wonderful things He did. Several of them came to Philip, who was one of Jesus' friends, and said, "Sir, we want to see Jesus." Philip brought the visitors to Jesus. Perhaps the visitors expected Jesus to work some wonder for them, as He had when He raised Lazarus from the dead. But Jesus never worked wonders just to satisfy a person's curiosity.

Instead, He talked to the strangers about seeds, and dying in order to bear fruit. "The time has come now," He said, "for me to be glorified. Unless a seed is planted in the ground so that it dies, it will always be alone by itself. But if it is planted and dies, it will bear much fruit. Every person who loves his life so much that he will not give anything up will lose his life in the end. Everyone who hates his life in this world will live forever. If anyone wishes to serve me, he will have to follow in the path of self-sacrifice which I am walking. If he does this, then he will be with me in heaven."

Father stopped reading a moment. "You know," he said, "Jesus was a real man, just like us, even though He was God too. It was not easy for Him to die. When He thought about dying, He said, 'My heart is troubled. Shall I pray, "Father save me from this hour!"'? But no, I came unto the world just for this hour, in order to die. Father glorify Your name.' Then there was a voice from heaven which said, 'I have glorified it, and will glorify it again.' Some of the people who were listening thought it thundered. Others said, 'An angel spoke to Him.' But Jesus said, 'If I am lifted up to die on the cross, I will draw all men to myself.' "

Father closed the book. Mother helped little sister to fold her hands, and they all bowed their heads and closed their eyes.

Father prayed: "Jesus, our Saviour, who loved us so much that You were glad to die for us, help us to be willing to die for You, so that all our angry, mean, selfish thoughts and acts may disappear, and some day we, too, shall be with You where You are, and see You face to face."

67

The Plots of Evil Men

Luke 22:1-6; John 11:47-53; 12:1-11

high up on the sacred level of the temple, where none but the priests might enter, the Jewish council met in secret session. The door was locked, and one of the temple police stood at the gate to keep out all intruders. The Pharisees were there, and all the chief priests. They met to decide a matter of the gravest importance.

This was not the first meeting the council had held to settle what should be done about Jesus. They had met several times before. They were all agreed that Jesus was a dangerous man. Or, if there were one or two of the seventy judges who were secretly interested in His teaching, they were afraid to admit it.

The problem was not whether Jesus was dangerous. The problem was what to do about Him. How could they stop Him? At first some thought it wisest to ignore Him. "This fad will die out of itself," they said. "You remember other popular leaders. How long did their popularity last? The common folk are very fickle."

But this was before Jesus had raised Lazarus from the grave. Ever since that day crowds of people had flocked to listen to His teaching. The Jewish court was seriously alarmed.

"What are we to do?" they asked each other. "If we leave him alone, before long everybody will believe in him. We will lose our important position."

"It is better that he should die," the high priest, whose name was Caiaphas, said. "He *must* die, in order to save the rest of us."

"Yes, yes!" the others agreed. "He must die."

"But we must not accuse him openly," another of the judges said. "Especially now, with the city full of visitors who have come for the feast. We must seize him secretly. Otherwise there will be a riot. This man has many sympathizers among the crowd."

"We will offer a reward," they finally decided. "Thirty pieces of silver to anyone who can give us information about his movements. There will be plenty among those who pretend to admire him who will sell him for money."

Not long after this Jesus was eating dinner at the house of one of His friends in Bethany. It really was a party given in Jesus' honor, because of what He had done for Lazarus. Lazarus was there among the guests, and Martha was helping to serve the meal.

If Mary had loved Jesus before He raised her brother Lazarus from the dead, how do you think she felt about Him now? Her heart was filled almost to bursting with love. Can you say just an ordinary "Thank you!" when a friend has given you such a present as this? No, no words could possibly begin to express what Mary felt.

Mary came into the room quietly. In her hand she carried a beautiful alabaster bottle. Standing behind Jesus, she broke off the top of the bottle and poured the perfume in it over His feet, wiping His feet with her hair. The fragrance of the perfume filled all the house.

The guests at the party were shocked. This perfume was spikenard, the most costly of all perfumes, brought from faraway India. It must have cost Mary every cent she had saved in a lifetime of putting aside one penny at a time.

"Why was not this perfume sold, and the money given to the poor?" It was Judas who asked this angry question. Not that Judas cared about the poor, but he was treasurer of the little group of disciples. He took care of the money. Judas loved to run the shining coins through his fingers. When no one was looking he put his hand into the purse, and took some of the money for himself. Yes, Judas was a thief.

Jesus understood the love that had prompted Mary to do this thing.

"Let her alone," He said. "She has done a good thing. You will always be able to help the poor, but you will not always be able to do a kind deed for me. Mary has done what she could. She has prepared my body ahead of time for burial. Wherever my good news is preached throughout the whole world, people will remember Mary's act of love."

Judas went straight from that house in Bethany to the palace of the high priest in Jerusalem. "How much will you give me," he asked, "if I show you where to find him?" The chief priest brought out the scale. He weighed thirty pieces of silver, and he offered the money to Judas. "It must be done quietly," the priest said, "where there is no crowd. We do not want a riot on our hands."

And so Judas and the high priest plotted. They little dreamed that God, and Jesus, knew about their evil plans. Jesus could read their thoughts — as He can read yours — and Jesus could see into the future too. He knew what was going to happen, and He was not afraid. For He knew that His life (like yours and mine) lay not in the hands of Judas, nor of the high priest. His life lay in the hands of Almighty God. And He knew that the one great reason He had come into this world at all was so that He might die for your sins and for mine.

68

Without Me You Can Do Nothing

Luke 13:6-9; John 15:5-15

*t*he tree in my front yard has grown so thick and so fast that now one great drooping branch hangs over the street. When the city bus comes rumbling down our hill, this branch brushes the top of the bus, and the tree goes *swish-swoosh* as the bus hurries past. I like to hear this *swish-swoosh* of the branch; even at night, when I am in bed, I can lie there listening to my tree *swish-swooshing* against the roof of the bus.

Apparently the bus driver does not like it. For today the city forester has arrived in my front yard, and he has brought with him the machine they call a cherry picker. A giant arm reaches up and out, an elbow bends in the middle of the arm, and where there should be a hand there is instead a basket. The forester stands in the basket, and the cherry picker lifts him into the very heart of my tree. He saws for just a moment, and then, crash! — my branch lies on the ground. A worker picks up the severed branch, tosses it into a truck, and it is hauled off to the dump. Already the green leaves are wilting. Just a moment ago this branch was alive, beautiful, shade-giving. Now it is fit for nothing but to be burned.

Probably you have never thought of yourself as a tree. And yet there are many things you can discover about how you ought to live, how to be happy and successful, how to do great things for God, just by looking carefully at a tree. This is not my idea. It is God's idea.

God says that you are like a tree. Not a wild tree, growing in the forest. For in the forest there is fierce competition for light and air and space. The giant forest tree drops thousands of seeds every year. Only a tiny fraction of these seeds ever comes alive. And of that tiny fraction, perhaps not more than half a dozen will grow to be full-sized trees. Some seedlings will starve to death, crowded out by more vigorous brothers and sisters. Some, after they are grown, will be blown down by wind, or split by lightning. Some will be eaten alive by insects, or fall victim to disease.

No, you are not a wild tree. You are a garden tree, planted in a favorable spot by the gardener, on a warm, southerly slope, where the rain waters your roots, and the soil is deep and fertile. Even so, with the best of care, a tree does not bear fruit immediately. And so the gardener waits patiently, and, year by year, he waters and fertilizes and prunes you. He waits patiently, but not forever. The day comes when the gardener expects you to show fruit on your branches. And if you do not, he says, "This tree has no fruit. I will not waste space on it any longer." And so he cuts you down, and you, like the branch of my front-yard tree, are hauled off to the dump to be burned.

This is one of the beautiful stories Jesus told. You — Jesus meant to say — are that garden tree. And the gardener who has so carefully chosen where you are to grow, and has patiently cared for you all these years, that gardener is God Himself. And the fruit He expects to find on your branches is not apples, or oranges, or figs. The fruit He is looking for is love, kindness, patience, gentleness, faithfulness, self-control, goodness, trust.

These are not easy fruits to bear. The garden tree seems to bear its fruit naturally, painlessly, easily. But love and unselfishness and trust are never natural to you and me, never easy, never painless. You can struggle all you like with your unruly heart, and the best that will come out is greed, anger, rebellion, pride, violence. What then are you and I to do? The Gardener demands fruit we cannot show.

Jesus told another story to explain this to us. When the branch was cut from my front-yard tree, the leaves immediately began to wilt. Why? Because the life-giving sap, which rose from the roots, was cut off. Just as long as the branch was part of the tree, and shared in the sap, it was green and alive. As soon as this connection was broken, it died.

In the second story Jesus speaks of you not as a tree but as a vine. A grape vine that bears luscious green or red or blue grapes. And the

root and trunk of this vine is, unbelievably, Jesus Himself. Our Saviour left the glory of heaven above to come down to earth, to be joined with you and me in a union as close, as intimate, as life-giving, as the union of root and branches. He became a man, like us, except without sin. He bore the punishment of our sin. And now from Him, our root, arises life-giving sap to each of us, His branches. And because His life-giving sap courses through our hearts, you and I have the power to bear that fruit for which God Himself planted us in the first place.

We have this power just so long as we remain joined to Him, one with Him. But if we allow ourselves to be separated from our only source of life, we will surely wilt, and die, and eventually be fit only for the dump and the fire. Just before He died, Jesus had a long, last talk with His followers. "Abide in me," He said to them, "for without me you can do nothing." *Abide in Jesus!* This is the secret of fruit-bearing, the secret of life, the secret of happiness, the secret of doing the works of God's kingdom.

69
Who Is the Most Important?

John 13:1-17

One picture, so they say, is worth a thousand words. Mother can talk and talk about playing with matches; but if you ever see a badly burned child, you will be more sure to remember than from all her warnings. One glimpse of a bad automobile accident will make you drive more carefully for a long time — and fasten your seat belts too. The picture of one dead soldier is more effective than all the statistics about the horrors of war.

That is because God made us that way. And having *made* us so, He also *teaches* us by pictures. He does not just tell us our sins are forgiven. No, He uses the water of baptism to show us how He washes us clean again. He does not just promise to feed our souls. He invites us to His supper, and breaks the bread for us, and pours out the wine before our eyes.

You might even say that one reason, one big reason, Jesus came to live among us was to show us what God was like, and how much God loved us. "He that hath seen me," He says, "hath seen the Father."

And so we should not be surprised that one of the very last things Jesus did before He died was to show us — not just in words but in action — how we ought to treat each other. It was the last night of His life on earth. Jesus knew all the agony that was coming. But He was not thinking about Himself; He was thinking about His friends. And His friends — were they thinking of what was about to happen? No, each of them was thinking about himself. They were quarreling, like naughty children, about which one of them was the most important.

In Palestine in Jesus' day people did not wear shoes such as you and I wear today. They wore open sandals, fastened to their feet by a strip of leather. The roads were hot and dusty, so their feet became dirty. When they came into a house, it was polite for the owner to see that their feet were washed. He did not do this himself. He had a slave attend to the washing of his guests' dirty feet.

Jesus and His disciples did not have slaves to do this for them. Probably the disciples took turns doing this for each other. But to-night not one of them volunteered to do this. They were too busy arguing who was the most important. None of them was going to act as a servant to the rest.

So Jesus Himself got up from the table. He took off His coat, wrapped a towel around His waist, kneeled in front of the disciples one by one, untied their sandals, washed their dirty feet, dried them with the towel, and put their sandals back on again.

The disciples watched Him with shame. They were too proud to do this slave's work for each other! So now their Lord and Master was doing it for them! Not one of them dared to speak. There was no sound in the room except the splashing of water, and the rustle of the towel, until Jesus came to Peter.

"Are You going to wash my feet, Lord?" Peter blurted out.

"You don't understand now what I am doing," Jesus answered. "You will understand later." But Peter answered, "I will never let

You wash my feet." Then Jesus said, "If I don't wash you, you have no part in me."

What was it Peter was going to understand later? Not just about the foot-washing — though Jesus was going to explain this in just a moment. Peter could not stand it to see Jesus so humiliated — to see Him dressed like a slave, on His knees, washing dirty feet. What Peter had to understand was that this was just the beginning of Jesus' humiliation. His beloved Master was going to suffer agony in Gethsemane, going to be mocked by the Roman soldiers, going to be condemned, crucified, dead, buried in the ground. And all of this Jesus was going to do willingly, we might even say gladly, because He loved Peter, and you and me, so much. If you cannot stand it to see your Master on His knees, Peter, how will you ever stand it to see Him on a cross? And yet, if Jesus does not die on that cross, you and I will never be washed clean of our sins.

After Jesus had washed the disciples' feet, He put away the pitcher of water, and the basin, and the towel. He sat down at the table again. "Do you know what I have done?" He asked His disciples. "You call me Teacher and Lord, and you are right, for that is just what I am. If I, then, your Teacher and Lord, have washed your feet, you also ought to wash each other's feet. I have given you this example so that you may do as I have done. I didn't come into this world to be waited on, but to do things for others."

Who is the most important? How can you tell? Is it the one who gets the best seat, who gets the first and biggest helping of food, who is waited on by all the others?

This is not the way it is in God's kingdom. The most important person in God's kingdom is the one who does the most for others. And this is because the secret password of God's kingdom is *love*. If we love God, we will love our brother, our neighbor. And if we love, we will not be thinking about ourselves, our pride, our importance; no, we will be thinking about what we can do for the person we love. And no task will be too dirty, too unimportant, too beneath us, if it can show our love.

How can we know all this for sure? We know just by looking at Jesus. He didn't just talk about love. He showed us what it is like. He left His wonderful home in glory. He came to our troubled earth as a tiny, helpless baby. He went about comforting the sad, healing the sick, teaching those who wanted to understand. And at last He gave up His life for us on the dreadful cross.

70
The Last Supper

Mark 14:22-31; John 13:21-30

Jesus did not have a home of His own. He had to borrow a room from some friend to celebrate the great Passover feast. He called Peter and John.

"When you come to the city," He said, "you will meet a man carrying a pitcher of water. Follow him, and when he goes into a house, say to the master of the house, 'The Teacher asks you for your guest room, to celebrate the Passover.' "

Peter and John did as Jesus told them, and they found the house. The owner showed them a large upstairs room, all furnished for the feast. There they got ready the things they needed: the bitter herbs which reminded them of their bitter years of slavery in Egypt so long ago, the unleavened bread which had no yeast in it because they had left Egypt in a great hurry in the middle of the night, and the lamb, which pointed forward to the true Lamb of God who would die to take away the sins of all God's people.

When it was evening, Jesus came with the rest of the disciples. As they took their places around the table, Jesus said to them, "I have very much wanted to eat this Passover with you before I suffer."

And then, as they ate, He went on, "I must tell you something. One of you is going to betray me." The disciples looked at one another with horrified suspicion. The one sitting next to Jesus at the table was John, the disciple Jesus loved. Peter whispered to John, "Ask Him which one of us it is." So John leaned over and whispered to his dearly loved Master, "Lord, who is it?" Jesus answered him, so quietly that the others did not hear, "It is the one to whom I give this piece of bread." And Jesus dipped the bread in the sauce and handed it to Judas.

Did Judas' heart smite him? If it did, he quickly crushed back these feelings. And even as he hardened his heart, Satan laughed. For Satan, too, was plotting to get rid of Jesus, just as Judas and the high priest were. And Satan, like the others, was riding hard for a dreadful fall. For the very thing they all thought would rid them of Jesus forever, His death on the cross, that was the very thing that would give the victory to Jesus, and glory to God, and new life to all who trust in our Saviour.

Jesus spoke to Judas. "What you plan," He said, "do it quickly." Judas got up from the table and rushed out. None of the others wondered where he had gone. They thought perhaps Jesus had sent him to make a gift to the poor. And so Jesus was left alone with the eleven friends who truly loved Him.

Then Jesus took the loaf of bread, and He broke it into pieces. He gave a piece to each of those around the table. "This is my body," He said, "which is given for you. When you eat this, remember me."

Then He took a cup of wine, and passed it around to all of them. "This cup," He said, "is my blood, which is poured out for you, for the forgiveness of your sins."

That was the last meal Jesus ate with His friends before He died. His friends did not forget what He had told them. After He had left them, they met around the table from time to time, and they ate the broken bread as they remembered that Jesus' body had been broken for their sins, and they drank the cup of wine to show that Jesus' blood had been poured out for them.

You, too, when you are a little older, and have confessed that Jesus is your Saviour, can sit at Jesus' table and share a meal with your blessed Saviour. And when you do, you will know that you are eating the very Bread of life itself, and that Jesus will surely feed your soul, as the bread and wine feed your body. And Jesus is present there at that table with you, even though you cannot see Him with your eyes.

After this last supper was finished, the little group in the upper room sang a hymn of praise to God. Then they went out into the darkness of the night. They went down the narrow, stepped streets to the lower city, passed through the gate, and crossed the brook that ran at the bottom of the ravine.

"Tonight," Jesus said to them as they climbed the hill, "tonight every one of you will falter in your faith. Every one of you will desert me."

"Even if everyone else deserts You," Peter said vehemently, "I will never desert You. My faith in You will never fail." Jesus looked at Peter. If he was not the bravest in the little group, he was surely the quickest to show his love.

"This very night," Jesus said, "before the rooster crows to tell that it is dawn, you will say you do not even know me, and that not once, but three times over!"

"I am ready to go with You both to prison and to death," Peter insisted. And all the others joined in. They meant it too. It was just that they did not know their own weakness.

71
The Will of God

Matthew 26:36-46

*T*he little garden grew on the hillside just outside the city wall. There were olive trees here, patches of fragrant herbs, and a little pool from which the gardener dipped water for the plants.

Jesus and His disciples often came here after supper. Sometimes they talked together as they walked back and forth beneath the trees. Sometimes — like tonight — they prayed. And sometimes they just sat, each one thinking his own thoughts, as they watched the city lights winking on below them.

Yes, they came here often, but tonight was different. It was different for the disciples. Something terrible was about to happen. They could not have told you how they knew. But they felt it in the cold, silent hatred with which the priests stared at them when they came into the temple. They heard it in the solemn, mysterious words their Lord spoke to them at supper.

Tonight was different for Jesus too, and He knew all too well why. He knew what the terrible thing was that was going to happen. Tomorrow He was going to die. And Jesus was afraid.

Every man has to die some time. And many men have willingly given up their lives for something they believed in. Perhaps you even know somebody who has done this. It takes a very brave man to say that he will die to help someone else. And Jesus was brave, the bravest man that ever lived.

Jesus was not afraid to die. That was not what frightened Him.

It was the anger of God that Jesus was afraid of. Tomorrow, when Jesus died, He was going to be carrying a terrible burden. He was going to be bent down to the ground beneath the load of my sins, and your sins, and the sins of every single man who ever trusted in God's salvation, every single one from the very beginning of the world to the very end.

Tomorrow, when God would look down on Jesus, as He hung on the cross, God wasn't going to treat Him like His beloved Son. He would treat Jesus like a sinner, like the worst sinner who has ever lived, like the one person who has committed all the sins every other sinner has ever been able to think up. It is a terrible thing, the Bible tells us, to fall into the hands of the living God. That was what was going to happen to Jesus. He knew it, and He was afraid.

And so they came to the garden. "Sit down here," Jesus said to His disciples. "I am going over there to pray." He took with Him the three who were closest to Him, Peter and James and John, and went on a little further. "I am terribly troubled," He said to these three close friends, "so troubled that my heart is breaking. Stay here, and watch with me while I pray." Then He went on still a little further, about as far as you can throw a stone.

Jesus threw Himself on the ground. "My Father," He cried out to God in great anguish, "if it is possible, let me escape from this experience. But, not my will, but Thy will be done."

After a little He came back to His three friends, and He found them all asleep. They had meant to pray with Him, but they were worn out with worry and grief.

"Could you not watch with me one hour?" Jesus asked them sadly. He went off again, and once more He prayed to God: "My Father,

if I must go through with this, Thy will be done." He came back again to His disciples, and again they were asleep.

But there was no sleep for Jesus, no more blessed sleep on this earth any more. He prayed again to God, in such terrible agony that His sweat fell on the ground as great drops of blood.

Did Jesus have to die? No, He did not have to die. He could still have said: "It is too hard. I am afraid. I will not do it." But that is not what Jesus said to God. All our life long you and I can thank God that that is not what He said. What He did say was this: "It is very hard, so hard that I would like to escape it if I can. But there is one thing I want even more than to escape dying, and that is to do what pleases You, my Father, no matter how much it costs."

God heard the prayer of Jesus, and He gave His beloved Son the second thing He asked for, but not the first. He sent an angel to comfort Jesus, and to strengthen Him. And, never forget, it is because God did not give Jesus the first thing He asked for, that you and I, sinners as we are, can become children of the holy God. God did not spare His own Son, but freely sacrificed Him for us all.

Yes, that night in the garden on the hillside, Jesus was unhappy so that you and I might become glad. He was afraid so that we should never have to be afraid again. He was condemned to die so that when God looks at us He should say, "That person is not guilty." He was forsaken by God so that you and I should never be forsaken by God.

Have you ever heard of such love? I do not know what answer we can make to our Saviour. But here is a prayer that you and I can say to Jesus:

> *What language shall I borrow*
> *To thank Thee, dearest Friend,*
> *For this Thy dying sorrow,*
> *Thy pity without end?*
> *O make me Thine forever;*
> *And should I fainting be,*
> *Lord, let me never, never*
> *Outlive my love to Thee.*

72

He That Spared Not His Own Son

Genesis 22:1-18; Hebrews 11:17, 18

Once, quite a long while ago it seems to you, your father was a boy, and your mother was a girl, like you. It is hard to imagine that there was once a time when your father and your mother did not know each other. It is even harder to imagine that there was once a time when they had never heard of you. You listen carefully when they talk about what they did when they were young, like you. You close your eyes and try to see that little girl and that little boy, who grew up to be your mother and your father.

Isaac liked to do this too. Perhaps because his parents were older than the parents of most boys his age, perhaps because he was their only child (he had had a brother once, but he had been sent away when Isaac was just a baby) they had more time to talk to him than many parents do. And they had so many things to tell!

Abraham and Sarah had traveled far and wide and seen many strange and wonderful sights. Abraham told about great cities, crowded with people and with high buildings reaching almost to the sky. Abraham and Sarah had met kings, and Sarah had even lived in a palace for a time. Abraham had fought a war and rescued his nephew Lot from the enemy.

But most of all, Abraham liked to tell about the times that God Himself had talked with him. And that was really what Isaac liked to hear best too. Because, you see, that is where Isaac first came into the story. Not as a baby yet. No, that was not till a long time afterwards. First Isaac was just a promise of God.

Isaac's father and his mother had been married a long, long time, and they did not have any children at all. They had almost given up hope of ever having any. And then came that strange and eventful day when God had first talked to Abraham. That was when Abraham, with Isaac's mother, was living in faraway Ur in the land of Mesopotamia. From there, God had sent Abraham on a long journey. And God had promised that the land he went to would belong to his children, and that some child, born long afterwards into Abraham's family, would bring blessing from God to all the people on the earth.

Yes, in those days Isaac was just a promise. But he was God's promise, and so his father and his mother believed the promise, even though year after year passed and still nothing happened — even when they finally became so old that it was no longer possible for them to have any children at all. No longer possible? There is not anything, not anything at all, impossible for God to do.

And that was the way it turned out too. When Isaac's father was a hundred years old, and his mother was ninety, Isaac was born, just as God had promised. Perhaps that was why the three of them, his father and mother and Isaac himself, loved each other so much. They had waited so long for one another. And certainly that is why they all loved God so much. God had never talked to Isaac himself, as He had so often talked to his father. But Isaac felt very close to God. And Isaac trusted the promises of God. He himself was a living proof that God was faithful, was he not?

And then something strange happened. God spoke to Abraham again.

"Take your dearly loved son, Isaac," God said, "and offer him to me as a sacrifice."

Abraham's heart shrank within him. His precious son, for whom he had waited so long, the one in whom all God's promises were to be fulfilled? How could God's promises come true if Isaac died? Abraham was torn with grief and with perplexity. He felt as if he was lost in a dark night and could not find his way. But there was one thing he knew. God was faithful. He clung to that truth. Somehow, God's promises would be fulfilled, no matter what happened.

Abraham got up early the next morning. He cut the wood he needed for the sacrifice and put it on the donkey's back. He took two servants along. Then, with Isaac and the servants, he set out on his sad journey.

For three days they traveled. Abraham felt that his heart was breaking. But he clung to God's promise. At last he saw the mountain God had spoken of.

"Stay here," Abraham said to his servants. "Isaac and I will go further and worship God, and come back again." Isaac carried the wood. His father carried the knife and the little pot of burning coals. Isaac was puzzled.

"Father?" he said. And Abraham answered, "Here I am, my son."

"I see the fire and the wood," Isaac said, "but where is the lamb for the sacrifice?"

"God will provide the lamb, my son," Abraham answered. Isaac was satisfied. He trusted God, as his father did. So they went on.

When they came to the top of the hill, Abraham took stones and built an altar. He laid the wood on the stones. Then he took a rope and bound Isaac. Isaac did not fight against his father. Whatever happened, he was sure — as his father was sure — that God would take care of him. Abraham placed Isaac on the altar. He took the knife in his hand and raised his arm to kill his son.

At that moment an angel spoke to Abraham out of heaven.

"Do not harm the boy," the angel said. "Now I know that you trust God, because you have not held back your only son from God." And Abraham looked up, and there was a ram caught by his horns in

the bushes. Abraham caught the ram, and bound him, and laid him on the altar, and offered the ram to God instead of his son.

That was a day that Abraham and Isaac never forgot. On that day

Abraham received Isaac back almost from the dead. On that day they learned all over again that, no matter how dark things may look, God never forsakes those who trust in Him, and His promises are forever sure.

Long, long after all this happened, there was another Father who had an only Son whom He loved dearly — far more dearly than Abraham loved Isaac. That Father also was willing to sacrifice His Son. He did it to fulfill the promise made long before to Abraham, that in one of his children's children all the nations of the earth should be blessed. And when that sacrifice was offered, there was no angel who spoke from heaven to save the Son's life. God really gave His dearly loved Son to death to save you and me from our sins.

73
The Betrayal

Luke 22:47-53

If tonight, when you come in from play, your mother should say to you, "Your little brother threw his softball through a window this afternoon, I am going to take your paper route money to pay for it," I think I know what your answer would be. You would say, "That is not fair!" And you would say it with some heat.

But it is just possible, of course, that if you are very fond of your brother, you might say instead, "My little brother has no money of his own. He could never pay for that window. I will help him pay for it."

But if, when he is older, your brother should take a rock and break a window, and steal a watch, and if the police should pick him up, and the judge should say, "Five hundred dollars fine!" would you say,

"My brother can never pay that fine. I will help him pay it."? Would you, to pay your brother's fine, sell the car you had worked and waited for so long?

And just suppose for a minute that, while he tried to rob that store, your brother was interrupted, and that he shot and killed the owner. Would you volunteer to go to the electric chair in his place? Do you love your brother that much?

"That," you say, "would take a lot of love."

You are quite right. It would. It would take the greatest love there is. And that is the very love God showed to you and to me on Good Friday. That is the day when Jesus stepped forward and said, "He can never pay for his crimes himself. I will take his place. I will bear his punishment. I will die in his place."

It was not easy for Jesus to do this. My crimes, and yours, are much greater crimes than murder, and the punishment the law requires is much worse than dying in the electric chair. And Jesus knew what that punishment was, every bitter moment of it. Yet He stepped forward and said, "I will take his place."

After Jesus had prayed in such agony in the garden and after the angel sent by God had strengthened and comforted Him, Jesus came back to His disciples. They were still asleep.

"Get up," He said, shaking them awake. "The man who is going to betray me is coming." The disciples started up, ashamed that they had fallen asleep. They rubbed their eyes. There was no one there but Jesus. The little garden slept peacefully.

There was still time to hide before it was too late! There was still a chance to escape! But Jesus did not run. He did not hide. And now they saw torches coming up the hillside. They heard the murmur of many voices, the heavy tramp of soldiers. Here came the servants of the high priest, and the temple police. Judas marched at their head.

Judas had given the priests a sign, so that they would not arrest the wrong man in the half-light of the torches. "The man I kiss is the man you want," Judas said. "Seize him!" So now Judas stepped forward. He kissed his Lord and Master.

"Do you betray your Lord with a kiss?" Jesus asked him. And then He said to the soldiers, "Whom are you looking for?" And they answered, "Jesus of Nazareth."

"I am He," Jesus answered. "If you are looking for me, let the rest of these men go in safety." The soldiers stepped forward to seize Him. Jesus did not lift a hand in protest. He was ready to go with them quietly. But not Peter! Peter pulled out his sword and struck out wildly at the man nearest him. He cut off the ear of the high priest's servant, Malchus.

"Put away your sword," Jesus said to Peter. "If even now I should ask my Father, He would send me thousands of angels to fight for me. But no! Instead, I am going to drink the cup my Father has given me to drink." Jesus spoke of His suffering and death as a cup offered Him by God. Then Jesus reached out His hand, and touched Malchus' ear, and healed it.

74

A Nighttime Trial

Matthew 26:57-75; John 18:19-23

When they saw that Jesus was not going to fight back, Jesus' friends all deserted Him. One by one they slipped away and disappeared into the shadows of the olive trees. Even Peter, who only an hour before had said, "I will go with You both to prison and to death" —even Peter turned tail and ran.

The soldiers closed in around Jesus. They bound His hands behind His back. They formed a square around Him, to prevent Him from escaping. They marched Jesus down the hillside, across the flooded brook, and through the city gate.

All Jerusalem was sleeping, except for one house. That house — the high priest's palace — was flooded with lights. The seventy judges of the great court were already there. It was against the law to try a man at night. They knew that. But they did not care. They hated Jesus so bitterly they could not even wait till morning to condemn Him to death. Yes, the death sentence had already been decided upon. The only thing left was to find some excuse for the sentence.

They had witnesses there too, waiting to testify against Jesus. Not witnesses who had seen Jesus do something wrong—for Jesus had never done any wrong. These were false witnesses, willing to lie to please the high priest. Perhaps the high priest had promised them a reward for their lies.

The soldiers brought Jesus in, and the witnesses stood up to testify against Him. The lying witnesses had invented many false accusations, but no two of their stories agreed with each other. The law was that a man could not be condemned unless at least two people had seen him commit the crime, and these two stories had to agree.

The high priest said to Jesus, "Are you not going to answer these accusations?" The high priest hoped Jesus would say something that might provide an excuse for His execution. Of course, this too, like the trial at night, was against the law. A man cannot be forced to testify against himself. But the high priest cared little for the law, if only he could get rid of Jesus. Jesus made no answer to the high priest's question. He made no answer at all to the lying accusations the witnesses brought.

"Tell me about your teaching," the high priest asked craftily.

"I taught openly in the temple," Jesus answered him. "I did not teach in secret. Ask the people who heard me what I said."

At these words the high priest's servant slapped Jesus across the face. "Is that the way you answer the high priest?" he asked.

Jesus answered quietly, "If I have said something wrong, say what it is. If I have not said anything wrong, why do you strike me?"

Meanwhile, out in the courtyard of the palace, the servants and the soldiers were waiting. The night was cold, and they had lit a charcoal fire in a little stove — something like the charcoal grill you use to broil a steak. They stood around the fire warming their hands.

I said that all the disciples ran away when Jesus was arrested. But Peter was not really a coward. He had not run far before he turned back again, and followed Jesus and the soldiers into the city. It was dangerous for Peter to be seen here in the high priest's courtyard, for Peter was the man who had cut off the ear of the high priest's servant. He was almost sure to be recognized here in the firelight. Though Peter knew this, he could not bear to leave. He, too, stood by the little stove warming his hands. One of the maids looked at him. His face seemed familiar. She looked more closely.

"This man," she said to the others, "was with the accused man."

Peter was frightened. He lied quickly. "I don't know what you are talking about. I don't even know the man."

Then he got up and left the fire. He went out onto the porch. But he could not escape so easily. This was Peter's time of testing. God was trying him. God was teaching him. He was showing Peter how weak he really was, how desperately Peter needed God's help if he was ever going to do the things he had promised to do! When troubles or temptations come in your life, remember that God tests and teaches you too.

Another servant saw Peter where he was trying to hide on the porch. "This man is one of the group," she said. Again Peter denied, this time with an oath. He called on God to witness that he had never known Jesus! A little later one of the men said, "You must be one of His followers. Your way of talking shows that you come from Galilee." Now Peter was really terrified. He began to curse and swear, saying over and over, "I do not know Him! I do not know Him!"

While he was still protesting, he heard the rooster crow for the first faint morning light. And instantly Peter remembered what Jesus had said to him that very night: "Before the rooster crows, you will deny me three times." Peter got up and rushed blindly from the palace. He threw himself on the ground and wept bitter, heartbroken tears. Ah, Peter, what would you not give now to take back those denials! But you cannot take them back! You can never undo the wrong that you have done! There is only one person who can undo it, and that is your beloved Master, the One you have denied. He is going to die to undo your wicked, faithless words.

The high priest was desperate. He said to Jesus, "Tell me whether you are the Saviour, the Son of God."

And Jesus answered, "It is even as you have said. Some day you will see me coming to judge the world on the clouds of heaven."

Then the high priest tore his clothes to show how shocked he was, or, at least, how shocked he pretended to be — and for a high priest to tear his clothes was also against God's law. "He is guilty of blasphemy! He pretends to be God!" he said. And all the seventy judges, except two, answered, "He must die for this sin."

75

Before the Roman Governor

Mark 15:1-19

It was very early in the morning. Only the first faint light showed in the eastern sky. The streets of Jerusalem were deserted.

Soon these very streets would be overcrowded with hundreds of thousands of pilgrims on their way to the temple. And mingled with the crowd would be the lambs, thousands and thousands of them too, also on their way to the temple to be sacrificed. For tonight, at six o'clock, the Passover began. And then all Israel set aside its usual work to remember that it was God who had saved them long ago, when they were slaves in Egypt. And to remind each other, that no one else but God could save them even now. And that God had promised that He Himself would provide the Lamb who would be sacrificed some day to pay for their sins.

But that was tonight. Now, at early dawn, the city was asleep. But see! Through the sleeping city there comes a strange procession. At its head marches the high priest himself, the religious leader of the nation. Behind him come the seventy judges who rule God's people. Look carefully at these important men. Do you see in their faces the love, the self-forgetfulness, the consecration to God that you ought to see in the leaders of God's people? Alas, no! Instead you see, if you look closely, greed, and selfishness, and love of power, and cruel ruthlessness.

Behind them there marches a troop of soldiers, and some of the temple police. They guard a prisoner. The prisoner droops with weariness. He has had no sleep. All night long the judges have questioned Him. They have hit Him, and spit upon Him, and lied about Him. But they have not succeeded in breaking His spirit. The prisoner is not afraid. Nor is He angry. There is only love in those tired eyes, and courage, and trust in God. The prisoner goes forward wearily, but willingly. He does not try to escape.

The procession comes at last to the palace where the Roman governor lives when he visits Jerusalem — the Praetorium, they call it. The soldiers pound on the gate, and the guard opens it. He recognizes the high priest and the seventy judges. They come into the courtyard. But they will not go into the palace itself. Only the guards and the prisoner go in. For these important religious leaders will celebrate the Passover tonight. They must keep themselves pure and holy for the feast!

The Roman governor comes out to speak to them. "What has the prisoner done?" he asks.

"He says that he is a king," they answer. "He does not allow his followers to pay taxes to our great emperor, Caesar." O lying tongues! And you wish to keep yourselves pure, to eat God's Passover? Pilate goes back into the palace.

"Are you a king?" he asks Jesus.

"My kingdom is not of this world," Jesus answers. "If it were, my servants would fight for me."

Pilate goes back to the priests. "This man has committed no crime," he says. The priests are furious. They begin, angrily, to make all sorts of lying accusations. "He is stirring up a rebellion," they insist.

Pilate returns to Jesus. "Do you hear what they say against you?" he asks. "Are you not going to answer them?"

But Jesus makes no answer.

Pilate is puzzled. He feels sure the prisoner is innocent. Why, then, does He not speak up in His own defense? There is a reason, but it is not one that Pilate would understand. Jesus does not answer because He wishes to die. He has chosen to be God's lamb, to die for the sins of His people.

By this time the city is waking up. A crowd has gathered before the palace. Pilate appeals to the people. "Every year," he reminds them, "I pardon one prisoner, at Passover time. Shall I release this man, or would you rather choose Barabbas?" Barabbas was a notorious criminal, a thief and a murderer.

"Not this man!" the people shout. "Release Barabbas!"

"What then shall I do with this prisoner?" Pilate asks.

"Away with him!" they shout. "Away with him! Crucify him!"

"But why?" Pilate asks. "What has he done that is wrong?"

The multitude will not listen to Pilate. Filled with hatred, and a lust for blood, they shout over and over, "Crucify him! Crucify him! If you let him go, you are no friend of Caesar." Pilate wants to do what is right, but only if it does not cost him too much; only if it does not get him in trouble with the emperor in Rome. He is certainly not going to risk his neck to save Jesus. He hands Jesus over to the soldiers.

While the captain makes the preparations for the execution, the soldiers amuse themselves by making fun of Jesus. They dress Him in a purple robe, such as kings wear. They put a crown of thorns on His head, and a stick in His hand for a scepter. Then they get down on their knees before Him and say, with cruel laughter, "Hail, King of the Jews!" They take the stick out of His hand and strike Him with it. They spit in His face. Jesus bears all this patiently, meekly, without a word.

Does it hurt you to see your Saviour standing there, the butt of the soldiers' jokes, with blood and spit running down His face? It hurts me so that I can hardly bear to look. And yet I need to look. For this dreadful treatment, this shame that Jesus bears so bravely, is really meant for me. My heart is so black, my sins are so great (and so are yours!) that I deserve all this and more. And Jesus knows this. That is why He chooses, of His own free will, to bear this too, for you and for me. So very much He loves us!

76
The Place of the Skull

Luke 23:32-43; John 19:17-27

The city is almost surrounded by cemeteries. It does not matter which gate you go through, or what road you take, you still must walk among the tombs. Some of these graves are very old. The people who live here will show you where King David was buried, and the boy-king Joash, and the wicked king Manasseh who made the streets of Jerusalem to run with blood. Some of the graves are recent; and still others have never been used at all. Their owners have prepared ahead of time these places where they wish to be buried.

Of all the cemeteries there was one more gloomy than the rest. Here, in the middle of the graves, there was a small hill. Many people said this hill resembled a skull, a ghastly death's head grinning at you mockingly from behind its empty eyes. It was not really a skull, of course. It was only a hill, and yet it was a place of horror. For on this hill desperate criminals were executed. Here they met the just reward of their wicked deeds.

This hill, then, was the spot to which Jesus came at last. It was a strange procession that wound through the city streets that Friday. The soldiers came first, their heavy boots clanking on the stone pavement. In the middle of the little group the condemned Man stumbled, bent low beneath the heavy wooden cross He carried. Behind them followed the crowd. Most of them were there out of idle curiosity, eager to enjoy the excitement of an execution. A few — these were the priests and the leaders — came with hearts filled with hatred. They could hardly wait to enjoy the sight of the condemned Man's last, gasping breath. And, behind all the others, there were a few, a very few, friends who were faithful to the end. Jesus' mother was there, and two or three other women who loved Him, and just a

single one of the followers who had shared the last three years with Him.

Jesus said once that there are many people who have eyes, but do not see. He did not mean that they are blind, but only that they do not understand the things they see. There were plenty of eyes in Jerusalem that Friday morning. But in all that crowd there was not a single person, except for Jesus Himself, who understood what it was that was about to happen.

And so the procession came at last to the hill that looked like a skull. The soldiers took away Jesus' clothes. If you look with the eyes of faith, you will see how poor your Saviour became so that you might become rich.

The soldiers nailed His hands to the crossbeam of the cross. They tied His feet to the upright. They raised the heavy cross, and set it in the ground. And then they sat down to wait until the end. While they waited, they amused themselves by dividing His clothes among themselves. When they got to the cloak, which was seamless, woven in one piece of cloth, each man wanted it.

"It would be a shame to tear it up," one of them said, "let us throw dice to see who gets it." Someone brought out a pair of dice, and so they gambled for the cloak.

The condemned Man hung on the cross. If there was ever a desperate moment in His life, it was this moment. This was the moment to cry out to God, to pray, as His great ancestor, David, had done so long ago, "Be not far from me, for there is none to help." But Jesus was not praying for Himself. "Father," He said, "forgive them, for they know not what they do." Did He pray for the Roman soldiers who sat there joking and tossing their dice? Yes, He prayed for them; but that was not all. Was it Pilate He meant, or the high priest and the Sanhedrin? Yes, but more than that. Was it the curious crowd, those who had shouted, "Crucify him!"? Yes, but even these were not all. If you really listen, listen with the ears of faith, and understand, you will see that Jesus was praying for you, and for me. He prayed about all those selfish, mean, disobedient things we have done, never realizing what our careless sins would cost our Saviour. For it was not the Roman soldiers, nor the Sanhedrin, nor the shouting mob that brought Him here. It was our sins, and His love for you and me.

Of all those standing beneath the cross, there was one whom Jesus loved dearly. It was His mother. He died for her sins, too, just as for yours and mine. But He had an extra care for this woman who once held Him on her lap, who guided His first uncertain steps.

"Woman," He said to her (for though she had been His mother, she would now become His child, His sheep, His friend), "see, there is your son, to care for you." And then He spoke to the disciple whom He especially loved, "Son, there is your mother; look after her." And so the beloved disciple took Mary into his own home from that day on.

The cross on which our eyes are fixed was not the only cross on the hill of the skull. There were two others, one on each side of Jesus. These men were really desperate criminals; they were murderers and robbers. The priests and the crowd mocked at our Saviour.

One of the crucified thieves joined in the mockery. But the other — he alone of all those people — saw, dimly, and yet truly, what was happening. "You and I," he said to his fellow murderer, "suffer what we deserve, but this Man is innocent." And then he said to Jesus, "Lord, remember me, when You come into Your kingdom." Jesus looked at him with love and compassion. "This very day," He answered, "you shall be with me in Paradise."

Can you see? Can you hear? And then understand as well? You and I do not have to pay for our own evil deeds. Like that dying thief, we have to bring nothing at all, nothing but sorrow for our sins, and simple, childlike trust in the One who hangs there on the cross in our place. It is a simple prayer, and yet it is the only prayer you need. "Lord, remember me." And if you pray it from a sincere heart, Jesus will never forget your need.

77
It Is Finished!

Luke 23:44-47; John 19:28-30, 38-42

Outside the city wall there is a hill, and on the hill there stands a cross, and on the cross Jesus hangs, dying.

Around the cross a crowd is gathered. Some have come to laugh; some, to pity; some, to stare.

Only a tiny handful of His friends are there, and they stand a little to one side. They are numb with the shock of what is happening. All their fondest hopes, everything that makes their lives worth living, has come crashing down around their heads this Friday.

They are numb with the shock, but they ought not to be. If only they had listened, and understood! For Jesus had warned them beforehand. "When a grain of wheat falls into the ground and dies," He said, "that is when it bears much fruit." He had even told them about the way in which He was going to die. "When I am lifted up," He said, "I will draw all men to myself."

Yes, now He is lifted up. And already He is doing just that —

drawing men to Himself, just as He said He would. There is another cross beside His. On it hangs a desperate criminal, a thief and a murderer. No man is less likely to turn to God, it seems. And yet this wicked man feels the pull of the Saviour who is lifted up. He has confessed his sins, and begged for mercy.

But Jesus' friends stand with bowed heads and bowed hearts. They do not understand that it is just *because* He dies that He can draw all men to Himself. The dying thief has already felt that amazing love tugging at his heart. And this is only the beginning. There will be more before this day is over.

It is noon. The sun ought to be directly overhead. But, strangely, it is not. No one can say where it is. It ought to be light. Instead it is dark — black dark, like a moonless, starless night.

The soldiers have to stay until the men on the crosses are dead. The strange darkness frightens them too. And now, to add to the terror of the scene, the ground beneath their feet begins to rock and shake. Why is it dark in the middle of the day? Who is this man that the ground should tremble when He dies?

The soldiers do not know. But you and I do. Beneath the curtain of that darkness, God is punishing your sins and mine. Jesus is suffering the pains of hell itself, for your sake and for mine. All the anger God feels towards cruelty and wickedness and sin is pouring down on our Saviour's head — so that you and I will never have to fear an angry God. So very much He loved us!

Out of the darkness a terrible cry is heard: "My God, my God, why hast Thou forsaken me?" This is just what sin does. It separates us from God. And Jesus took this terrible lostness, this awful aloneness, for us too. He was forsaken by God, so that we, who deserve to be forsaken, might never be. Was there ever love like His love?

Out of the darkness, the horrifying aloneness, Jesus speaks again.

"I am thirsty," He says. There is a jug of sour wine standing there, for the soldiers to drink. One of them dips a sponge in the wine, and holds it up to Jesus' mouth.

It is now three o'clock. Jesus says simply, "It is finished!" What is finished? His suffering? Yes, but He is thinking not of Himself, but of us. It is the dreadful payment for our sins that is finished. All the wicked thoughts that I have thought (and will think, still), all the wicked words I have spoken (and continue to speak, alas), all the vile deeds I have done (and go on doing), and all your sins, and the sins of every person who trusts in Jesus since the world began, all of these, every single one, have been paid for.

And now His work is finished. He can return at last to God. "Father," He prays, "into Thy hands I commend my spirit." And then He bows His head and dies — willingly, gladly, trusting in God, His Father.

The captain of the soldiers has been watching all this. Never has he seen a man die like this man. There is a strange stirring in his heart, the pull of something he hardly understands.

"Truly," he says, "this was a good man. This was the Son of God." This is the second man Jesus drew to Himself when He was lifted up on the cross.

There are still two others to come. The Jewish law was that dead bodies could not be left hanging on the cross after sunset. Who will take down the body of our Saviour and bury it? All His friends have run away in fear. Must He be thrown into a common criminal's grave? No, now that there is no one else to help, two men come forward — Joseph of Arimathaea and Nicodemus. Both of these men are rich, and both are powerful. In fact, they are members of the Jewish court, the Sanhedrin. They alone, among the seventy judges, had opposed the crucifixion of Jesus. But neither one had dared to speak openly for Jesus.

But the marvelous power of the dead Saviour draws them. They come forward boldly, and ask for the body. They wrap it in linen cloths, and sprinkle it with costly spices. Then they lay it in a new grave, cut out of the rock of the hillside nearby, a grave Joseph had intended for himself, when he should die. They roll a great disc of rock in front of the grave, to keep out wild animals.

The priests are not done yet with their hate. They go to Pilate.

"Set a guard of soldiers," they say. "Otherwise his friends will steal the body, and will claim he has come back from the dead." So Pilate sealed the grave shut with his official seal, and he sent a company of soldiers to watch the grave, to prevent the dead body from being stolen.

78
The Empty Grave

Mark 16:1-8

If tomorrow, when you come home from school and call your mother, there is no answer, and if you find a note on the kitchen table saying "Mother has gone to the hospital," you would be frightened. But if Mother had told you beforehand that she was going, and that she would be home again in two or three days, you might be lonely when you found the house empty, but you would not be afraid. If something unpleasant is about to happen, it often helps to know about it ahead of time. It is still unpleasant, but it is not such a shock.

Jesus knew this too. And so He had told His friends that He was going to be arrested, and brought to trial, and executed. He had told them over and over again that He was going to die, and that three days afterwards He would rise again.

But sometimes, if you are enough afraid of the thing you see ahead of you, you just close your eyes and pretend it isn't there. You tell yourself that the horror will go away if only you do not look at it. That is what the disciples of Jesus did. They had heard what He said all right, but they refused to understand. Not one of them could bring himself to believe that his beloved Master was going to die.

And so, when it happened, it was a dreadful shock to all of Jesus' friends. Everything that made life worth living for them came to an end that Good Friday afternoon. Friday night, and the endless aching hours of Saturday, and all Saturday night, they were sunk in gloom. And Easter day — the happiest day of all the year — was a day of hopeless grief and black despair for Jesus' friends.

If only they had *really* listened to what Jesus had said! What a terrible mountain of useless fear and grief they would have been spared! For right now, while they sit in that upstairs room, too sunk in sorrow to talk, to eat, or even to pray, right now God is working, almost before their very eyes, the greatest miracle that ever happened.

But do not be too quick to blame them. Has it never happened to you that you have been afraid just because you forgot the promises of God? It has happened to me many times. Oh, I had heard those promises often enough. Many of them I knew by heart. I learned them — some of them when I was younger than you are. But when trouble came, how quick I was to forget! How quick to tremble and to doubt!

But now it is Easter morning, that very first Easter in all the world. A little group of women walk slowly through the city streets. It is still dusk; the first morning light is just beginning to glimmer in the east. They are carrying spices to spread on the dead body of their Master. It is the only thing left that they can do for Him, to show how much they love Him.

Their eyes are red and swollen, but they are not crying any more. When there is no hope at all, it does not help even to cry. They do not talk much, but now and again one of them asks, "How are we going to move that big stone in front of the grave?" No one answers. No one knows.

They pass silently through the city gate, and so they come to the cemetery. Oh, women, women, who love Jesus, and whom Jesus loves! Lift up your gloomy eyes, for you are going to see something such as you never dreamed could happen!

But what is this? The stone is rolled away already! How did this happen? The women are too deep in grief even to ask.

The grave is not such a grave as you and I are used to. Instead, it is a rock cave, cut out of the hillside, and in this cave the body of our Saviour had been laid.

The women have forgotten the promises of God, but God has not forgotten the women. He sees their grief. He knows how much they love the Saviour. He has sent a special messenger to comfort them, to remind them that their God is always faithful.

The women step into the cave. The body of Jesus is not there. Instead, sitting on the shelf where the body had been laid, there is an angel, wearing a robe as white as snow, and with a face so dazzling bright it hurts to look at him. The women are terrified. They fall on the ground and hide their faces.

The angel speaks to the women. "Do not be afraid," he says. "You are looking for Jesus, who was crucified. He is not here; He is risen. Look! this is the very place where they laid Him! Don't you remember," the angel went on, "how He told you beforehand that He was going to die, and to rise again on the third day? Go and tell His disciples. He will meet you in Galilee, just as He promised."

When the angel finished speaking, the women turned and ran as fast as their legs could carry them. Fear, and doubt, and a wild, new hope were all mixed up inside of them.

But even as they ran, the Holy Spirit whispered in their hearts: *"Don't* you remember He *did* tell you He would rise again." At last, completely out of breath, their steps slowed, and then they stopped. And one of them said slowly, wonderingly, "I do remember. He did say He would rise again." And another answered softly, "Why, yes, that is just what He promised."

79
Mary Magdalene

John 20:1-18

*t*here was once a money-lender," Jesus said to His disciples while He was still on earth, "who had two men that owed him money. The one owed five hundred pieces of silver, the other fifty pieces. Neither of them could pay back what he owed, and so he forgave both of them their debt. Which of the two will love him the most?"

And His listeners answered, "The one, I suppose, whose debt was the greater."

"You are right," Jesus answered. "And so, too, the person who is a great sinner, and has been forgiven by God, will love God more than the person whose little sins have been forgiven."

Mary Magdalene was one of those who had had great sins forgiven. God has not told us what Mary's past had been. We only know that Jesus had driven seven devils out of her, and that she had followed Him ever since.

Mary was one of the women who came with Jesus to Jerusalem that last week of His life, one of those who took care of Him, as women have always cared for the people they love. These women washed His clothes, and cooked His meals.

All that dreadful Friday, when the world seemed to come to an end, these women stood near the cross. They could hardly stand it to watch, and yet they could not bear to leave either. Not even after it was all over, after Jesus had gasped His last breath, and His soul had returned to God, and only His lifeless body hung on the cross — not even then did they leave. They were still there keeping their loving watch when Joseph and Nicodemus took the body down and laid it in the grave.

Mary Magdalene was one of the women who came early Sunday morning to anoint Jesus' body with spices. She was one of those who ran in mingled fear and hope from the grave. They were not sure themselves what the angel had said. And who could believe such a story? Who would believe it?

Not the eleven disciples who had known Jesus best! When at last the women had retraced their steps to Jerusalem, and tried to tell, in confused excitement, what had happened in the cemetery, the disciples turned away indifferently. "You are out of your heads," they said to the women. "Where did you dream up such an idle story?"

Only Peter, the impulsive one, and John, the beloved disciple, went to the cemetery to see for themselves. And Mary Magdalene followed them. Not that she hoped any longer to find even the dead body of Jesus. But, since this was where His body had last been seen, this was where she wished to be.

Peter and John stooped down and looked into the grave. The linen cloths in which Jesus' body had been wrapped lay neatly folded on the shelf. The body itself was gone. Troubled, puzzled, not knowing what to think, they went slowly back to the city.

But Mary Magdalene could not bear to leave. She stood there crying. Once again she leaned down to look into the grave. Two angels were now sitting where the body of Jesus had lain. They were dressed in white, shining with an unearthly light. Mary was so sunk in grief that she did not even stop to wonder about the angels.

"Woman, why are you crying?" one of them asked.

"They have taken away my Lord," she answered, "and I do not know where they have put Him."

Mary turned away, and saw Jesus standing beside her. She did not recognize that it was Jesus. Perhaps her eyes were too full of tears to see clearly. Or perhaps it was because Jesus now appeared to her in His glorious new body, His resurrection body.

"Woman," Jesus said, "why are you crying? Whom are you looking for?" Mary thought this must be the gardener.

"Sir," she begged Him, "if you have moved the body, tell me where you have put Him, and I will take Him away."

Jesus answered with just one word. "Mary!" He said, calling her

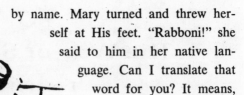

by name. Mary turned and threw herself at His feet. "Rabboni!" she said to him in her native language. Can I translate that word for you? It means, "My Master, my Lord, my Saviour, my Teacher!" It means, "If You are indeed here, all is well, no matter what else happens. If You are gone from me, nothing can ever be well again!" Mary reached out to clutch at Jesus' feet.

"Do not cling to me," Jesus said to her gently. "I must still ascend to my Father. But go and tell my brothers that I am going up to my Father and your Father, to my God and your God."

So now Mary stumbled back to the city, through the gate and up the endless steps. She did not really see where she was going, not because she was crying, but instead because of the dazzling light of a new life shining in her heart. It would be a little while before she understood it all. For now, it was enough that she knew her Saviour was alive.

All of this happened long ago and in a distant country. And yet it is not so far away as you might think. For though you do not stand beside Joseph's grave weeping, you, too, are often sad, and afraid, and ashamed of things that you have done. It will never be right with you until, like Mary, you hear Jesus speak to you, calling you by name; until you turn and suddenly recognize your Lord, your Teacher, your Saviour; until you know for sure that He is alive forevermore, and that all your sins are paid for in His death.

80
The Way of Suffering

Luke 24:13-33

It was late in the afternoon when Cleopas and his friend left Jerusalem. They had seven miles to walk before they got to Emmaus, where they planned to spend the night. But they would not have minded the miles. It was the heaviness in their hearts that made the way seem long.

They did not notice the setting sun or the late afternoon breeze. Their faces were drawn with sorrow. Their feet dragged, and their shoulders sagged because of their grief. As they walked, they talked sadly to each other.

"I just don't understand it," Cleopas said. And his companion answered, "After all our high hopes, such a bitter disappointment!"

What was it that filled these men with sorrow and perplexity? These men were followers of Jesus. Just a week ago Jesus had come riding into the city, surrounded by the happy shouts of His friends. "Blessed is the King who comes in the name of the Lord," they shouted. Were Cleopas and his friend in that happy crowd? Very likely they were. Very likely they, too, took off their coats in their excitement, and spread them on the ground for their new King to ride upon.

But since that day, just one week ago, something terrible had happened. Their new King, from whom they had expected so much, had been arrested, tried, and at last executed on the cross like a common criminal.

And when His lifeless body was taken down and placed in the grave, all hope had died in the hearts of His followers. For who can argue with death? Death is the end of every man's work! Death is permanent!

As Cleopas and his friend walked and talked sadly together, another traveler came up behind them. "What is it you two are talking about?" He asked. "Why are you so sad?"

The two friends stared at Him in surprise. "Are you the only person in all Jerusalem who does not know what has happened?" Cleopas asked. And the traveler answered, "What is it that has happened?"

"Why," they said to him, both now talking at once in their astonishment, "the things that happened to Jesus! He was a prophet who spoke wonderful words, and did wonderful things. But our priests arrested and killed Him. And we had so hoped He was the One sent by God to save His people! And there is something else that is very strange. Some of the women of our company were at the grave very early this morning, but they could not find His body. They came back saying they had seen a vision of angels who said Jesus was alive again. But, of course, they did not see Jesus Himself."

Then the Stranger said to them, "O foolish men, and slow of heart to believe what the prophets have said about the Saviour! Don't you see that suffering was the way by which the Saviour entered into His glorious kingdom?" And He began right then and there, as they walked along the road, to explain to them what God had said about the Saviour, from the beginning of the Old Testament to the very end.

There was something about what He said, and the way He said it, that caught at their minds, until, at last, their hearts began to burn with excitement, with joy, with new hope. But still they never suspected who the Stranger was. For men do not expect to meet along the road a man who has died. And Cleopas and his friend had not yet heard about Easter.

By this time they were approaching Emmaus, where they lived. They begged the Stranger to come home with them, and spend the night. They could not bear to let Him out of their sight. And so they all went into the house, and sat down to supper.

Then the Stranger bowed His head, and asked a blessing on the meal. He picked up the loaf of bread, and broke it, and gave each of them a piece to eat. At that very instant their eyes were opened, and

they recognized Him. This was Jesus! He *was* alive, just as the angels had said! And even as they recognized Him, He vanished from their sight.

They got up immediately and started back to Jerusalem. For they had something to tell the others that could not wait until tomorrow.

81
The First Easter

John 20:19-29; Revelation 5:9, 10

*T*here had been many celebrations in heaven, but never another one like this one. When God made the heavens and the earth, the angel choirs sang with joy. The night that Jesus was born, there had been rejoicing and songs of praise. But this was the gladdest, the most wonderful celebration of all.

They were all there, the people who had trusted in God's salvation. Adam was there, the first man of all, and Noah who had spent so many weeks and months in the ark, and Abraham who left his own country because he trusted God's promise; and David, and Elijah, and Daniel, and many, many others, more than you could ever count. But most of all, the reason for all the rejoicing, Jesus was there, sitting on the great white throne, by the side of His Father. Jesus in His beautiful new and glorious body, the body that had no flaw or weakness, but only beauty and marvelous perfection, such a body as you and I are going to have some day too.

The saints of God, as they walked the golden streets, said to one another in wonder and delight, "It is finished!" And another answered, "Just see what it is that God has done!" And the great angel choirs, standing on either side of the throne, sang their new song, the song that they had learned just for this special celebration:

"Worthy art Thou," they sang to Jesus our Saviour, "to receive power, and honor, and glory, and blessing, for Thou wast slain, and didst purchase unto God with Thy blood men from every tribe and tongue and people and nation."

Yes, that was a wonderful celebration, a day of great delight and joy. For that was the first Easter day in all the world.

But back on earth, among those very people whom Jesus had purchased with His blood, it was not a day of celebration, but instead a day of weeping and of sorrow. It is true, the women had heard the message of the angel, and now they almost dared to hope. But the disciples still sat there in that upstairs room, and when the women told them about the angel's message, they answered gloomily, "You are out of your head. Who ever heard of such a thing?"

But for all their grief, they remembered to lock the door. The truth is, they were afraid, afraid that they might be the next ones to hear the tramp of armed soldiers in the street, the pounding of armed fists on the door.

They were all there except Thomas, who had gone off to grieve by himself. And, of course, Judas, the traitor, wasn't there either. He could no longer be considered one of the friends of Jesus, not since the awful moment in the garden when he planted that lying kiss on Jesus' cheek.

One moment they sat there, staring at the floor, each thinking his own dark thoughts. And the next moment everything was changed. Suddenly ten heads lifted, as if Someone had whispered in each heart, "Look now! He is here!"

And there, standing in the middle of the circle, was Jesus Himself. The disciples were terrified. Their eyes grew wide and staring; they shrank back in their chairs. Surely this was a ghost!

"Peace be to you," Jesus spoke quietly. "Why are you so troubled? Look at my wounded hands, and my torn side. See! It is I myself, and not a spirit!" And now a wild, new joy showed in their faces. It was their own Lord and Master, come back to them from the dead!

"My Father sent me," Jesus went on, "and I am sending you to carry my good news to the ends of the earth. You must tell everybody what you have seen. And the Holy Spirit will live in your hearts, and go with you, to teach you, and to give you power."

In that moment, life changed for the friends of Jesus. Nothing was ever the same again. Their Lord had come back to them. Wonder of wonders, Jesus had conquered even death itself!

But Thomas was not there. He had missed this marvelous reunion. When the others told him about it, he answered bitterly, "I will never believe that could happen, unless I put my own fingers in the nail marks in His hands, and feel with my own hand the wound in His side."

The next Sunday night they were together again, and this time Thomas was there too. Again Jesus came through the locked door to stand among them, saying, "Peace to you!" And now He spoke especially to Thomas:

"Reach out your finger and put it in the nail holes in my hands," He said, "and put your hand into the hole in my side. Do not doubt, but believe." Thomas was overcome. He did not need to feel of Jesus.

He knew! "My Lord, and my God!" he cried out.

"Because you have seen me, you have believed," Jesus said. "Happy are the ones who have never seen me with their eyes, but still have believed."

Do you know who those happy ones, those blessed ones are? Jesus was talking about you and me. We have never seen that blessed body that was sacrificed for our sake (though we are going to see it some day). But, seeing Him with the eyes of faith, we have believed that Jesus is the Son of God, who died for us and rose again; and in Him we have life everlasting.

82
Breakfast on the Beach with Jesus

John 21:3-17

By evening the beach was usually deserted. Those who were going fishing had already left. The others were at home. Tonight, however, a little group of men stood on the sand. The water lapped softly at their feet. On the further side of the lake the cliffs rose steeply from the shore. The men were lost in remembering.

"Right there," Peter said, "is where we were standing when He first spoke to us."

"Yes," echoed his brother Andrew, "and do you remember how He used our boat to teach the crowd on the shore?"

"And out there," said another one, "is where He spoke to the winds and waves, and the storm obeyed Him."

"And that," said Andrew, looking at the green hills across the lake, "is where He fed the five thousand people with five loaves and two fish." They had come back north from Jerusalem because Jesus had told them to. "Tell my brothers that I will meet them in Galilee," He had said to the women on Easter morning. So now they stood again on the shore of the lake where so many wonderful things had happened.

"I am going fishing," Peter said now. And the others echoed, "We will go with you." They ran the little boat down the sand and into the water. They rowed out to deeper water, and threw in the nets. By now it was dark — a good time to fish. But you can never tell just where you will find fish. After a while they pulled the empty net back in, and moved the boat to another spot. No fish here either!

What did they think about as they sat there in that little boat in the dark? I cannot say for sure. But I do know there was one of them who had something special on his mind. That one was Peter. When Jesus told them about His approaching death, it was Peter who promised he would never leave his Master, but would even die for Him if necessary.

How bitterly those empty boasts stuck in Peter's heart now! For he had broken those well-meant promises. He had denied the Master he loved, not once, but three times over. Could he ever forgive himself?

Just as the first streaks of light appeared in the sky, they noticed a man standing on the beach. "Do you have anything to eat?" the man called to them. "No, we have not caught anything," they answered. "Throw your net on the right side of the boat," the man said. And so they threw their net on the right side, and suddenly it was full of fish, so many fish, they could not pull it out of the water into the boat. John guessed at once who the man must be.

"It is the Lord," he said to Peter. Peter could not wait to row to shore. He wrapped his outer garment around him, jumped into the

water, and waded to shore. The rest of them rowed the boat in, dragging the net full of fish behind them.

When they got to the beach, they found a fire burning. Fish were cooking over the fire, and a loaf of bread was set beside it. "Come and eat breakfast," Jesus said. The men sat around the fire silently. Their Saviour, the Lord of heaven and earth, had cleaned and broiled fish for their breakfast, and kneaded and baked bread for them to eat! They were amazed, and you and I are amazed too. Never, never forget that Jesus loves you so much that He Himself sees to all your smallest needs.

After they had finished breakfast, Jesus turned to Peter. "Peter," He said, "do you love me more than these others do?" Once Peter would have answered at once that he did. But not any more. "Yes, Lord," he said humbly, "You know that I love You."

"Then feed my lambs," Jesus told him. Jesus had work for Peter to do — as He has work for you and me. Peter was to be a shepherd, working for Jesus, the Good Shepherd. He was to lead and feed the lambs of Jesus' flock.

Jesus spoke to him again:

"Peter, do you love me?" Peter answered again, "Yes, Lord, You know that I love You." Again Jesus gave him work to do. "Take care of my sheep," He said.

Then Jesus asked him a third time, "Do you love me?" Peter felt bad that Jesus asked him this three times. "Lord," he said, "You know all things. You know that I love You." Once more Jesus gave him a task to perform for his Lord. "Feed my sheep," He said.

Would Peter ever forget what he had done? No, I don't suppose he ever forgot. But he no longer brooded about it. Jesus had given him three chances to say that he loved Him, and Jesus had given him work to do for the Master he loved. Peter was ready to work for Jesus. He was ready because he no longer trusted in his own strength. He knew now that he was not as brave, and not as faithful, as he had boasted he was. But he knew, too, where to look for help and strength.

I know that there are things you have said and done that you wish you could take back. I know this because I have looked into my own heart; I remember my own sins. You cannot go back and undo what you have done, however much you want to. But God can. This is exactly what God did when Jesus died on the cross. He paid the whole price of your sin. He took a sponge and wiped the blackboard clean. Do not wait another day to take the help He offers. Kneel down and say, "Father, forgive me for the sake of Jesus' death."

If you do this, then God will *forget* your sins. And when God forgets your sins, you, too, will be gloriously free of guilt and of regret. Then to you, as to Peter, your Saviour will assign a share in His work. "Come, my son, my daughter," He will say, "I have work for you to do. If you truly love me, you can tell others the wonderful news about my death. Lean on me for strength. I will never let you down."

83
The Great Commission

Acts 1:1-11

Jesus chose twelve men to help Him, and today we call them St. Peter, St. James, St. John, and so on. But we must not suppose that they were saintlike when He chose them. These men were no supermen. They were just ordinary folk like ourselves, and among the twelve of them you would find nearly every weakness and sin you and I show. Some of them were proud and ambitious, eager to get ahead, to promote themselves. Some were timid and doubting. One was skeptical, unwilling to believe unless he could see with his eyes and touch with his hands. One was boastful and overconfident, a man who spoke without ever stopping to think what he said. All twelve of them were cowards, and one was a thief.

Would a general ever have chosen such a group of volunteers? Would a business man have selected such helpers? Surely not! But with Jesus it was different — quite different. For He intended to make these men over, to transform them, to empty them of themselves and to fill them with His power. He was going away, and these men were to take over His work. But not in their own strength. They were going to work in His strength. They were going to be taught what to think and what to do by the power of the Holy Spirit.

Not one of them understood this yet. Just as you and I do not understand what it is that God is going to do with our lives that we have dedicated to Him. When Jesus' dead and broken body was taken down from the cross and placed in the grave, these men felt an awful sense of loss and despair. Everything that had made life worth living had been buried with their Master. How could they ever go on living? How go back to the empty lives they had known before they met Jesus?

Three days later their world was turned upside down. And when they actually saw their Lord again, when they discovered that He had not only died, but had come back to life again, had risen from the grave, had conquered death, then they could hardly contain their joy. Their Master no longer spent all His time with them, as He had done before Good Friday and Easter. He came to them, He talked to them, He even ate with them. But always He went away again. He came through locked doors, and then He disappeared again mysteriously, before their very eyes.

They knew another parting lay ahead, and they listened carefully to every word Jesus said. When a private in the army becomes an officer, we say that he has received a commission. The commission means new work, new opportunities to be of service, new responsibilities. It is a great honor too. Before He left them, Jesus gave His followers a commission too. He gave them new work, new responsibilities, and the great honor of serving as His mouth in telling the Good News of salvation, and as His hands in helping those in trouble or in grief.

"You must tell people," He said to them, "about my life, about my death, and about my resurrection. Start right here at home in

Jerusalem. Then you must go out and tell what you have seen and heard in Judaea, and in Samaria, and go on telling what has happened until you have carried the news to the very ends of the earth."

These words were not meant just for the disciples. They were to start telling the story. But all Christian people are expected to help in carrying the story of Jesus to the ends of the earth. You and I too.

At last the day of parting came. Jesus led His disciples outside the city. "Stay in Jerusalem," He said to them, "until the Holy Spirit comes." Then Jesus raised His hands to bless His disciples. And even while He was blessing them, He vanished out of their sight in a cloud. The disciples stood there looking after their Master. Suddenly two angels stood beside them.

"Why are you looking into heaven?" the angels said. "This same Jesus, who has just gone to heaven, will come back to earth again some day."

Then the disciples worshiped Jesus. I think perhaps they bowed their heads and got down on their knees. It was almost as if they had been given a little glimpse of that other world we all hope to see some day. They were overcome with wonder and surprise. After a little while they got up again. They went back to Jerusalem, not weeping as they had on Good Friday, the day Jesus died; not stunned with grief and fear about the future — no, they went back to Jerusalem with great joy.

For they knew their precious Lord would come again to take them to Himself. And while He was gone He had given them work to do for Him. They were eager to begin that work, to show by their faithfulness, while He was absent, how much they loved Him.

And Jesus — what happened to Him? Jesus sat down in glory at the right hand of God, His Father. But you must not think of Him as just sitting there, listening quietly to the songs of the angels. Jesus is very busy. He is working all the time. He is working for you, and me, and all His loved children.

What is He doing? He is ruling the whole world. The lives, the hearts, the decisions of all men lie in His powerful hands. Nothing, not one solitary thing, can happen to you by accident. Jesus controls everything in your life.

Yes, and Jesus is praying for you. He knows you better than you know yourself. He knows what you want. He knows what you need. He knows what the purpose of your life is.

And He is very close to you, never far away. You can talk to Him any time, any place, and He will listen and answer.

And there is something more than this. He is expecting you to join Him there in that blessed world. He is busy getting a place ready for you, so that you can always be where He is. And while Jesus is busy getting your place ready, you can be busy telling other people the Good News.

84
The Gift of Courage

Acts 2

My name is Peter, and I have a message for you. It is not a formal message, but just the story of something that happened to me. I have been asked to hand it on to you, and perhaps you in your turn can some day hand it on to someone else.

At first I would have been ashamed to tell you about how it all began. That was before I understood that it *had* to start right there. I *had* to know the truth about myself, bitter as this lesson was. I had to see that I was really a coward, before I could start to be a brave man.

Once I had been a fisherman, but for the last three years I had followed Jesus. I had boasted loudly of my loyalty. "Even if everyone else deserts You," I had said, "I will never desert You. I am ready to go with You both to prison, and even to death itself." How sure I was of myself when I spoke those foolish words! How little I knew about the treachery of my own heart!

For I ran away, just as all the others did. Indeed, I sank lower than the others. It was I, and I alone, who swore with oaths and cursing, that I had never known my precious Lord. Yes, when the test came, I forgot all that I had promised. I thought only about how to save my own skin.

That dreadful Friday when we thought everything had ended turned out instead to be the beginning, not the end. No man had ever heard of such a thing, but it happened just the same. We saw it with our own eyes. That is why we know for sure. Jesus, our Master, the Son of God, conquered death. He came alive again, after He had been dead and buried three days.

The days that followed were doubly precious to us. We knew that our Master could not stay with us. He had finished His work here on earth. He was going back to His Father in heaven. How we cherished every moment we saw Him! How we hung on His every word!

"You must travel all over the world," He told us, "and tell people everywhere about me." I was to tell people about Jesus? I, Peter, the one who had been afraid to admit I even knew Him? I meant to do better the next time. But would I? Or would I run away again?

"I am going away," He told us. "But I am not going to leave you alone. I am going to send my Spirit to strengthen you and to teach you. Do not try to tell other people about me yet. Wait in Jerusalem until God's power comes upon you."

Then He led us out of the city to the hilltop that overlooks the little village of Bethany. He lifted up His hands to give us a blessing. And as He was speaking a cloud came over Him, and He disappeared. We did not see Him again. But we were not sad as we were that

Friday when He died. We knew that He would always be with us as we went about His work. And that some day we would see Him coming back to earth on the clouds of heaven. We went back to Jerusalem. We waited for the Spirit He had promised. And while we waited we talked to our Lord in prayer.

Now it was feast time again. There were many strangers in the city, strangers from everywhere, come to thank God for the harvest. But I and my companions did not mingle with the crowds. We stayed mostly in the upstairs room, waiting and praying for God's Spirit.

Suddenly we heard a rushing sound, as if a powerful wind were blowing through the sky. In a minute the whole house was filled with the whistling wind. And then on the head of each one of us there appeared tongues of burning fire. And at that very moment all of us began to talk about the wonderful things God had done. But there was something very strange about what we said. We did not talk in our own language, which we had always spoken together. Each of us spoke in a different language, languages we had never learned to speak.

A great crowd collected in front of the house, to see what was going on. There were people from many different countries there, and each of them heard us speaking in his own language. "What is going on here?" one of them asked. And somebody answered, "These men are drunk!"

I had been a coward once. I had been afraid I might be a coward again. But suddenly I was not afraid any longer. My heart was full of courage, not my own courage, but the courage given me by God's Holy Spirit. I stood up in the middle of the crowd.

"We are not drunk," I said. "This is the pouring out of God's Holy Spirit which the prophets promised long ago. God worked many wonderful miracles through Jesus. You people did not pay any attention to these signs of God's power. You killed Jesus on the cross. But God raised Him from the dead, and now He is Lord in heaven."

It was not the words I spoke, but the Holy Spirit Himself that awoke their sense of guilt. "What shall we do?" they asked. And I said, "Be sorry for your sins, and be baptized in the name of Jesus. God will forgive your sins, and give to you also His Holy Spirit."

That day the Holy Spirit added about three thousand persons to the number of those who believed in our Lord Jesus.

And now I would like to say a word to you, my friends, who are far away, whom I have never seen. God's promise is for you too. If you are sorry for your sins, and trust in our Lord Jesus, God will forgive you also. God will give to you His powerful Holy Spirit.

God's Spirit will live in your heart. He will teach you what you need to know. He will give you courage and strength to do God's will. He will put the right words into your mouth when you tell others about Jesus.

And He will bless, with His wonderful power, the words you speak for Jesus, so that many others will be added to those that love the Lord.

85
Stephen Sees Heaven Opened

Acts 6, 7

It isn't easy to be a Christian. It has never been easy. It wasn't easy for the early Christians either.

After the death of Jesus the early Christians were driven from town to town. They were thrown into prison. They were cruelly beaten. Many of them were killed.

And yet those early Christians were not discouraged. There was a reason why they bore this all so bravely. They were looking for a reward, a gift from God, a reward they wanted so much that the sufferings they experienced hardly seemed to count. What was that reward?

When you are a little older, and you fall in love, you will discover that the thing you want most of all is just to be near the person you love. It doesn't matter where you are, or what you are doing. The only thing that really matters is being together.

That was the reward the early Christians were longing for. They loved Jesus so much they wanted more than anything else just to be with Him. They loved Jesus so much they gladly suffered beatings, prison, even death itself. You see, they had seen with their own eyes, many of them, how much more, how very much more Jesus had suffered for their sakes. They were willing to follow in their Master's footsteps, and to suffer a little bit for Him.

One of these early Christians was Stephen. Stephen was an unusual man. He was different from his fellow Christians. And yet, I don't think he started out different. To begin with, I think he was just an ordinary person, much like you or me.

Stephen was unusual because he had yielded his heart so completely to God's Holy Spirit. The Bible tells us that Stephen was *full* of the Holy Spirit. And because the Holy Spirit is so powerful, His power showed in Stephen's life too.

The Jewish leaders thought that as soon as they killed Jesus, His followers would forget His teachings. But this did not happen. Just the opposite happened. The disciples, who had been frightened and timid while Jesus was alive, now became bold. They talked to people everywhere about Jesus. It was the Holy Spirit that made them brave.

The Jewish leaders were very angry that the disciples preached about Jesus. They were especially angry about Stephen, because he spoke so well that no one could answer what he said. They persuaded some wicked men to tell lies about Stephen. The priests paid them money to do this.

Stephen was arrested and brought before the Jewish court. The lying witnesses accused him of teaching that Jesus was going to destroy the temple, and change the laws of Moses. The judges sat in a circle, and they all looked at Stephen. There was something strange about Stephen's face. It did not look like the face of an ordinary man. It looked like the face of an angel. So completely was Stephen's heart yielded to the Holy Spirit that you could even see the glory of the Holy Spirit shining through his face.

"Are these accusations true?" the high priest asked Stephen.

"God does not live in a temple made with men's hands," Stephen answered. "God made a promise to Abraham long before there was a temple. He appeared to Moses before there was a temple. But you Jewish people have not listened to God's messengers. You did not listen to Moses or the other prophets. And now God has sent you His own Son, and you have killed Him too!"

This made the Jews very angry. They knew in their hearts that what they had done to Jesus was wrong. But Stephen was not afraid of anything the Jews could do to him. And God gave him a special vision, a little glimpse beforehand of what awaited him.

"Look!" Stephen cried, "the heavens are opened, and I see Jesus standing at the right hand of God!"

This made the Jews even angrier. They shouted loudly so they would not have to hear what Stephen said. They put their hands over their ears to shut out the sound of his voice. In a blind fury they rushed at Stephen, and dragged him out of the city. They threw great rocks at him.

"Lord Jesus," Stephen prayed, "receive my soul!" Then, as the rocks flew all around him, he kneeled down and said, "Lord, forgive them for this sin." And as he said these words, he closed his eyes and died. When he opened his eyes an instant later, he was with his precious Saviour.

Perhaps God will never ask you to die for Him. But He is going to ask you to do things that are hard for His sake. If you want to do them gladly, happily, bravely, as Stephen did, you must know Stephen's secret. You must pray for God's Holy Spirit to come into your heart, and to fill your heart to overflowing with love for Jesus. Then nothing will seem too hard for you to do for your precious Saviour who did so much for you.

86
God Turns a Man Around

Acts 9:1-25

If your doorbell rings, you can answer it or not, as you choose. If you do not answer it, the person on your doorstep will go away after a while. But you cannot get rid of God like this. There are some people, the Bible tells us, who have ears but cannot hear. Or, perhaps we should say, they *will* not hear. For you and I are quick to close our ears when God tells us something we do not wish to hear. But if you do not answer when God calls, He will speak to you in a voice that cannot be ignored, perhaps in a great crash of events.

He reaches down into your life, and turns you right around. And this is just what happened to Paul.

Paul thought he was running as hard as he could toward God. And all the while he was running away, closing his ears, when the one thing in the world he wanted most of all was to hear the voice of God speaking to him.

But it was not only his direction that was wrong. Paul was dead wrong about himself as well. Paul was a proud man. Not proud of his intelligence, or his education, or his Roman citizenship — though he had good reason to be proud of any one of these. No, Paul was proud of how religious he was, of how hard he worked to obey the tiniest dot and comma of the law of God, of how much better he was than most other men. He was going to make himself over into the kind of man God would be pleased to talk to. He was very sure he could manage this. And yet, no matter how hard he tried, he found no peace of mind.

When Stephen, the first Christian martyr, was stoned, Paul sat watching. If there was any whisper of doubt in his heart about this wicked deed, he did not listen to it. After the death of Stephen, Paul persecuted the church with new fury. He went from house to house, and street to street in Jerusalem. His foot upon the step, his knock upon the door was almost a death warrant for the Christians who hid inside. Man or woman, they were dragged off to judgment, and there were few who escaped alive from that court. Paul saw to that.

Now this deeply tormented man, who longed for God but did not know how to reach Him, was on the way to Damascus. A little band of police officers from the high priest were with him. In Damascus, too, they would hunt down the Christians, and drag them back to Jerusalem to stand trial.

It was almost a hundred and fifty miles from Jerusalem to Damascus. Paul had been on the way nearly a week, but he was now in sight of the city. It was noon, the hottest time of the day, when travelers usually rest a bit. But Paul pressed on.

Suddenly a dazzling light shone all around him. Paul was terrified.

He fell to the ground and hid his face. A voice spoke to him out of the light.

"Paul, Paul, why do you persecute me?" the voice asked. Paul did not know who this could be that spoke to him.

"Who are you?" he asked.

"I am Jesus," the voice replied, "whom you are persecuting."

Paul was struck with terror and amazement. Jesus was dead, wasn't He? He had died on the cross some months ago. If this was Jesus speaking, then Jesus must be alive. Suddenly Paul realized that everything he had thought he knew so well was wrong. He had been completely mistaken in his ideas. His whole life was turned upside down.

"Go into the city," Jesus told him, "and you will be told what to do." Slowly Paul got up from the ground. He opened his eyes, but he did not see anything. He had been struck blind by the dazzling light of Jesus in glory. The men who were with him took him by the hand and led him into Damascus like a little child. For three days Paul could not see. He did not eat or drink anything those three days either. He was too shocked to eat.

After three days God appeared in a vision to a Christian in Damascus named Ananias. "Go to Straight Street," God said, "and ask at Judas' house for Paul. He is praying, and he, too, has had a vision. He has seen you coming to lay your hands on him so that he can see again."

Ananias was afraid of Paul. "Lord," he said, "this man has done a lot of harm to Christians in Jerusalem. He has come here to imprison everyone who believes in Jesus."

"Go," the Lord said to Ananias. "I have chosen Paul to carry my name to those who are not Jews, and to appear before kings for me." So Ananias did as he was told. He went to Straight Street, to the house of Judas. He came into the room where Paul sat praying.

"Brother Paul," he said, "the Lord, who appeared to you on the road, has sent me so that you may be able to see again, and so that you may receive the Holy Spirit."

Immediately it was as if scales fell off the eyes of Paul. He could see again. He got up from where he was sitting. The very first thing he did was to be baptized in the name of Jesus. After that he had something to eat.

Paul could have slipped quietly out of Damascus soon after he had been converted. No one except a small handful of Christians would have been the wiser. But that was not Paul's way. Paul felt that he must make a public statement about how wrong he had been. He must now preach about Jesus as openly as he had persecuted Him.

And so, on the Sabbath morning, Paul went to the synagogue. He walked down the aisle and took his seat. The Jewish leaders gloated in their hearts when they saw him. "Now," they thought, "we will be rid of these troublesome Christians. He will carry them off, bound hand and foot, to Jerusalem."

Their smug satisfaction did not last long. Presently Paul was asked to say a few words to the congregation, as important visitors often were in those days. Paul came to the front. He spoke boldly, persuasively. "Jesus," he said, "is the very Son of God. He is the Saviour whom God promised to send. No one can be saved unless he trusts in the death and resurrection of Jesus, not in his own good works."

After the service the angry leaders collected outside. This man had been sent to help them, but he was a traitor to the cause. He had joined the enemy. Death was too good for men like him. So they plotted together. They set a special watch on the city gates, to be sure Paul did not escape their angry revenge. Paul was a trapped man.

"Thou shalt not be afraid of the terror by night, nor for the arrow that flieth by day. . . . For He will give His angels charge over thee. . . . They shall bear thee up in their hands, lest thou dash thy foot against a stone." Did Paul think about these words of the Psalmist that night of danger?

Late that night, when all the city was asleep, there still burned a light in one house, though the windows were carefully shaded. Down that Damascus street, one at a time, came those Christians who trusted in God, and the house door was opened to them silently, secretly.

This was a Christian home and, in the amazing providence of God, it was built right on the city wall. The Christians took a large basket. They tied a long, strong rope to each corner. They put the basket out of the window that hung over the city wall. They worked very quietly. No one spoke out loud. Paul climbed out of the window into the basket. He did not look at the dizzy depths below him! Instead he looked up to God. Carefully the disciples lowered the basket to the ground. When morning came Paul was already far from the city. He had escaped from the fury of the Jews in Damascus. This was the first narrow escape Paul had after he became a Christian. It was not the last — far from it. But Paul was not afraid. For he knew that, as he carried God's Good News to the ends of the earth, he was doing God's work, and that God was watching over him.

87
God's Doors

Acts 16:6-15

It was a sand road, hardly more than a fire trail, and it led through unbroken forest. Every mile or so it branched. There were no signs. We had come to another of these intersections, and were sitting in the car, staring bewildered at the three roads ahead of us. They all looked alike. Which was the main road?

Then we noticed an old man sitting by the side of the creek, fishing, sitting so still he almost seemed part of the foliage. "Which is the main road?" we asked. He shrugged. "It depends on where you want to go." We laughed uneasily. "We're not sure just where we are going," we admitted. "We are just out for a ride. But we do want to stick to the main road. We don't want to get lost in the forest."

It was a moment before he answered. "Well," he said at last, "on the left-hand fork there is a bridge out a mile or so south of here. The right fork is blocked by a fallen tree. If you want to get anywhere at all you had best stick to the middle road."

We took the center fork, and we did at last come to the edge of the forest. Later we laughed about our experience. And much later it occurred to me that this is just the way God often leads His children. "I'll go where You want me to go, dear Lord," we sing. But just where *does* God want us to go? It is not always easy to tell. Even Abraham, you remember, was not told where he was going. He was just commanded to leave home and start traveling. "And he went out, not knowing whither he went."

Often the place God wants us to go is not at all the place we have figured out we want to go. And God directs us by opening and closing doors — or roads, if you like. We have to keep our eyes and ears open to discover where God is leading. And we have to be willing to give up our own plans when it becomes clear that God has closed the door we wanted to go through, and has opened another door before us — sometimes a door we are reluctant to enter.

And this is how it was when Paul was traveling from place to place telling people about Jesus. On this particular trip he was visiting all the new churches he had set up when he came this way the year before. I wonder if you can imagine what a reunion that was! What happy preparations were made when they heard that he was coming! How they hung on every word he said when at last he arrived! Never was a pastor more loved by his converts than Paul was! These tiny bands of Christians, who lived in the midst of a threatening heathen world, had first heard the Good News about Jesus from this man. And some, newly born into the church, had never seen him at all, though they had certainly heard the older members repeat over and over everything he had said and done.

Paul loved these people as dearly as they loved him. But he could not linger. There were so many who had not heard the Good News yet! Where should he go next? The Roman province of Asia and the great city of Ephesus lay directly ahead. But God closed that door in Paul's face. We do not know how he closed it — whether by a washed-out bridge, or a fallen tree, or in some quite different way. But Paul was watching for God's leading, and he turned obediently aside. Ephesus was part of God's plan, it would take an important place in His church, but not yet. Something else came first.

So Paul went north instead, thinking perhaps Bithynia was where God wanted him to work. But again God closed the door. Bithynia, too, was to be part of God's church, but God had chosen Peter, not Paul, to work there. And so, since there was no other road open, Paul came to Troas, on the coast. Here he could take a ship for almost any place in Europe, even for Rome itself. Where did God want him to go? And now, just when it was needed, God spoke.

Paul was asleep at night. He saw a vision from God. It was the coast of northern Greece that he saw in his vision. A man stood on the hillside, a Macedonian man, and beckoned to him. "Come over and help us," the man begged.

The very next morning Paul and his fellow missionaries took a ship for Macedonia. They landed at Philippi, the largest city in that part of northern Greece. There was no Jewish synagogue in Philippi where Paul could preach to those who already knew about the one true God. And so, on the Sabbath morning, he went down to the riverside, and there he found, as he had hoped to, a little group of people praying. Most of them were women.

Paul sat down with these women, and talked to them about God and about Jesus. And God Himself opened the hearts of these women, so that they listened to Paul and believed. One of them was Lydia, a business woman of some importance in Philippi. She imported and sold purple dye and purple cloth, a color so expensive that only rich men and kings could afford to wear it.

Lydia was the very first convert to the Christian church in Europe. And that, in a very real sense, makes her the spiritual mother of us all, for it is by way of Europe, as you know, that the Christian faith came to America. She and all her family were baptized. And then she begged Paul and his fellow missionaries to come and stay at her house.

Of course, all this happened long, long before you and I were born, or even thought of. But the thing I want you to remember is that when God opened the door for Paul to go into Macedonia, and when He opened the heart of Lydia to believe the Good News, He was thinking even then of you and me. He was planning how He would draw you and me into the circle of His love. And now He expects us to spread the Good News to others who have not yet heard. And if you listen carefully, as Paul did, you will find that God will lead you, too, opening and closing doors before you.

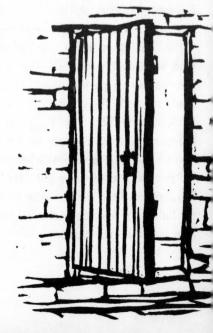

88
The Sound of the Last Trumpet

Matthew 25:1-13

In Palestine a wedding is a big event. All of the family is invited — uncles and cousins and aunts. Some of them travel great distances to share in the celebration. Family friends are there also, and, if the village is small, all the villagers are guests too. There are games, and singing, and feasting, and all of this lasts for several days. Yes, a wedding is a time of great rejoicing.

On this particular wedding day there were ten people who had a special reason to be excited. They were the girl friends of the bride, and they had been chosen to be her bridesmaids, and to take part in the ceremonies. How many excited, whispered conferences there had been among them, as they helped the bride to plan her wedding day! None of the bridesmaids was married yet, and I suppose each one thought in her heart, "Perhaps the next wedding will be mine!" And so their joy was partly for the bride, and partly because each girl hoped soon to be herself the central figure of a wedding just like this one.

Each bridesmaid had a new white dress, and each one had a lamp to carry. They did not take part in the bridal procession, as bridesmaids do in our country. Instead, they waited at the bridegroom's house for the procession to arrive, and then they went into the house with the procession, and stood around the bride, holding their shining lamps, while she watched the singing and the games, and thanked each person who had brought a gift for the new home. Five of the bridesmaids had taken care to bring along oil for their lamps; the other five, whether from carelessness or from excitement, had quite forgotten that a lamp needs oil if it is to give light.

And so now they were waiting outside the bridegroom's home, and because they were so eager, the time seemed long to them.

"They must be almost there," one of them said. "How excited

our friend must be!" The bridesmaids were pretty excited themselves.

"Now she will be coming out of the house," another said. "See! the veil is over her face. She is getting into the litter!" A bride was not expected to walk to her own wedding. Her bridegroom and his friends carried her in a special chair, with handles on the sides, and a curtain overhead to shade her.

"Yes," added a third, "they are forming the procession. I think I can hear them singing." The others laughed excitedly.

"Don't be foolish," they said. "You know you could never hear the singing. It is much too far away for that." At last they were quiet. And then, worn out by all the excitement, they fell asleep.

It was quite dark by this time. The moon came up slowly in the east. The girls slept quietly. Suddenly, at midnight, there was a shout: "Look, the bridegroom! Come out to meet him!" The ten bridesmaids scrambled up, and hurried to smooth their hair and light their lamps. One of them cried, "I have no oil! Give me some of yours!" A second girl said, "I forgot to bring oil too. Let me borrow from your lamp." And so a third, and a fourth, and a fifth.

But the other five bridesmaids said, "If we do that, there will not be enough left in our lamps for the feast. Go, rather, and buy oil for yourselves." The five careless bridesmaids rushed off to look for oil. While they were gone, the procession arrived. The five with the lighted lamps went in with the bride to the wedding feast, and the door was shut behind them.

After a little while the five foolish bridesmaids returned. They had found oil, and their lamps were now lighted. They knocked on the door.

"Lord! Lord!" they called. "Open the door and let us in!"

But the bridegroom, inside the house, answered, "I do not know who you are!"

A sad story, you say, with an unhappy ending. But it is more than just a story. And the unhappy ending is there for a special reason. It is a warning to you and to me.

For the bridegroom who speaks these words is our Lord and

Saviour, Jesus Himself. And the wedding feast that all ten of the bridesmaids had so longed to share in, the wedding feast is heaven. And you and I are the bridesmaids, waiting eagerly, longingly, for the day when our Saviour comes again. And the shout that went up at midnight, "Look, the bridegroom!" — that shout is the sound of the last great trumpet.

When we hear that sound, echoing from heaven to earth and back again — and every single one of us is going to hear it some day — then the sky is going to be rolled up like a scroll of paper. Then the hearts of all men will tremble with fear, for, looking up, they will see descending to the earth Jesus Christ, the One who was crucified. In that day it will not matter any longer whether you are rich or poor, whether you are popular, or successful, or have many friends. The only thing that will matter will be whether you have trusted in the death of Jesus Christ as your Saviour, and obeyed Him as your Lord. If in all the excitement and fun of your life you have forgotten to attend to this, then you, too, will find the door shut against you, and will hear the dreadful words, "I do not know you." But all of those who have taken refuge in Jesus will be caught up to meet Him in the air, and so they will forever be with the Lord they have loved.

89
The Promise of His Coming

Matthew 25:31-46

The first time the King came, He came quietly, almost secretly, His dazzling glory disguised by the form He took. For He took off His royal robes, and laid aside His many crowns, and appeared among His people as a poor carpenter.

Instead of riding down the city streets in the royal coach, with a herald to go before Him, shouting, "Bow the knee! Bow the knee!" He walked along the roads with the common people, His feet in the dust. And at night when He grew tired — for even kings grow tired — He lay down on the ground to sleep, as other poor travelers have to do.

And so, His glory being hidden, there were many who did not recognize Him as their King. When He told them who He was, they laughed in scorn. "We know who you are," they said. "You are only a carpenter, and the son of a carpenter." And others became angry. "How dare you say you are the King?" they shouted. "We will kill you for this lie."

There were only a few who, with the eye of faith, recognized who He was.

That was the first time He came.

The second time He comes will be quite different. There will be nothing hidden this time. His glory will be plain for all to see. The trumpet will thunder through the sky with a note that awakes even those long since dead. The archangels will shout, and the King will descend on the clouds of heaven, with all His great host of angels attending Him. Every eye will see Him, even those whose sins have driven the nails into His hands. Those who refused to have Him for their King will cry to the mountains to fall on them and hide them from His face.

Then the King will sit down on His throne. And all the people that have ever lived will be gathered before Him. And He will divide them into two groups as a shepherd divides the sheep in his flock from the goats. The King will set the sheep on His right hand, and the goats on His left.

And the King will say to those on His right hand, "Come, you blessed of my Father, inherit the kingdom made ready for you before the foundations of the world were laid. For once I was hungry, and you fed me. I was thirsty, and you gave me a drink. I was a stranger, and you invited me to your house. I was naked, and you provided me with clothes. I was sick, and in prison, and you came to see me."

And those on His right hand will answer Him in surprise, "Lord, when did we see You hungry, and fed You? Or thirsty, and gave You a drink? When did we see You a stranger, and invited You to our house? Or naked, and gave You clothing? Or sick, or in prison, and came to see You?"

And the King will say, "Truly, since you did it to one of my brothers, even the least important of them, you did it to me."

And then He will say to those on His left hand, "Depart from me, you cursed, into the everlasting fire. For I was hungry, and you refused to give me anything to eat. I was thirsty, and you would not give me a drink. I was a stranger, but you did not invite me to your house. I was naked, but you did not bother to give me something to clothe myself with. I was sick, and in prison, and you never came to see me."

And these also shall say, "Lord, when did we see You hungry, and refused to give You something to eat? Or thirsty, but did not give You a drink? When did we see You a stranger, and did not bother to give You clothes? Or sick, or in prison, and did not come to see You?" And the King shall answer, "Truly, since you did not do it to one of the least of these my brothers, you did not do it to me!" And all these people, who turned their backs on their brothers and sisters — no, who turned their backs on the King's brothers and sisters who were in need — all of these will go away to everlasting punishment. But the righteous shall inherit everlasting life.

That is how it will be the second time that the King comes.

And you and I — we will be there on that day. We will see His glory, and we will hear His voice. Will we be among those who are called *righteous?*

There is not one of us who can earn that title. No matter how hard we struggle, we will never deserve to be called "righteous." Only those who trust in the death of their Saviour-King, who wash their robes white in His blood shed on Calvary, are righteous.

But while we await His coming again, trusting only in Him, He Himself has given us this touchstone that will help us to be sure whether or not we truly love and trust Him. For all the unfortunate, the hungry, the poor, the strangers, the sick, the imprisoned, stand in His place. And the one who does not love his brother or sister whom he has seen, cannot love God, whom he has not seen.

90
We Wait for Jesus

Abraham, and later his son Isaac, and still later his grandson Jacob, lived for about two hundred years in a tent, because they were homesick. Not homesick for Ur, the city they had left behind when God called Abraham. No, it was the beautiful garden they longed for, the place where God had once walked and talked with men.

Perhaps you wonder why they had to live in a tent, just because they longed for heaven. They lived in a tent because they had a message they wanted to leave behind for all who came after them. And that includes you and me. They did not write their message down. Instead they lived it. That tent which they moved from place to place, always wanderers, always homeless — that tent was their sign that they had discovered something better than anything earth had to offer. It was their way of telling us that he who has tasted the precious friendship of God will never be really happy until he comes at last to the city where God Himself lives among His people.

Moses, too, longed for that city, and David, and Isaiah, and many thousands of others, most of whom we do not even know by name. All of them died without having seen the Saviour God had promised. For all of them the Saviour was only a distant vision, almost a dream. And yet it was a dream certain to come true, because it rested on the promises of God.

You and I do not live in a tent; yet we, too, are only passing visitors on this earth. We know far more about God's Saviour, Jesus, than did those people who lived before He was born. But what we know does not content us; it only increases our homesick longing for His return.

You may not ever have thought about it, but home is not so much a place. Home is most of all a person. Home is wherever you can be with those you love the most. Even Jesus was homesick here on earth, homesick to return to His Father whom He loved so dearly.

God has not told us much about the second coming of our Saviour — when He will come, and how — or about the new heaven and the new earth which He will bring with Him. For God expects us, like the people who lived before Jesus was born, to walk by faith, not by sight, trusting in the promises of God.

He has not told us much, but He has promised that we are going to see our Saviour face to face. "I go to prepare a place for you," Jesus said, "and I will return to get you, so that where I am there you may be also."

In that beautiful garden so long ago God was present only part of the time. In the evening, in the cool of the day, He came to the garden and walked and talked with Adam and Eve. It will not be that way in the place Jesus is preparing for us even now.

When that wonderful day arrives, God is going to live among His people. He Himself, with His own hand, is going to wipe away the tears from our eyes. And this is not all. God will draw even closer than this. For God has promised that He is going to spread His own tent over us, to shelter us. He is going to take us into the very place where He Himself lives. And so we shall be forever with our Saviour.

"Watch therefore," Jesus tells us, "for you do not know in what hour your Lord will come." And again He says, "Behold, I come quickly, and my reward is with me." And we answer, with our eyes fixed on that city where we shall at last be at home, "Even so! Come quickly, Lord Jesus!"